SEXUAL CRIME

Selected Titles in ABC-CLIO's
CONTEMPORARY
WORLD ISSUES
Series

For a complete list of titles in this series, please visit
www.abc-clio.com.

Books in the Contemporary World Issues series address vital issues in today's society, such as genetic engineering, pollution, and biodiversity. Written by professional writers, scholars, and nonacademic experts, these books are authoritative, clearly written, up-to-date, and objective. They provide a good starting point for research by high school and college students, scholars, and general readers as well as by legislators, businesspeople, activists, and others.

Each book, carefully organized and easy to use, contains an overview of the subject, a detailed chronology, biographical sketches, facts and data and/or documents and other primary-source material, a directory of organizations and agencies, annotated lists of print and nonprint resources, and an index.

Readers of books in the Contemporary World Issues series will find the information they need to have a better understanding of the social, political, environmental, and economic issues facing the world today.

SEXUAL CRIME

A Reference Handbook

Caryn E. Neumann

**CONTEMPORARY
WORLD ISSUES**

A B C ☰ C L I O

Santa Barbara, California
Denver, Colorado
Oxford, England

Library of Congress Cataloging-in-Publication Data

Neumann, Caryn E., 1965-
    Sexual crime : a reference handbook / Caryn E. Neumann.
        p. cm. — (Contemporary world issues)
    Includes bibliographical references and index.
    ISBN 978-1-59884-177-0 (print : alk. paper) — ISBN 978-1-59884-178-7 (ebook : alk. paper)   1. Sex crimes.   I. Title.
    HV6556.N48   2009
    364.15'3—dc22   2009043177

14   13   12   11   10   1   2   3   4   5

This book is also available on the World Wide Web as an eBook. Visit www.abc-clio.com for details.

ABC-CLIO, LLC
130 Cremona Drive, P.O. Box 1911
Santa Barbara, California 93116-1911

This book is printed on acid-free paper ∞

Manufactured in the United States of America

Contents

Preface

R ape is a problem as old as humanity. It is referenced in ancient
art and in the Bible. Yet it is also paradoxically a topic that
remained off the public agenda until the rise of the women's
movement in the late 1960s and early 1970s. Everyone knew that
rape existed but no one wanted to acknowledge it. The silence
aided rapists and furthered the suffering of victims. Myths
about rape were allowed to flourish because everyone knew
that they were true while no one investigated them to see if they
were indeed true.

The attitudes toward sexual crime have changed dramatically in just the past few decades. As this book went to press, representatives of the Catholic Church in Ireland publicly apologized
for the sexual and other types of abuse that boys and girls under
its care suffered from the 1930s to the 1990s. The Commission to
Inquire into Child Abuse, created by the government of Ireland,
made the abuse public. In earlier eras, the sexual abuse would
have remained a forbidden topic allowed by silence to continue,
as it clearly did for at least 60 years in Ireland. Sexual crime is no
longer a taboo subject.

Rapists are no longer excused for their actions. *Saturday Night
Fever* is a landmark 1977 movie that made John Travolta into a star
while popularizing disco. Everyone of a certain age remembers
Travolta's white suit, his moves on the dance floor, and the Bee
Gees soundtrack. Few recall that Travolta's Tony Manero character tried to rape his dance partner or that two of Manero's friends
gang-raped a young woman. The boys were just being boys and the
girl got what she had asked for. The sexual attacks were simply not
important enough to most viewers to be remembered. It is doubtful
that filmgoers of the 21st century would have the same dismissive
reaction. We know enough about rape today to condemn it.

Sexual crime victims are no longer shamed into silence. The media traditionally has not reported the names of rape victims to protect the victims from public embarrassment. Victims were once thought to be so ruined by a rape that their lives would be destroyed if the fact of the rape became public knowledge. Increasingly, however, rape victims are coming forward to tell their stories and they ask the media to use their real names. These individuals, such as child victim Paul Martin Andrews and prison rape victim Stephen Donaldson, are angry at the fact that they were attacked by sexual predators. They typically speak out to encourage other victims to come forward or to make certain that the criminal pays for his crimes. They also seek to draw attention to types of rapes that have received comparatively little attention, such as sex trafficking. Several high-profile victims of rape, such as legal scholar Susan Estrich and Cambodian antiprostitution activist Somaly Mam, have done much to reform the treatment of rape victims. It is clear that many rape victims believe that shame should attach to the rapist and not to his or her victim.

Yet major issues clearly remain. Movies and television shows teach women that rapists are strangers, but most rapists are known to their victims. The abuse of alcohol makes someone more likely to be a victim and more likely to be an attacker. Native American women are three-and-a-half times more likely to suffer sexual assault than white, black, Latina, or Asian women, partly because of the high rate of alcohol abuse in Indian country. However, comparatively little antirape activism has focused on substance abuse. Meanwhile, everyone knows that real men cannot be raped. So, rape centers cater explicitly or implicitly to women, leaving male victims of rape shut out and further victimized. Victimization is more than just physical, though these injuries can be severe. Victims can suffer psychologically, socially, intellectually, and financially long after physical wounds have healed. These other wounds have received comparatively little attention because they are less obvious.

This book is an objective introduction to contemporary issues surrounding sexual crime. It is designed to provide a broad range of information about an issue that may touch the lives of many Americans. Interest in the study of sexual crime has grown tremendously in the last few decades. The identification of date or acquaintance rape as a social problem, in particular, has prompted high schools and colleges to implement rape education or awareness programs. Self-defense classes for women have become common. Yet no comprehensive reference handbook on sexual crime has existed to help educators, activists, or students. The best defense against sexual crime is knowledge.

This book is divided into eight chapters. The first chapter covers the history of sexual crime and discusses the various rape myths that have persisted over the years. It identifies the various types of rapists. This chapter provides historical context for students to understand the current issues relating to sexual crime. The second chapter is split into sections on victims, attackers, after the attack, law enforcement, and the judicial system. It provides the latest findings as well as a discussion of controversies and problems in the reporting and prosecution of sexual crime. The third chapter focuses on sexual crime in Africa, Asia, Europe, and Latin America. It provides information about the key issues relating to sexual crime in these regions, such as rape as a war crime and forced prostitution. A chronology of events relating to sex crime is provided in the fourth chapter. The fifth chapter includes over 20 short biographies of antirape activists and policymakers around the world, including Andrews, Donaldson, Estrich, and Mam. Important statistics and data about sex crimes can be found in chapter six. The last two chapters are devoted to resources. Chapter seven is a directory of selected public and private organizations that address sex crime. Chapter eight contains an annotated bibliography of print and film resources, including popular films and documentaries.

I have many people to thank for their help in this project. Sandra Carrigg, Pam Hipple, Dr. Susan Cratty, and Dr. Sara Jane Rowland provided research assistance. The librarians of Miami University of Ohio at Middletown kindly thanked me for boosting their circulation numbers. I appreciate their good humor. I am quite delighted to be part of the Miami of Ohio family. I am also grateful to be a graduate of The Ohio State University and to have worked under the guidance of Dr. Susan M. Hartmann. Holly Heinzer of ABC-CLIO suggested that I write this book. Lauren Thomas and Kim Kennedy White, both at ABC-CLIO, were patient and enormously helpful. Any errors, of course, remain my responsibility.

This book is dedicated to all victims of sexual violence and to the people who fight against this violence.

1

Background and History

Sexual crimes historically have not been as easy to classify as other offenses. Both the definition of the crime and the victim of the crime have changed over the years. The act that one person views as a violation may be seen by another as something natural and certainly permissible. The physical reality of rape has not changed over time: the penetration of a vagina or other orifice by a penis or other object without the consent of the man, woman, or child being penetrated. Definitions of rape, ideas, perceptions, and applicable laws have all shifted over the years.

Legal perceptions of rape are shaped by time and place. For much of history, women have been regarded as the property of men. Wulfstan, the Archbishop of York, relates in the *Lupi sermo ad Anglos* in 1014 the plight of an Anglo-Saxon who is shamed by the gang rape of his wife by Vikings. Wulfstan focuses only on the man's shame, ignoring the woman's pain. Medieval law in Burgundy, *Lex Gundobada,* states that a woman who rejects the man to whom she is married shall be put to death in mud (Taylor, 2002, p. 161). While rape within marriage is probably the most typical age-old example of a sexual attack permitted by legal authorities, rape has not always been regarded as a criminal act. Historically, slaves have been used for sexual purposes. The Arabic word *jariyah* means slave girl or concubine, while the word for slave boy, *ghulam*, has homosexual connotations (Taylor, 2002, p. 87).

Since women were essentially the property of men, the rape of a woman became a crime committed against her father or husband. His authority as head of household was undermined whether or not prosecution proved successful. An acquittal of an accused rapist pointed to a man's inability to control his wife's or daughter's sexuality, while a conviction would show that another man had successfully overcome his ability to protect the members of his household. Men, expected to be strong enough to defend themselves as well as to be sexual aggressors, were simply not considered as rape victims, particularly in eras when homosexual activities were taboo. Modern laws in the United States recognize that both men and women can be raped.

History of Sexual Assault

Sexual Assault in the 17th Century

Seventeenth-century colonial America consisted of a long strip of sparsely populated land along the Atlantic seaboard of North America. The separate colonies had legal institutions that were shaped by both their historic relationships to Europe and their own particular ethnic mixes. In addition to Native Americans, the population consisted of Europeans, some free and some indentured servants, and Africans, some free and some in bondage. Together these factors make discussion of rape in 17th-century America a complicated one.

Befitting their close ties with Mother England, British colonies adopted English law with respect to rape. The legal statutes of Virginia are typical. Convicted rapists faced the death penalty since rape was a capital offense. Accordingly, the evidence against the accused first had to be heard by a grand jury. Juries were all-white and all-male. If the grand jury concluded that the prosecutor had sufficient evidence to secure a conviction, the case was tried by a petit jury, or trial jury, in the Virginia General Court. The jurors had to reach a unanimous verdict for conviction. Conviction required two witnesses to the fact of penetration, an almost insurmountable barrier to successful prosecution. Further, if the victim was not a minor, independent proof of force was usually required to back up the victim's claim that she had not consented. A woman's word counted for little. To make matters even more difficult, force was defined as physical brutality, not economic or emotional power.

The paucity of sources makes it difficult to provide an example of a rape from the 17th century. However, Martha Ballard, a midwife who kept a diary, reported an attack that may well be typical of earlier rapes on the frontier. Ballard lived in the late 18th century in a sparsely settled area of Massachusetts. She provided medical care to a woman who claimed that she had been sexually assaulted in her home by a prominent man in the community while her husband was away. The victim did not press charges but Ballard clearly found her to be credible. Considering the isolation of many colonial homes, the vulnerability of women, and the prevalence of acquaintance rapes in the modern era, it is reasonable to suspect that rapes were not unknown in the 17th century.

In the absence of legal protections, few women were willing to charge rape. The surviving Virginia General Court records reveal no such cases prior to 1670, and only one has been found at the county level (Smith, 2004, p. 177). Women who charged rape risked the loss of their reputations and the destruction of their marriages if their husbands did not believe in their innocence. The results could be personally and financially devastating, as divorced women lost the custody of their children along with their major source of income. Additionally, many women were indentured servants. A servant who became pregnant could legally have years added to her term of servitude as punishment. Well-off white southerners also believed that poorer women, especially those without husbands, were innately depraved. There is also evidence that southern magistrates simply did not believe women's accusations, unless they were against black or Native American men. Taken together, such factors and fears provided a decidedly cold climate for women who wanted to charge men with rape or attempted rape.

Rape, according to legal statutes, happened to women or girls only. A 1699 Massachusetts legal statute defined rape as sexual intercourse committed by a man on a woman against her will or sexual intercourse committed by a man against a girl under the age of 10 (Block, 2006, p. 56). There was no provision for same-sex rape, although men who engaged in sodomy could be prosecuted.

Sexual Assault in the 18th Century

Eighteenth-century Americans understood rape as always including sexual intercourse between a man and a woman. Sexual intercourse between men, or sodomy, whether forced or consensual, was always a sexual crime. Sexual intercourse with girls under 10 years of age was considered to be rape regardless of their degree of consent. Marital rape simply could not occur—married women gave their perpetual consent to sex with their wedding vows. For most of the 18th century, as in the 17th century, rape was a capital crime, punishable by execution. Only after the American Revolution did some states begin to eliminate the death penalty for rape.

However, early American courts only rarely executed rapists. Courts were especially hesitant to execute upstanding white men for rape. Slaves brought before the courts in general were dealt with more harshly than the white population and slaves accused of rape were no exception. The majority of cases brought before the Massachusetts Superior Court involved defendants of low social standing, including Native Americans and African Americans. In such cases, rape was an assault upon the dignity of higher-ranking men who should be able to protect their women against harm by servants, transients, and laborers. Rape attacked the authority of patriarchs. Most rape prosecutions were structured along racial lines. Cases involving white women were much more likely to be prosecuted than those involving women of color. Conversely, nonwhite males, especially African American men, were far more common targets of rape prosecutions than were white men. These distorted prosecutions contributed to the still common myth that black men were more likely to rape white women.

The American colonists of European descent stereotyped black men as animal-like beings who were oversexed, brutal, and especially dangerous to white women. Colonial and early American rape law mandated either castration or death for blacks convicted of sexually assaulting or attempting to sexually assault white women. (Castration did not necessarily have sexual connotations. Slaveholders and local officials typically utilized castration as a means to control difficult slaves. As one example, in South Carolina, slaves who ran away for a fourth time could be castrated.) The 1738 case of Jemmy is representative. Jemmy, a slave owned by James Holman of Goochland County, Virginia, died by hanging for raping Elizabeth Weaver (Clinton & Gillespie, 1997, p. 79). In some cases, mere execution did not seem to be enough of a deterrent to would-be black rapists. In 1702, a Virginia slave hanged for the rape of a married woman suffered the additional punishment of having his head cut off and placed on a pole as a warning to deter other slaves from committing a similar crime. In 1777, the body of Titus, a North Carolina slave, was burned after he was hanged for committing a rape (Clinton & Gillespie, 1997, p. 80).

However, the courts apparently preferred castration or a lesser punishment than execution because the government would not have to compensate the slave owner for his loss of property. In an attempt to reduce the huge sums paid in compensation for executed slaves, the North Carolina legislature in 1758 passed a law that substituted castration for execution in all but cases of murder and rape. Historian Diane Miller Sommerville reports that 16 slaves were castrated during the five years in which the law remained on the books. When the financial strains created by the French and Indian War ended, the North Carolina assembly repealed the law and resumed executing slaves (Clinton & Gillespie, 1997, p. 78). Lynching a black man accused of rape did not become as popular as it was in the latter part of the 19th century partly because slave owners did not received compensation for lynched slaves.

Many men had concerns about the propriety of castration as an acceptable form of slave control. A North Carolina physician in the 1790s was pressured by a slave owner into castrating a slave who repeatedly made sexual attacks upon female slaves. The physician refused to accept payment because of his unease over the procedure (Clinton & Gillespie, 1997, p. 79). In 1724, a Virginia court convicted Caesar, a slave owned by Gawen Corbin of Spotsylvania Country, for the attempted rape of a four-year-old white girl. Caesar received 21 lashes, a half-hour standing in the pillory, and both ears severely cropped. A person who stood in a pillory faced verbal abuse and thrown objects from the citizenry, but such treatment, although brutal, is still quite far from being hanged. In 1742, a Virginia slave named Jack went on trial for raping a white woman. Convicted of simple assault, he received 39 lashes. A Maryland slave owner in the 1750s successfully received a pardon for his slave, who had been convicted for breaking and entering, stealing, and attempting to rape a white woman. The master received a pardon with the provision that his slave leave Maryland within 10 days (Clinton & Gillespie, 1997, p. 80). It is probable that the slave owner acted to save his money rather than out of any humanitarian concern for the slave.

It is a misconception that black males were the only ones to face castration for rape. Pennsylvania law permitted the castration of white male rapists, though there is no evidence that the sentence was ever carried out on whites. Georgia, Maryland, and North Carolina were the colonies that treated black and white rapists differently with respect to legally mandated punishment (Clinton & Gillespie, 1997, p. 79).

Black men had much in common with black women. Both received harsher treatment from the legal system. All women in 18th-century American might fall victim to a sexual assault, but some women enjoyed far better protection than others. African American women had the least legal and social protection from rape. Slaves did not legally own their bodies; their masters did. Male slaves could be ordered by their masters to impregnate female slaves to improve the stock. Female slaves also lacked the power to refuse sexual relations. As a result, the sexual assaults of slave women by masters, sons of the masters, and friends of the masters were simply not regarded as criminal acts. William Byrd (1674–1744), the Virginia planter and diarist, wrote of engaging in sexual relations with slaves, though he personally disliked the institution of slavery. Thomas Thistlewood (1721–1786), a Jamaican slave-owner, boasted in his diary of his numerous rapes of slave women. Thistlewood habitually raped slave women because a white man could do so without fear of any consequences and because he needed to demonstrate his domination of slaves. Byrd and Thistlewood were unique only in that they recorded their sexual activities.

Legally, a white man could be prosecuted for raping a slave woman. However, many colonies passed laws that prevented slaves from testifying against whites in court. Since a victim's testimony was usually crucial to a successful prosecution, few slaves could win a rape prosecution against any white man. Even free African American women could rarely bring a rape prosecution against white men because early Americans believed that black women were naturally promiscuous and thus unlikely to resist a rape. Accordingly, there is no known conviction of a white man for raping a slave or free black woman in the 18th century, even though it is known that many white men forced slaves to have sexual relations.

Although white women had more legal protection after a rape, reporting and prosecuting a sexual assault was never easy. A victim had to convince her guardian—husband or father—to take her to court to complain about the attack, then had to tell a magistrate what had happened, and then had to repeat her story to courtroom lawyers, jury members, and judges. Many legal officials believed that women often lied about rape, so would try to disprove women's stories whenever possible. A 1739 English news item, widely reprinted in the colonies, depicted a woman who had complained to her town's justice of the peace in the middle of the night that her husband had abused her. The justice, reluctant to lose sleep, told the woman that her husband would immediately be castrated. Confronted with this possibility, the woman abandoned her case. The news item portrayed sexual assault within marriage as properly a private matter—and women who thought otherwise as foolish. Since respectable women were supposed to resist sexual relations with men that they had not married, legal officials also believed that women would charge men with rape to preserve their reputation when they regretted having illicit sexual relations. However, there is little evidence of false rape charges in early American court records (Foster, 2006, p. 6).

Eighteenth century people expected men to engage in moderate behavior. Men who took sexual advantage of those under their care, such as servants, jeopardized their professional standing. Public knowledge that a man could not control himself could be emasculating and socially unbearable. In 1781, newly-wed Elizabeth Bemis of Lexington, Massachusetts received a divorce on the grounds of cruelty because her violently abusive husband had sexually assaulted her and given her a sexually transmitted disease. Samuel Bemis had violated his position as husband, to the disgust of his neighbors who testified against him (Foster, 2006, p. 102).

Men accused of rape in the 18th century typically simply denied the charge. Given the difficulty of proving rape in the absence of force, most men apparently did not feel the need to resort to the strategy of openly denying the victim's charges by claiming that she had invented the attack or had invited sexual relations. A simple denial depended on the popular image of a woman as untrustworthy and unreliable.

Sexual Assault in the 19th Century

Attitudes toward rape changed little between the 17th and 19th centuries. Legal codes continued to define rape as the unlawful carnal knowledge of a woman by a man forcibly and against her will. The prosecution of sexual criminals remained as difficult as it had been in the previous centuries. The major change that took place occurred after the Civil War when women and girls of color obtained the legal right to charge a man with rape.

Men continued to be highly suspicious of women who brought a rape charge. Nineteenth-century legal and medical writers frequently invoked the advice of Sir Matthew Hale, a British judge of the 17th century, who warned that women tended to charge rape out of spite or embarrassment. Some legal authorities insisted that women accused men of rape to blackmail them into marriage, to obtain money, or to exact revenge. They feared that a woman might claim rape as a sort of buyer's remorse when she had merely been seduced by a man. The possibility of false accusations concerned many legal officials, because if jurors—and only men served on juries in the 19th century—allowed their emotions to govern their intellects, they would convict innocent men of rape. For this reason, judges created exceptional rules of law, intended to protect defendants in rape cases while modifying generally accepted legal doctrines to make it difficult for a woman to prove that she had been raped. Essentially, women were presumed to be liars until they demonstrated otherwise. However, no one provided any proof that women were in the habit of falsely charging rape.

Not surprisingly, rape convictions were difficult, though not impossible, to achieve in the 19th century. Two key elements of the crime of rape were force and resistance. To meet the legal definition of rape, the courts required proof that the defendant had used physical force and that he had penetrated the woman with a penis. Penetrating a woman with an object other than a penis did not qualify as rape. Merely threatening a woman with a knife or a gun did not suffice as the kind of force that the law demanded for a rape conviction. Threatening loss of income did not qualify as force. To qualify as force, the man had to physically wound the woman. To qualify as resistance, a woman had to fend off her attacker successfully, unless she could show that an extenuating circumstance had prevented her from so doing. In essence, the law required an unarmed woman to battle a man with a gun or a knife to prove that she was a virtuous woman worthy of being believed.

If a woman submitted to a rapist for fear of being maimed, judges and jurors regarded consummation as consent. Judges devised the "half consent" and the "ultimate consent" doctrines for cases where women claimed they had resisted to the utmost of their abilities, yet the man still managed to complete the sexual act. Under the half consent doctrine, defendants argued that if the woman's resistance was equivocal, it amounted to a partial consent, which was as good as a whole consent. Defendants used the ultimate consent rule to assert that even though their accusers initially resisted their efforts at seduction, they eventually surrendered and ultimately consented.

Race is linked to sexual crime in the 19th century in a range of ways. After Emancipation, black females were no longer property to be used at will by white men. The change meant that white men began to use rape as an instrument of terror in the Reconstruction South to intimidate both black women and their families. In 1866, officials of the Freedmen's Bureau reported that Ku Klux Klan (KKK) members robbed, assaulted, and shot a black preacher from Bath County, Kentucky before raping his wife. Hannah Tutson, a middle-aged black woman living in Clay County, Florida, became the target of whites who wanted to force her off land that she had purchased. One night in 1866, the KKK invaded Tutson's home, carried her about a quarter-mile away, whipped her repeatedly, and then raped her. The injuries left Tutson barely able to walk. After raping a black woman in Georgia, white attackers vowed revenge against family members of those who had served in the Union Army. In 1871 Governor Rufus B. Bullock of Georgia offered a $5000 reward for information about the band of nearly 40 men who stormed the plantation of a Colonel Waltemire, who had fought for the Union army during the Civil War. The attackers whipped and beat two black servants and raped three young black girls. Federal records contain numerous cases of African American females who were sexually attacked during Reconstruction (Sommerville, 2004, p. 148–149). The attacks reasserted the sexual and racial power of whites over blacks while taking away the manhood of black men.

Race continued to be a factor in convictions and punishments for rape both before and after Emancipation. Whites and blacks received different punishments for statutory rape. Rape law defined sex with female children under a specified age of consent, usually 10 or 12, as rape even in the absence of force or resistance. While today such an act is referred to as statutory rape, in 19th-century legal terms such a crime was known as the carnal knowledge and abuse of an infant female. Slaves in Arkansas, Mississippi, Tennessee, Texas, and Virginia who were found guilty of having sexual intercourse with white female children could receive the death penalty. White men, by contrast, received prison sentences of 5 to 21 years. Missouri punished white offenders with a minimum prison sentence of five years while slaves were to be castrated. North and South Carolina did not make racial distinctions. White and black men who had carnal knowledge of white girls would be condemned to death (Clinton & Gillespie, 1997, p. 77).

The allegation that black males were prone to rape white females is a rape myth that originated after emancipation of the slaves in the mid-19th century. Following emancipation and until about 1960, black men were subject to extralegal murders called lynchings, allegedly for the rape of white women, but often without formal rape charges and always without a court conviction. Determined to end these brutal killings, African American investigative journalist Ida B. Wells combed through newspaper accounts, visited death sites, and interviewed witnesses to determine that most lynchings could be credited to economic competition and racial control rather than a defense of southern white womanhood. In 1892, she published an editorial that revealed that most "rapes" were in fact often consensual liaisons between black men and white women. In that same year, she published *Southern Horrors*, with the pamphlet's title mocking Southern honor as the commonly cited justification for lynching. Wells documented that only a third of the 728 lynching victims between 1884 and 1892 were even accused of rape.

Sexual Assault in the 20th Century

The 20th century brought tremendous changes in every aspect of the laws concerning rape, but these improvements came largely in the last third of the century. The law gradually became more respectful toward women, making it somewhat easier for women to charge rape, to appear in court, and to obtain a conviction. A scientific approach to the collection of evidence, especially the introduction of rape kits and the use of DNA, resulted in higher rates of conviction for rapists. The public eventually condemned marital rape, acknowledged the existence of acquaintance rape, accepted that not all force involved a gun or knife, and generally displayed more kindness towards the victims of rape.

In the first half of the 20th century, rape continued to be seen from the perspective of the perpetrator rather than the victim. Psychology developed as a field only in the 20th century but it had a great impact upon criminology. The view of the pioneering

Austrian psychologist Sigmund Freud heavily influenced legal and public attitudes toward rape. Freud and his followers defined rape as the action of a mentally ill individual with uncontrollable sexual drives. Rapists were sick men who needed sympathy along with psychological treatment. The victims of rapists were essentially forgotten.

However, this sympathetic view of rapists extended only to white attackers. With respect to race, the myth of the black rapist continued to thrive as it was fed by some notorious media portrayals such as D. W. Griffith's blockbuster silent film *Birth of a Nation* in 1915. The case of the Scottsboro Boys illustrates the continuing challenges faced by black men with respect to rape. In 1931, two young white women charged with rape a group of nine African American youths traveling illegally on a train. The youths, who ranged in age from 12 to 20, were arrested in Scottsboro, Alabama, and 8 were subsequently convicted. The youngest boy received a mistrial because of his age. The other boys received death sentences. The case became a cause célèbre as northern newspapers and activists described it as a legal lynching. The U.S. Supreme Court overturned the convictions in 1932. A year later, one of the women recanted her testimony, claiming that she and her friend had fabricated the charges in an effort to escape being arrested for vagrancy. After a series of trials, the state of Alabama dropped charges against the four youngest defendants—Leroy Wright, Montgomery, Roberson, and Williams. The others received prison sentences of varying lengths, with the last released in 1950. In 1976, Alabama Governor George Wallace pardoned all of the Scottsboro Boys.

Until legal reforms of the 1970s, most states had laws that required corroboration, or independent evidence, of rape claims before a case could be tried. As the Scottsboro Boys case illustrates, this burden did not always apply to white women charging black men but it did apply to the majority of rape cases. Many state laws required judges to instruct juries that rape charges were easy to make and hard to prove, no matter how innocent the accused. All states exempted husbands from rape charges and, in practice, this exemption was extended to the boyfriends of sexual assault victims. Women who brought rape complaints found their own sex lives scrutinized for signs that they had been sexually active prior to the rape; those who had not remained pure could not expect prosecutors to move forward with rape charges or juries to convict. Even if such cases went to trial, victims could expect defense attorneys to present evidence of their previous sexual experiences, creating the impression that a woman who has said "yes" to sex would never say "no" again. Rape trials typically focused more attention on the victim than the alleged assailant.

Changes in the perception of rape were fueled by social and cultural changes. In 1964, while 38 witnesses ignored her screams for help, Kitty Genovese was raped and stabbed to death in New York City by Winston Moseley, a married business-machine operator with no criminal record. The case became symbolic of the refusal of Americans to get involved. It also reflected the increasing fears of Americans about crime. Genovese's neighbors were afraid of being attacked by the thug, but the public condemned them because anyone could have been Genovese. As the crime rate skyrocketed in the 1960s and 1970s, criminals received less and less sympathy. Audiences who watched Charles Bronson in the 1974 film *Death Wish* cheered as his vigilante character shot muggers and rapists. Meanwhile, women influenced by the rise of feminist movement began to speak out about their experiences with rape.

The antirape movement of the 1970s challenged common knowledge about rape. The movement grew out of the feminist mobilization of the 1960s that challenged sexism and discrimination against women in all aspects of society. Based on the testimonies of victims themselves instead of psychological research or racist stereotypes, the antirape movement redefined the crime from the victim's point of view . In rape speakouts and Take Back the Night marches, victims dispelled many of the myths that had surrounded rape. Women did not ask for rape by the way that they dressed or behaved. No one sought to become the victim of a violent crime.

Rape, as the feminists of the 1960s and 1970s stressed, is not a crime of sexuality and passion but one of violence and control. Antirape activists, such as author Susan Brownmiller, lobbied to enact such reforms as the rape shield law, which limited the evidence of a victim's sexual past that could be admitted at trial. The movement also sought to remove the marital exemption for rape, to develop a degree structure for rape, and to remove evidentiary roadblocks to prosecution such as corroboration requirements. All of these initiatives were an attempt to create victim-friendly rape laws that would force the legal system to take sexual assault seriously. As a result of these efforts, all of the

50 states have reformed their laws pertaining to sexual crime. The federal government has even enacted legislation to protect victims of rape, such as the 1996 Drug-Induced Rape Prevention and Punishment Act that makes a certain type of rape into a federal crime worthy of 20 years imprisonment.

Sexual Assault Myths

Despite the successes of the antirape movement, common myths about sexual assault still abound. These myths punish the victims for being victims and permit sexual criminals to continue their activities. Such myths make victims reluctant to seek treatment, to prosecute, and to take other steps to recover. These myths, most of which are age-old, are not as powerful as they were only a few decades ago but they still remain in the public consciousness.

Myth: Sexual assault results from uncontrollable sexual desire.

Fact: Rape is a crime of power. It is an act of aggression that uses sexuality as a weapon to unleash anger, to control, degrade, humiliate, and otherwise harm the victim. Sex is not the primary desire in a sexual assault.

Myth: Rape usually involves an attack by a black male upon a white victim.

Fact: Most crimes occur within racial boundaries with whites preying upon whites and blacks playing upon blacks. Black men usually rape black women, Latino men rape Latina women, and white men rape white women.

Myth: Most rapes occur at night in deserted areas such as parking garages, dark alleys, and parks.

Fact: Most rapes are acquaintance or date rapes. These attacks occur in the home of the victim, with homes of friends of the victim and cars as other popular locations for sexual assaults.

Myth: If a man spends a lot of money on a woman or a woman changes her mind after beginning foreplay, the man has the right to some form of sexual intercourse.

Fact: A man cannot buy a woman's sexual services without her consent. Most women are not prostitutes. Sexual relations without consent constitute a crime. The woman has the right to say "no."

Myth: If no semen is present, no sexual assault took place.

Fact: Sexual assaults may involve inanimate objects, such as bottles. Studies of convicted rapists have also found that many experience sexual dysfunction in the form of impotence, premature ejaculation, or retarded ejaculation, thus accounting for a lack of semen on the victims. In cases where an assault was disrupted by external factors or victim resistance prior to ejaculation by the rapist, semen is not present.

Myth: Most rapes are committed by strangers.

Fact: Most victims know their assailant. The most common estimate is that about 80 percent of all sexual assailants are known to the victim.

Myth: A husband cannot be found guilty of raping his wife.

Fact: By 1993, all 50 states had removed the "spousal exemption" from their legal statutes on rape and sexual assault. A husband can be convicted of sexually assaulting his wife.

Myth: Rapists do not look like normal people.

Fact: As the scandal about sexually abusive priests in the Catholic Church demonstrates, sexual criminals can appear to be respectable citizens. Rapists come from all walks of life, including firefighters, police officers, teachers, nurses, and ministers. Rapists are also all ages, from 10-year-old boys to elderly males.

Myth: A rapist is starved for sex.

Fact: Sexual assault is not a crime of passion. The majority of convicted rapists have had regular sexual outlets, in the form of spouse, girlfriend, or significant other. They attacked for the emotional gratification of committing an act of violence.

Myth: A rapist cannot control his sexual desires.

Fact: Rape is most often a premeditated crime. It is an act of aggression and sexual violence, not an expression of sexual desire.

Myth: No woman can be raped against her will. It is physically impossible to rape a woman against her will.

Fact: Rape is a physical assault. Anyone can be physically assaulted. Any person, male or female, can be intimidated into submission by a weapon or a threat.

Myth: Rape only happens to young, sexually attractive women who put themselves in dangerous situations.

Fact: Infants, nuns, and elderly women have been sexually assaulted. Victims of sexual attacks come from all ages, races, classes, ethnic groups, sexual orientations, and religious persuasions. Rape victims are of all physical descriptions. Victims are chosen for their vulnerability.

Myth: Women who are sexually assaulted asked for it by dressing provocatively or walking on the street without a male protector.

Fact: Victims of muggings and other types of assault are generally not accused of asking for it. Victims of sexual assaults are no different. No one asks to suffer an attack that can leave lifelong psychological and physical injuries. Such an assumption removes responsibility from the criminal who planned and carried out an attack.

Myth: A male cannot be raped.

Fact: Men can be raped but they are even more reluctant than women to report such attacks. While it is estimated that between 50 and 90 percent of female rapes are never reported, there is no estimate for attacks upon males. Numerous studies have indicated that between one in five and one in seven males have been sexually abused by their 18th birthday.

Myth: A woman cannot become pregnant from a rape unless she enjoys it.

Fact: In the female body, an orgasm is not required for conception to occur. Additionally, while orgasms by victims during sexual attacks are rare, such responses are physiological events rather than an expression of pleasure. Direct stimulation of the genital area can produce a physical response. There have also been cases of heterosexual males who had an unwanted orgasm as the result of the assailant masturbating them. There have also been cases of male children who got and maintained an erection as the result of adrenaline during the stress and fear of a sexual attack.

Sexual Crime Categories

There are as many different categories of sexual assault as there are types of victims and types of perpetrators. Some of the categories overlap, with serial rapists, as one example, known to have preyed near college campuses.

Campus Rape

Campus rape is a sexual assault that is associated in some way with a college or university. The victim or perpetrator is usually a student, with the attack occurring on or near campus. Accurate statistics about campus rape are hard to obtain, because many women and men do not report such assaults. Campus rape is underreported for several reasons. Many victims appear to believe that they are at fault for the attack, perhaps because they were consuming alcohol. Many women do not report their assaults for fear that they will be subjected to further pain and humiliation at the hands of the college authorities or police. They fear that authorities will not take their assault seriously or will consider them to be responsible for the attack. Additionally, some students do not report rapes because they do not want their parents to know, while others do not even realize that a lack of consent always constitutes rape.

Colleges and universities have used a variety of strategies to address and prevent campus rape. Many schools have created clear policies about unacceptable sexual behavior that include strict penalties. All members of the campus community, including faculty and staff, have been educated about the policies. Acknowledging that most campus rapes are not stranger rapes, many students receive acquaintance rape education both at first-year orientation and throughout their college careers. Men are educated about what constitutes rape and the importance of verbal consent.

Child Rape

Children have traditionally been viewed as innocent beings in need of special protection. One way in which societies have tried to protect young girls is through laws that designate a statutory age of consent. Such laws prohibit men from having sexual contact with females under a specified age on the legal theory that they are too young and immature to make informed decisions and, therefore, are incapable of giving a legal consent. Historically, the age of consent was set somewhere between 10 and 13 years, depending on the era and the culture, and tending to coincide with female puberty. In the modern United States, the age of consent ranges from 14 to 18 years with 16 years as the standard. Child rape laws punished men who had sexual relations with females younger than the designated age of consent on par with the crime of rape, even if the girl consented and the man used no force.

Historically, male youths have been seen as far less likely to need protection as girls. However, sodomy laws were often used to punish the adult participant in homosexual activities while not holding the male minor criminally liable.

Date Rape/Acquaintance Rape

Acquaintance rape is most broadly defined as any situation in which the requisite elements of the crime of rape are satisfied and the victim and attacker know each other. This prior relationship between the parties—which can range in degree of familiarity from fellow classmates who have never spoken to one another to a couple involved in a long-term relationship—is the only difference between acquaintance rape and stranger rape.

Date rape is a form of acquaintance rape, though the two phrases are often used interchangeably. Date rape refers to a rape scenario in which there is some sort of romantic relationship between the two parties. Date rape is a particular problem on college campuses, where it frequently occurs in situations involving alcohol or date rape drugs, such as ketamine or "Special K" and gammahydroxybutyrate or GHB.

Acquaintance rapes are rarely reported to the authorities. If victims do report these assaults, rape is most likely to be charged and tried only when the following conditions are met: a prompt report to the police, the existence of witnesses who can testify to similar crimes committed by the suspect, physical injury to the survivor, and corroboration of the individual's story. This differential treatment of survivors of acquaintance rape has been documented by a number of researchers studying different aspects of the criminal justice system. The thoroughness of a police investigation, the choice of whether or not to prosecute a charge, the likelihood that the defendant will be convicted, and the likelihood of incarceration have all been shown to vary significantly along acquaintance rape/stranger rape lines.

Forcible Rape

Forcible rape is the sexual knowledge of a male or female against his or her will. The question of force is problematic because the threat of harm is strong enough to frighten the victim into acceding without physical resistance. The definitions of "force" and "without consent" are fuzzy because legal statutes vary. Force can be used at any stage in a rape, from a logistical advantage such as ambush to overt aggression if a perpetrator does not obtain verbal consent.

Foreign-Object Rape

Foreign-object rape refers to the placement of an object into the vaginal, rectal, oral or other orifice of an individual. The object appears to represent a virile penis for the perpetrator who would otherwise be impotent. Raping with objects further humiliates the victim while amplifying the power of the attacker. The choice of object could be opportunistic or symbolic. If the rape is followed by murder, the object, as part of the crime scene, can provide information about the perpetrator.

A variety of legal definitions abound in the United States with regard to foreign-object rape. In New York State, digital rape (using a finger) is included in the foreign-object category. In Pennsylvania, foreign-object rape is considered deviate sexual intercourse. In Georgia, foreign-object rape is classified as "aggravated sexual battery" (Smith, 2004, p. 79).

Statistics about foreign-object rape are difficult to obtain. In one study done on 30 men classified as sexual sadists, foreign-object penetration was the least common sexual activity of the four studied (anal, forced fellatio, vaginal, and foreign-object). However, the majority of the men subjected their victims to three of the four acts (Smith, 2004, p. 80). The decision a victim makes to report a rape with a foreign object is difficult to make, just as reporting other types of rape varies with the victim's motivation to undergo the stresses involved in the legal process.

Gang Rape

Gang rape involves two or more assailants. Gang rapes are a frequent occurrence in wars and with gangs. They are used as a method of punishment, social control, bonding, and as rite of passage. They also increase the ties among the assailants. Gang rapists do not necessarily always commit an assault with any of these consequences in mind, and it is important to distinguish the act of violence and the conscious goals from the resultant effect for all involved. The intentions of each individual rapist may vary. In some cases, the attack is the result of a group decision. In other cases, the assault is initiated by the leader or small group of those involved. Sometimes, it is crime of opportunity, while in other cases the victim has been sought out. Some victims, particularly those involved with gangs, participate willingly while others are coerced.

Gang rapes are even more difficult to prosecute than rapes involving only one assailant, but successful prosecutions will usually result in a harsher punishment. Assailants may provide alibis for each other or offer differing versions of events, making it hard for the authorities. Victims of such attacks are often reluctant to report it because they fear reprisal from more than one person. When gang rape is a form of initiation for either an assailant or victim, silence is the price of inclusion.

Homosexual Rape

Homosexual rape refers to coerced, nonconsensual sex between members of the same sex. This term has been used mistakenly to describe the sexual orientation of either the perpetrator or the victim. This is particularly the case for male rape, when a male attacker is labeled homosexual because of the homosexual nature of the act. Studies have shown that heterosexual men, not homosexual men, generally rape men. Rape is not a sexual crime but a crime designed to diminish the victim.

One of the reasons that homosexual rape has been harder to study and understand is that traditional definitions of rape do not easily lend themselves to same-sex situations. By defining rape as a sexual act between people without freely given consent, legal systems can better address the range of sexual experiences that mark individual lives. Research into the causes, occurrence, and consequences of homosexual rape is minimal, but early findings have raised critical questions about the complex relationship between power, violence, gender roles, and sexuality.

Woman-to-woman sexual assault among strangers is still largely undocumented. That women can and do rape each other has been hard for many to believe. In a heterocentric, phallocentric society, even defining what constitutes sexual relations between two women has been widely misunderstood outside of the lesbian community. The homosexual rape between women that is documented often occurs within a lesbian relationship. Homophobia, misinformation about lesbian sex, and disbelief that women hurt other women in relationships all contribute to the general silence that characterizes this issue. Domestic violence and rape crisis centers rarely provide the support and information needed by female survivors of homosexual rape, perpetrating their isolation and confusion.

Stranger rape among men is more common and better documented. Throughout American history, forced sex between men has been characterized as sodomy but not rape. Early studies of male-on-male rape employed a similar model of analysis as that developed by feminists studying rape of women by men: Rape is about exerting power, not about sexual desire. Following this, it was held that rape between men was predominantly by heterosexual men against homosexual men. Gay men who cruise public places looking for casual sex partners are more susceptible to these kinds of attacks. One reason for the predominance of stranger rape over acquaintance rape between men was the focus of early studies—prisons, military settings, and other single-sexed but not explicitly gay situations. More recent studies which focused on men in the gay community reveal a higher rate of rape between gay men than was previously thought. Male rape is dramatically underreported, by gay and straight men alike. Gay men often expect that they will be blamed for being raped, or worse yet, accused of enjoying it. Studies confirm that when the victim of male rape is homosexual, he is more likely to be blamed for the encounter than a heterosexual man in the same situation.

Incest

Incest is the sexual abuse and rape of a child by a family member. While many forms of incest undoubtedly exist, by far the most common is the assault of a daughter by a father. Although incest has probably existed since ancient times, the definition of incest and the social reactions to it have changed markedly over time. Many historians believe that the modern definition of incest only emerged in the 19th century, as conceptions of childhood and adolescence changed and as the government increasingly intervened in family life.

Incestuous activities were rarely pursued by early American authorities because of reluctance to interfere with paternal authority. Cases came to the attention of authorities because the victims had become pregnant by their fathers, stepfathers, or uncles. Once in court, the law was not on the victim's side. Judges did not comprehend the helplessness of the incest victim, who was caught between devotion to a parent or guardian and the blatant disregard for the child's well-being. Preindustrial science claimed that a female could only become pregnant after achieving orgasm, and thus pregnancy was for the judges a sign of consensual sex. A failure to immediately report the incident also was received skeptically by the judges. Sentences for those men convicted were generally light.

Most historians note a dramatic shift in society's reaction to incest between 1880 and 1920, during the Progressive Era. Although scholars cannot measure changes in incest activity itself, they argue that a more concerted effort was underway to protect children from sexual crimes. American culture began to emphasize the innocence of childhood, with many Americans working to protect children from social evils. Governments became concerned about future generations of citizens. Reformers, such as the New York Society for the Prevention of Cruelty to Children, lobbied governments for child protection laws and established networks of inspectors and caseworkers alongside the police force. Reformers sought, above all, to protect the morality of young girls, believing that social problems resulted from crimes committed against girls that ruined their sexual virtue.

In the last three decades of the 20th century, awareness of incest increased dramatically. Feminist groups spoke out against family violence while a number of television shows and novels broached the subject. As a result, incest accusations climbed astronomically among all socioeconomic levels and ethnic groups. Anecdotal evidence suggests that some of the increase can be attributed to divorcing parents lobbying charges in the midst of ugly child custody battles. Since the 1990s, psychiatrists and psychologists have helped victims recall earlier crimes committed against them that they had expunged from their memories because of the trauma involved. Such remembered memories, however, have been hotly disputed in the courts as being inaccurate and the result of suggestion.

Interracial Rape

The term "interracial rape" refers to cases of rape that involve perpetrators and victims of different racial or ethnic descent. While interracial rape is statistically known to be the exception, not the rule, the term clearly underscores that discussion of sexual crime is highly racialized. The predominant view of the rapist as black or ethnic "other" who attacks white women has not only tended to draw attention away from cases of sexual assault involving white middle- and upper-class perpetrators. It has also pushed African American female rape victims out of public view. Black-on-black sexual violence is the most common form of sexual attack for black rapists.

Marital Rape

In the United States, wives were long viewed as the property of their husbands under the concept of coverture, meaning that a woman was legally "covered" by her husband when she married. Thereafter, she ceased to have a separate legal existence. Since a wife was owned by her husband, he had inherent rights to her body. In most states, a husband could beat his wife with impunity. He also had the right to forced sexual relations.

In 1975, John Rideout became the first man to be charged with raping his wife while he was still living with her. According to his wife Greta, Rideout was addicted to violent sex, which he frequently demanded several times a day. In October 1975, Greta Rideout fled from her abusive husband, but John followed her.

He locked her in their apartment and beat her until she agreed to have sex with him. After Rideout was acquitted of the rape charge, the couple reconciled but later divorced. Much criticism was directed at Greta Rideout throughout the trial, with observers frequently arguing that she could not have returned to the marriage if she had truly been raped. Studies on marital rape show that most wives who are raped are also battered, as was the case with Greta Rideout.

By 1993, all 50 states and the federal government defined marital rape as a crime punishable by law. In most states, married women who are raped by their husbands also have the right to bring civil suit and may recover medical and legal expenses, as well as damages for pain and suffering.

Prison Rape

While incarcerated in detention facilities, men, women, and youths can be subjected to sexual harassment, sexual brutality, and rape. Rape within a prison setting can happen through multiple combinations of circumstances and perpetrators. Prison rapes can be prisoner-on-prisoner, in which either a single individual or a gang of individuals is responsible for the rape of another inmate. In addition, prison staff may sexually abuse individuals under their control.

Although anyone can become a victim of sexual abuse, prisoners with mental disabilities or small size or male prisoners with characteristics perceived as feminine are major targets for sexual violence in prison. Among male and female prisoners, often the newest inmates who may have yet to form the protection of gangs, who are younger or who are lacking other resources for defense, become those prisoners facing the most potential risk for sexual victimization.

Secondary Rape

"Secondary rape" is the term used to describe the process of investigation that agencies, institutions, or individuals perform when questioning a rape victim. It is considered secondary rape because the experience has the same characteristics of the primary or original rape: it exerts power, it is invasive, it is destructive of privacy, and it denies the victim of a sexual crime control over his or her own body. For these reasons, some women also use the term secondary rape to describe being forced to give birth after conceiving from a rape.

An example of secondary rape occurs when police question the victim in a way that treats him or her as a perpetrator rather than a person who was injured. Officers might use language that casts doubt on the victim's complaint, is accusatory, or insinuates that the victim did something to instigate and cause the rape. Women of color, poor women, or women viewed as promiscuous are often not believed.

During the processing of the sexual crime, the victim goes through many stages of secondary rape. She or he is questioned and subjected to inspection and photography of the body parts that were penetrated, touched, injured, or covered with semen or other body fluids. The bright lights and awkward positions put the victim in the same vulnerable circumstances from a psychological point of view as the original rape, or more so. Once again the privacy and integrity of the individual is compromised and invaded. Getting evidence in a rape case results in a secondary rape for many individuals because it contains many of the elements of the primary rape.

After law enforcement and medical personnel question and obtain evidence from the victim, a period of time elapses while the legal system arranges for identification of the perpetrator and for a court hearing. During this time, the victim is urged to seek professional help in dealing with the trauma. As the event fades from the present, healing begins to take place. However, since the law requires the victim to testify against his or her attacker, the shock of going to court and reliving the crime may reawaken the profound psychological distress. The victim is forced to undergo the rape again, this time in public.

Serial Rape and Serial Rapists

Serial rape, a type of criminal offense that only became recognized by the general public in the 1970s, involves sexual attacks upon 10 or more stranger victims. The reluctance of victims to report rapes and the absence of effective police procedures may mean that this type of rape is an old phenomenon only recently identified. Stylized verbal scripts demanded from the stranger victim, sadistic or violent behavior, the rapist's inability to penetrate his victim or to climax, and the collection of souvenirs, are all marks of serial attacks.

The few studies conducted upon serial rapists show that these men, particularly the most violent ones, are usually white males of European ancestry who target white females. Black serial rapists, by contrast, are known to cross color lines. The majority of offenders enjoy stable employment, live with someone, and have been married at least once. Significant numbers of these men experienced troubled childhoods, with many reporting juvenile alcohol abuse, cruelty to animals, fire setting, stealing, and assaults against adults. A majority of rapists, 68 percent, began their sexual predation as voyeurs. (Smith, 2004, p. 221).

The Federal Bureau of Investigation (FBI) has used interviews with serial rapists to group this type of offender into four camps: power-reassurance, power-assertive, anger-retaliatory, and anger-excitation. All of the men in the categories share a psychosexual trait that drives them to repeatedly attack. Unable to match reality to their sexual fantasies, the men feel the need to try again, thereby creating a process that results in serial sex crime. The pattern of behavior of serial rapists is similar to that of serial killers, since many murderers begin their criminal careers as rapists and often intersperse murders with non-lethal sexual assaults (Rossmo, 2000, p. 54).

The power-reassurance attacker is the most common type of serial rapist. Often referred to as the gentleman rapist, he bolsters his masculinity through the exercise of power over women. Victims are preselected through surveillance or peeping activities, surprised, and usually attacked in the evening or early morning. The rapist may have several potential victims, all in the same vicinity, lined up. If one potential assault is foiled, the rapist will often seek another victim nearby on the same night. He will take souvenirs from his victims and keep a record of his crimes.

The power-assertive rapist, the second most common type of serial rapist, uses his attacks to express his natural dominance over women. Unlike the power-reassurance rapist, this rapist is regarded as a selfish offender who is unconcerned over the welfare of his victim. He will often use a con approach and then force the victim to engage in repeated sexual assaults. The victim is often left in a state of partial nudity at the assault location, which will be a place of convenience and safety for the offender.

The anger-retaliatory rapist is motivated by feelings of rage and retaliation: he wants to get even with women. The victims are symbols of someone else, often exhibiting certain appearance, dress, or occupational similarities. Sex is used to punish and degrade and the attacks are typically frenzied with excessive levels of force. Since the attacks occur as the result of an emotional outburst, they lack premeditation. There is little planning or advance victim selection. The attacks are sporadic and can occur at any time of the day or night.

The anger-excitation rapist, the least common type, achieves sexual excitement from observing the victim's reaction to physical or psychological pain. The rapes, characterized by fear and brutality, may involve torture. The offender uses a con approach, attacks and binds the victim, and then takes her to a preselected location that offers privacy. He will usually keep her for a period of time and may make a visual or audio record of his activities.

Contrary to public perception, most serial rapes occur in the homes of the victims. According to FBI researchers, only six percent of rapes occur in streets or alleys, with another six percent of victims attacked in parking lots or on highways. Serial rapists are more likely to attack in the summer in neighborhoods characterized by ethnic diversity, high population turnover, and multiple unit dwellings.

The study of serial rape is still in its infancy. Difficulty in recognizing the presence of a serial rapist and difficulty in capturing such an attacker have resulted in a lack of knowledge about such predators.

Statutory Rape

Statutory rape is sexual intercourse with an unmarried individual who is under the age of consent. As the crime rests solely on the age of the victim, force is not required. The laws are supposed to protect youths from engaging in potentially coercive sex, which may not be recognized as meeting a legal definition or popular perception of forcible rape, before they are physically or emotionally ready. As such, these laws are often used to prosecute the sexual abuse of young children and teenagers. The wording of the legislation also allows the prosecution of consensual sexual relationships between any underage person and any other person if they are not married to each other.

The implementation of statutory rape laws sometimes undercuts their stated purpose of protecting the young and vulnerable. If someone underage is married, his or her sexual activity is not illegal regardless of the character of the relationship. Furthermore, some states still retain the "mistake of age" defense, so that young people who appear older or who try to act older are outside the law's protection. Additionally, some states still allow the prosecution of a perpetrator, always a male, who is the same age as or younger than the victim. An underage participant cannot stop a prosecution by claiming that the he or she regarded the activity as consensual. Males in committed relationships with underage females may have to register as sex offenders and thus be barred from seeing their partners, approaching places where their own children gather, and living in certain areas.

Conclusion

The difficulties in halting sexual crime are rooted in historical views of sexuality and complicated by enduring myths about sexual assault. Until the public is better educated about sexual crimes, such attacks will continue to be common and victims will continue to be victimized.

Further Reading

Bevacqua, Maria. *Rape on the Public Agenda: Feminism and the Politics of Sexual Assault.* Boston: Northeastern University Press, 2000.

Block, Sharon. *Rape and Sexual Power in Early America.* Chapel Hill: University of North Carolina Press, 2006.

Brownmiller, Susan. *Against Our Will: Men, Women, and Rape.* New York: Simon and Schuster, 1975.

Carter, Dan T. *Scottsboro: A Tragedy of the American South.* Baton Rouge: Louisiana State University Press, 1979.

Clinton, Catherine, and Michele Gillespie, eds. *The Devil's Lane: Sex and Race in the Early South.* New York: Oxford University Press, 1997.

Estrich, Susan. *Real Rape: How the Legal System Victimizes Women Who Say No.* Cambridge, MA: Harvard University Press, 1987.

Foster, Thomas A. *Sex and the Eighteenth-Century Man: Massachusetts and the History of Sexuality in America.* Boston: Beacon Press, 2006.

Godbeer, Richard. *Sexual Revolution in Early America.* Baltimore: Johns Hopkins University Press, 2002.

Herrup, Cynthia B. *A House in Gross Disorder: Sex, Law and the Second Earl of Castlehaven.* New York: Oxford University Press, 1999.

Koehler, Lyle. *A Search for Power: The Weaker Sex in Seventeenth-Century New England.* Urbana: University of Illinois Press, 1980.

Lockridge, Kenneth A. *The Diary, and Life, of William Byrd II of Virginia, 1674–1744.* Chapel Hill: University of North Carolina Press, 1987.

McMullen, Richie J. *Male Rape: Breaking the Silence on the Last Taboo.* Boston: Gay Men's Press, 1990.

Parrot, Andrea, and Laurie Bechhofer, eds. *Acquaintance Rape: The Hidden Crime.* New York: John Wiley, 1991.

Rosenthal, A. M. *Thirty-Eight Witnesses: The Kitty Genovese Case.* Berkeley: University of California Press, 1999.

Rossmo, D. Kim. *Geographic Profiling.* Boca Raton, FL: CRC Press, 2000.

Smith, Merril D., ed. *Encyclopedia of Rape.* Westport, CT: Greenwood Press, 2004.

Somerville, Diane. *Rape and Race in the Nineteenth-Century South.* Chapel Hill: University of North Carolina Press, 2004.

Taylor, Timothy. *The Buried Soul: How Humans Invented Death.* Boston: Beacon Press, 2002.

Ulrich, Laurel Thatcher. *A Midwife's Tale: The Life of Martha Ballard, Based on Her Diary, 1785–1812.* New York: Vintage, 1991.

Wells, Ida B. *Southern Horrors and Other Writings: The Anti-Lynching Campaign of Ida B. Wells, 1892–1900.* Edited by Jacqueline Jones Royster. Boston: Bedford Books, 1997.

2

Issues, Controversies, and Problems

The U.S. Department of Justice estimates that more than 270,000 men, women, and children are the victims of sex crimes each year. Many victims do not report the crimes. Many attackers do not believe that they have committed crimes. The response of the criminal justice system to sex crimes has historically been poor. Every step in a sexual attack and the responses to the attack trigger debate. This chapter examines issues, controversies, and problems that surround victims, attackers, the period after the attack, law enforcement, the judicial system, and the correctional system.

Victims

At the most basic level, confusion exists over rape. Contrary to the popular belief that many women are eager to embrace the identity of rape victim for the sympathy that it purportedly brings, many rape victims do not label their experience as a rape. The phenomenon, known as unacknowledged rape, has clear ramifications in the underreporting of sexual attacks and the resulting inability to deter attackers from repeating their behavior.

Rape Myth Acceptance

Common rape myths can be found in chapter one. Many women do not report rapes for the main reason that they believe these myths about rape. Zoë D. Peterson and C. L. Muehlenhard (2004), writing in the journal *Sex Roles*, report that many women believe that rape must involve fighting back and that rape can only involve the insertion of a penis into a vagina. If nonconsensual behavior does not include these two events, then it is not rape. Barrie Bondurant (2001) reached the same conclusion as Peterson. She found that college women were more likely to acknowledge rape if the incident involved violence, a blitz attack rather than an acquaintance assault. Women did not blame themselves for inviting the attack. Rather, they displayed a very low amount of self-blame.

Women do seem to have abandoned the once-popular myths that women invite rape by dressing provocatively, flirting, or behaving in some inappropriate manner with a man. The attitude of women may reflect decades of feminist lobbying that a woman should not be blamed for being a victim of rape any more than a man should be blamed for being the victim of an armed robbery. Robin Warshaw (1988) spoke with a middle-aged woman for her book, *I Never Called It Rape: The Ms. Report on Recognizing, Fighting, and Surviving Date and Acquaintance Rape,* who had once accepted rape myths and paid dearly for her mistake. Ruth married the man who raped her on their second date after she had passed out from too much drinking. She related to Warshaw, "In my naivete, I thought that he truly did care for me and I blamed myself for what happened. I wish I had known about date rape then; maybe I wouldn't have felt like I was such a tramp, that it was my fault . . . We were married for 10 years. I found out after the divorce that he had tried this [getting a woman drunk and then trying to rape her] on both of my sisters too" (Warshaw, 1988, p. 44). Date rape only became the focus on considerable public attention in the 1980s, long after such knowledge would have benefited Ruth.

The woman who is most likely to be raped is not the woman who dresses suggestively or flirts. The most likely rape victim is the woman who drinks. According to the research, such women commonly underestimate their risk of being sexually assaulted. They view themselves as more competent to resist rape than they are in reality. In a 1991 interview with the *Washington Post*, Sybil R. Todd, who worked with victims of date rape in her capacity as the associate dean of students at the University of Virginia, stated that alcohol has been involved "in every instance" of date rape on campus. "I don't know of any [date rapes] that involved hallucinogens," she added.

The fact that alcohol is a legal drug may mask its dangers. People who know that methamphetamine or cocaine use is dangerous may not fully realize that alcohol use can also significantly damage their lives. In fact, according to the Injury Prevention Network Newsletter in 1992, alcohol is associated with almost every cause of serious injury, including "fires, drownings, falls, shootings, homicide, suicide, child abuse, rape and battery." A 1994 study by the Columbia University Center on Addiction and Substance Abuse concluded that that 90 percent of all reported campus rapes occurred when alcohol had been used by either the assailant, the victim, or both. In addition, 60 percent of college women with sexually transmitted diseases, like herpes or AIDS, were drunk at the time of infection.

As many women as men are reported to be problem drinkers, who drink to get drunk. Psychologists Jenna McCauley and Karen S. Calhoun (2008), who examined the effects of binge drinking upon college women in a 2008 essay for the journal *Addictive Behaviors*, suggest that women should be made explicitly aware of alcohol's impact on their rape resistance ability. Pepper spray and mace are not as effective in preventing rape as remaining sober.

Who Is Likely to Be Raped?

The likelihood of becoming a victim of sexual assault is greater for nonwhites than whites. According to the 2000 National Violence Against Women Survey, 34 percent of Native American women reported being raped in their lifetimes versus 18 percent of white women. Amnesty International reported on the incidence of rape and sexual violence among American Indian and Native Alaskan women in 2007. In Anchorage, Alaska, such women were 10 times more likely to be attacked than women of other races. Alaska has the highest per capita rate of rape. Overall, Amnesty International found that American Indian women are three-and-a-half times more likely to suffer sexual assault than white, black, Latina, or Asian women.

Why are American Indians more likely to be raped? Nicole P. Yuan (2006) and three colleagues investigated this question. In an essay for the 2006 issue of the *Journal of Interpersonal Violence*, Yuan reported that predictors of sexual assault among women were marital status, childhood maltreatment, and lifetime alcohol dependence. Separated or divorced women were more likely to be raped. The second predictor is not uncommon among victims of rape. Sexual revictimization occurs when a survivor of childhood sexual abuse or rape is victimized again in adulthood.

Alcoholism or problem drinking determines victims across all racial lines. The vast majority of Indian country crime has historically been the product of alcohol abuse. Nationally, substance abuse is closely linked with domestic violence, including marital rape. Shira Rutman and several colleagues surveyed risky behavior in urban American Indian youth from 1997 to 2003. Native Americans were twice as likely as white youths to engage in such behaviors as illegal drug use and alcohol consumption. Probably as a direct result, American Indian youths were also twice as likely to experience rape and other forms of sexual crime. Native American girls and women seem to be suffering from a trifecta of woes that, together, make them more vulnerable to sexual assault

Other personal characteristics contribute to a higher likelihood of being sexually assaulted. Ronet Bachman and Linda Saltzman (1994), in their book *Violence Against Women*, reported that women between the ages of 19 and 29 are the most likely to become victims of a sexual attack by an acquaintance or relative. Widowed women over the age of 65 are least likely to be victimized. Such attacks are not unknown though. The Philadelphia Assault Victim Study, which spanned the years 1973 to 1975, included an 84-year-old rape victim. The Center for Rape Concern at Philadelphia General Hospital assisted a 97-year-old rape victim in 1976.

While elderly women are least likely to be victimized, they may have the most difficulty in responding to an attack. Older women may have trouble talking about sex. They find even the exam needed to collect evidence of the crime "very degrading," as Tammy Taylor informed a reporter for the *St. Petersburg Times* in 2004. Taylor works as an outreach clinical supervisor and sexual assault counselor for Sunrise of Pasco, an agency that works with victims of sexual abuse. "They are from a generation that typically doesn't discuss sexual issues at all, so they feel a heightened sense of shame and embarrassment over being raped," Nancy Bell, a research psychologist explained to the *Times* reporter (*St. Petersburg Times*, May 17, 2004, p. 1B). As a result of their difficulties discussing sexual matters, elderly victims are also less likely to report the crime or to seek counseling. A rape can also take away that sense of independence that most elderly women prize dearly.

Marital status, race, and money also indicate likely victimization. Poor women are more vulnerable to sexual assault than middle class or wealthy women. Divorced or separated women are more likely than married or single women to be attacked, presumably by their estranged or former spouses. In her book *Rape in Marriage* Diana Russell (1990) declared that an estimated 14 percent to 25 percent of women experience forced sex at least once during their marriages. In the Philadelphia Assault Victim Study, three times as many African American women as white women reported being raped. Children in low-income, single-mother homes are more likely to be sexually assaulted and by people that they know. In Philadelphia, adolescents were typically raped outside the home, unlike younger and older victims.

Individuals who suffered childhood sexual abuse are more likely to be raped as adults, as psychologists Terri L. Messman-Moore (2009) and her colleagues related in their 2009 article in the *Journal of Interpersonal Violence.* Women with a childhood history of sexual abuse are 4.7 times more likely to be subsequently raped, according to a 1997 Naval Health Research Center report. The reasons for this increased risk of attack are not clear but appear to be linked to substance abuse and posttraumatic stress. People with developmental disabilities also have an increased vulnerability to sexual assault, probably because they are seen as easy marks.

Male Victims

Male rape seems to be the last taboo. Most studies of sexual assault pay no attention to male victims. Until fairly recently, many people even doubted that a male could be raped. While men are more likely than women to be victims of violent crimes, rape and domestic violence are two of the few exceptions to this likelihood.

Yet male rape is a topic that deserves greater attention than it has so far received. Studies estimate that 5 to 10 percent of reported rapes involve males, as Michael Scarce (1997) noted in his book *Male on Male Rape: The Hidden Toll of Stigma and Shame.* Many men do not report, however, making it impossible to determine accurate numbers of male rape victims.

Men and boys who are sexually assaulted are usually too ashamed to speak out, though society is not inclined to listen to them anyway. Male victims face skepticism, criticism, and disbelief, as well as a near total absence of support services. Rape centers very rarely cater to men and often show a reluctance to let them in the door since men are more often the abusers than the abused.

A case of male rape in Baton Rouge, Louisiana, in 1995 illustrates the problem of male rape. Police arrested a 58-year-old apartment complex security guard for raping an 18-year-old man after offering him a ride home from a local laundry. Instead, the guard drove the young man to parking lot and raped him at knifepoint. A police officer publicly commended the rape victim for stepping forward and reporting the crime, since male rape is probably the most underreported violent crime.

The perception that real men cannot be raped remains very strong, despite some portrayals of normal male rape victims in popular culture, such as the blockbuster movie of the early 1970s, *Deliverance*. Sandy White and Niwako Yamawaki examined the effects of homophobia on the perception of male rape victims in a 2009 essay that appeared in the *Journal of Applied Social Psychology*. Victims were assigned more blame in acquaintance rape than in stranger rape, with gay men blamed more for their sexual victimization than heterosexual victims. Gay men, apparently reflecting internalized homophobia, also tended to blame themselves for being attacked at a greater rate than heterosexual victims.

Male victims of rape tend to be in their late teens to late 20s. More African Americans than members of any other racial group report being sexually assaulted. Gay men seem to be raped in higher numbers than straight men, but there is a chance that gay men are more likely to report. As in cases of women raped by men, sexual attraction appears to have little to do with rape. It is a crime of violence. Rapists of men tend to identify as heterosexual. Virtually every study indicates that men rape other men out of anger or an attempt to overpower, humiliate, and degrade their victims. The stigma and shame associated with male rape shows that rapists often succeed in their goal.

Victims of Same-Sex Rape

Men rape men and women rape women. Such violence may take the form of date or marital rape. Gay, lesbian, bisexual, and transgendered (GLBT) victims of same-sex domestic violence often feel very isolated because of a lack of support from both the wider community and the GLBT community. Many gay, lesbian, bisexual, and transgendered people believe that if domestic violence exists within the GLBT community, it takes the form of mutual fighting and does not reflect the same power and control as heterosexual domestic abuse. Just like many straight men, many gay men believe that men are supposed to be able to defend themselves from other men's violence. Men are not supposed to be victims. Harkening back to a distant past when many people believed that two women could not have sex with each other because no penis was present, some people believe that one woman lacks the ability to rape another.

Sexual violence within same-sex relationships has been particularly difficult to acknowledge. Gay culture often holds that men are supposed to want and enjoy sex pretty much whenever it is available from someone that they are attracted to. Patrick Letellier, a rape survivor, related his story in *Same-Sex Domestic Violence: Strategies for Change.* "I called it rough sex," he wrote before adding, "Forcing himself on me. Being selfish and inconsiderate, a beast, a monster. He called it getting what he wanted. What he was entitled to . . . [I] occasionally tell a sexual partner that sex can be difficult for me because I was . . . raped. They almost always furrow their eyebrows. Gay men don't use that word when they talk about themselves" (Leventhal, 1999, p. 74).

Among women, attitudes toward butch/femme roles can lead to unintended support for the attackers. Batterers can play on the misassumption—both within and outside of the lesbian community—that butch is the same as male. A femme can abuse her butch partner by forcing sexual activity that her partner does not want. The abuser can deflect responsibility by claiming that the victim is just not butch enough. A butch woman may have her bad behavior excused as being just a part of being butch.

Attackers

Rape Myth Acceptance

The United States has a rape culture, as some antirape activists have argued, because of the wide acceptance of rape myths. Beliefs about rape allow some individuals to justify engaging in sexually aggressive behavior, including rape. Research on date rapists and "real" rapists show that the belief systems of these men foster rape. There is no significant difference between the two groups.

Both believe that women are complicit in rape and that rapists are entitled to attack.

Some attackers believe that since they do not fit the rape myths, then they are not participating in a real rape. Martha R. Burt, in a 1980 article in the *Journal of Personality and Social Psychology*, offered that adversarial sexual beliefs are tied to rape myth acceptance. Such beliefs hold that sexual relationships are fundamentally exploitative and that each party is too manipulative to be trusted. Fourteen years later, Kimberly A. Lonsway and Louise F. Fitzgerald (1994) concluded in a *Psychology of Women Quarterly* essay that negative and stereotypical attitudes toward women have been found to be associated with rape myth acceptance.

Many of the most persistent rape myths address marital rape. Men, as a whole, are more likely to minimize the seriousness of all forms of rape. Individuals of both sexes tend to minimize the seriousness of a rape perpetrated by a husband versus one committed by a stranger. Margaret Gordon and Stephanie Riger, in their 1989 book *The Female Fear*, reported that 64 percent of men and 63 percent of women surveyed did not characterize unwanted sexual assault between a husband and wife as rape. In a 1987 study for *License to Rape: Sexual Abuse of Wives*, David Finkelhor and Kersti Yllo asked people to rank the severity of 140 crimes. "Forcible rape of a former spouse" ranked at number 62, below selling marijuana and stealing $25. Abused wives have reported that their husbands thought that they could do anything to their wives—cut them, beat them, and rape them—because of the marital relationship.

In her book *Wife Rape*, Raquel Kennedy Bergen (1996) quoted two women who made the point that rape is rape, no matter who commits it. Karen said, "It was very clear to me. He ripped off my pajamas, he beat me up. I mean some scumbag down the street would do that to me. So to me it wasn't any different because I was married to him. It was rape—real clear what it was. . . . I guess I can't say I would have been more fearful with a stranger because I didn't know when he was going to stop or if he was going to kill me." Wanda, another victim of wife rape, stated, "This is a crime, no matter if your husband does this or not. Nobody has the right to drag me by my hair into the room and do that. There's such embarrassment and degradation you go through because you're a wife and some stranger didn't do" (p. 36). Researchers have tried to determine why people think the way that they do about rape.

By identifying the roots of rape myths, researchers Shelly Schaefer Hinck and Richard W. Thomas hoped to reduce the prevalence of myths such as the ones that excuse marital rape and reduce the overall rate of rapes. In 1999, Hinck and Thomas asked 158 male and female college students whether they agreed with various statements about rape. The statements included: "you cannot be raped by someone you know," "it would do some women some good to get raped," "many people secretly desired to be raped," "rape of a woman by a man she knows can be defined as 'a woman who changed her mind afterward,'" "the degree of a woman's resistance should be the major factor in determining if a rape has occurred," "rape only really occurs when a rapist has a weapon," and "if a woman says 'no' to having sex, she means 'maybe' or even 'yes.'" The results, published in the journal *Sex Roles*, indicated that specific factors such as victim blame, sex role expectation, misinformation, and communication skills all contributed to an individual's rape-supportive attitudes. Hinck and Thomas concluded that attendance at a rape prevention workshop might reduce the risk of rape by making potential rapists aware of their faulty thinking.

Student Athletes

Some subcultures seem to justify violence against women through group activities, language, practices, and rituals. These groups, which include the military, college fraternities, and male athletic teams, may foster violence against women through narrowly defined notions of masculinity that include dominance, aggression, and competitiveness. Athletes have come under particular focus by rape researchers.

There is a debate over whether an athlete is more likely to commit an act of violence than an ordinary man or whether an athlete is more likely to be reported for his bad behavior because of his celebrity status. Some studies have found that there is no difference in violent tendencies between athletes and nonathletes. Other studies, however, have found that male athletes are overrepresented among rapists on college campuses.

Such men also accept rape myths at a higher rate. Scot B. Boeringer found, in a 1999 essay for the journal *Violence Against Women*, that male college athletes responded positively to rape-supportive statements 56 percent of the time, while a control group of male students believed rape myths at only an 8 percent rate.

To explore the meaning and role of rape myths, Sarah McMahon spoke with 48 male and female student athletes. All played at a Division I school, a large public university in the Northeast. The athletes played football, soccer, lacrosse, wrestling, and volleyball as well as track. They tended to believe that female athletes were invulnerable to rape and that some women provoke rape. They misunderstood consent while believing that "accidental" rape could be falsely charged rape. The young men claimed that some women fabricated rape because of feeling vengeful or regretful in the morning. In McMahon's 2007 *Affilia* essay, "Understanding Community-Specific Rape Myths: Exploring Student Athlete Culture," she quoted one athlete: "As long as they're [women] conscious, it doesn't matter how drunk they are. . . . Unless they're drugged and unconscious, they're capable of saying 'no.' And if they don't, it's a mistake." The same young man also tried to get women drunk so that they would have sex with him. The female athletes believed that some women invite rape by their style of dress. One commented, "When we go out to parties and I see girls and the way they dress and the way they act and then how close the guys come up to them, and just the way they are under influence . . . I honestly always think it's their fault" (McMahon, 2007, p. 360, 367).

Such beliefs by the athletes justify rape and help explain why many women do not report rape. The ideas that "she was asking for it" and "she could have said no" remain strong in some subcultures. There is clearly a need for rape prevention groups to focus their educational efforts upon student athletes of both genders.

Several universities have already taken steps to reduce the potential for rape among student athletes. At the University of Arkansas, this has meant setting up workshops on date rape and making attendance mandatory for athletes. St. John's University has mandatory seminars on sexual ethics and drug and alcohol abuse for athletes and all fraternity and sorority pledges. The National Collegiate Athletic Association (NCAA), which governs college sports, has no programs addressing sexual assault, preferring leaving it up to individual institutions.

Tom Jackson, the director of the program at Arkansas, told a reporter for the *St. Petersburg Times* in 1992 that his research did not indicate that athletes commit a disproportionate number of sexual assaults. Jackson established the date rape program at his university because the lifestyle for many athletes does have potential for sexual abuse problems. The idolatry heaped on athletes and their isolation from other students on campus poses particular problems. "My goal has been to help athletes understand their special circumstances," Jackson said. "I believe there are more opportunities for male athletes to engage in various types of interaction with women, and they must be aware of the basic causes of date rape" (*St. Petersburg Times*, June 28, 1992).

Fraternities

Men in campus fraternities may not be among the individuals in need of rape education, contrary to popular belief. Fraternity men—at least the ones who remain sober—may simply be victims of erroneous assumptions.

There is considerable literature, especially in popular culture, suggesting that fraternity men are particularly likely to victimize women on college campuses. Fraternities have historically occupied a privileged place in campus social life. The isolation of fraternities may enhance their sense of entitlement that spills over into interpersonal violence against female party guests. The list of schools that have had highly publicized instances of fraternity gang rape include the University of Pennsylvania, Notre Dame, Morehead State University, and the University of Tennessee at Chattanooga.

However, Martin D. Schwartz and Carol A. Nogrady have challenged the idea that fraternity men are more likely to rape. In a 1996 essay for the journal *Violence Against Women*, they did not find evidence that fraternity men differed from their male peers in their support of rape myths. They discovered that men who drink heavily are more likely to victimize women. Schwartz and Nogrady advised that antirape efforts include alcohol education. Some studies have shown that more than half of convicted rapists were drinking at the time of their crime

Anthropologist Peggy Reeves Sanday (2007), a longtime antirape activist and author of *Fraternity Gang Rape*, offers additional support for the need for alcohol education, albeit unintentionally. Most of the cases that she profiles in her book involve excess consumption of alcohol by men who then behave badly. Sanday, who seeks to change the fraternity subculture, argues that status among the brothers depends on how many girls that a fraternity member has bedded. She also states that most of the attacks involve party settings with men plying women with drinks. It appears that drunken men rape drunken women and that rape myths excuse such behavior. Fraternity membership may be incidental to the crime.

Clergy

The notion that a man of the cloth would sexually molest a woman or child once seemed patently ridiculous. Survivors of such abuse have related tales of being punished by their parents for supposedly lying about what the priest had done. In 2002, the widespread abuse of boys by Catholic priests suddenly became public knowledge as two priests, John Geoghan and Paul Shanley, faced charges of molesting great numbers of boys. In subsequent years, the Catholic Church would deal with many more sex abuse scandals, as would every other major denomination.

Contrary to public perceptions, most victims of clergy abuse are grown women and not boys. A United Methodist Church survey found that 1 in 15 women reported to church officials that they were being abused by a clergy member. Women simply do not get media attention, with newspapers and television shows preferring to focus on the more dramatic and terrifying stories of pedophile priests.

The effect of clergy abuse on victims can be deeply traumatic. Kathryn A. Flynn related in her 2003 book, *The Sexual Abuse of Women by Members of the Clergy*, that the 25 women she interviewed were disbelieved, discredited, blamed, and ostracized by the very group that they expected to minister to them spiritually: their clergy members and congregation. As with the Roman Catholic Church before its problems became very public, all of the churches covered up the abuse.

Stranger Rape

The stereotypical image of a rapist is of some mysterious stranger who lurks in the shadows waiting to pounce on a vulnerable woman who walks by. The stereotype does not match reality. Nicole P. Yuan, who heads the Rape Prevention and Education Program (RPEP) in Arizona, also considered perpetrators of sexual crime in her essay for the *Journal of Interpersonal Violence*. Her team found that most Native American female victims of sexual assault were attacked by male relatives or romantic partners. For American Indian men who were victimized, the most common attackers were male relatives followed by strangers.

Other researchers have come to the same conclusions, albeit with other populations of people. Keith Bletzer and Mary P. Koss, in their 2006 article "After-Rape Among Three Populations in the Southwest," in *Violence Against Women,* asked low-income Southwestern Native American, Latina, and white women about their experiences of rape. Most of the women were assaulted by men that they knew, often long-term acquaintances, such as classmates, boyfriends, and cousins.

Female Sex Offenders

American society has been very reluctant to acknowledge that women can commit sex crimes. A small but significant percentage of sexual violence involves female perpetrators. In 1988, the National Center for Juvenile Justice estimated that women were responsible for eight percent of the total number of sexual offenses committed against boys and girls. In 2000, the Bureau of Justice Statistic estimated that about two percent of violent sex offenses were committed by women. These sex criminals can be the mothers, older sisters, aunts, or other relatives of the victim.

Female sex offenders exhibit several similarities when compared with male offenders. Common characteristics include secrecy, deception, manipulation of the victim, gradual escalation of sexually abusive behavior, abuse of power, social isolation, distorted thinking to justify the behavior, and the likelihood of reoffending. Female offenders may groom teenage male targets in ways that make their sexual conduct appear normal. Subtle but escalating forms of direct physical contact and of improper sexual exposure are common. The grooming process may begin with inappropriate hugs and kisses, peeping, and apparently accidental rubbing against the boy's genitals. The female sex criminal progresses to erotic talk, undressing in front of the boy, showing pornography, masturbation, and intercourse. A common tactic is for abusive women to engaging in provocative acts with the hope that the boy will make the first move. If the boy approaches the woman, she can claim that he started the affair. Such an argument convinces the boy that he is responsible for what happens next.

Women who prey upon young male victims challenge conventional thinking about gender norms. Victims of incest typically receive sympathy. Boys who engage in sexual conduct with their older stepsisters or stepmothers are not necessarily seen in a sympathetic light. Even if many people recognize that sexual molestation of boys can involve female perpetrators, this same behavior is rarely defined as abusive once these males enter puberty. Adolescent males who are having sexual relationships with an older female are not seen in an especially sympathetic light. Many people believe that there is no harm in such a relationship, which emphasizes the heterosexuality of the boy. The boys are not victims, they are lucky.

Such behavior is abusive because it fulfills the needs of the female perpetrator and not the boy victim. The power differential between the two people is also not the same. To be manipulated and used as a sexual object by a more powerful person is the very definition of abusive behavior.

Mother-daughter incest is not unknown but little has been written about it. It seems to distress people even more than attacks by pedophiles on little boys. The bond between mother and child, especially a daughter, is supposed to be sacred. When a mother sexually abuses her daughter, the relationship is a severe violation of trust.

Beverly A. Ogilvie interviewed 62 adult female survivors of mother-daughter incest for her 2004 book, *Mother-Daughter Incest: A Guide for Helping Professionals*. The survivors ranged in age from 19 to 56 and experienced anywhere from 1 to 40 years of sexual abuse. The average length of abuse was 11.5 years. Ogilvie reported that the mothers who committed incest provided their daughters with no nurturance or sense of safety. Many of the perpetrators felt that their own mothers hated them. The daughters described them as lonely, miserable, isolated, cold, insecure, inadequate, unstable, unempathetic, unable to keep friends, mean, and vindictive. Others in the community, however, viewed the mothers as good parents who kept their daughter clean and well-dressed. These mothers seemed to feel that they had to display and protect their maternal image. They also made their daughters responsible for their happiness, often turning the daughters into caregivers.

Although Ogilvie never says so, she gives the impression that she regards mother-daughter incest as the very worst form of sexual abuse and the one that is most difficult to treat. The daughter is robbed of an essential part of her identity and is left very vulnerable.

After the Attack

Providing Rape Services to Victims

Most rape victims do not obtain help for their injuries. Only about 25 percent of women who are raped seek out medical treatment, according to a study published in 2000 in the *American Journal of Preventive Medicine.* The numbers are undoubtedly lower for male victims because of the stigma of such assaults. The College of Emergency Physicians recommends that rape victims obtain medical treatment immediately and within five days at the latest. Delays can result to further harm to the victim as well as complicate any prosecution of the assailant.

It is no easy matter to report a sexual assault. The time following a sexual attack has been deemed the second rape because it can be nearly as traumatic as the rape. Insensitive medical personnel and police may blame the victim for the attack. The victim may not receive the services that will help him or her to heal both physically and psychologically. The United States is better than most countries in its provision of care but there is significant room for improvement. Several studies have illustrated the problems with institutional responses to rape.

In the wake of a rape, victims must be carefully examined to provide evidence that may result in the conviction of the attacker. Just as crucially, victims need treatment for physical and psychological injuries as well as protection against pregnancy and sexually transmitted infections such as HIV, gonorrhea, chlamydia, and syphilis. Some medical providers focus on the forensic examination to the exclusion of the health services that are needed. The forensic examination has largely been standardized in the form of a rape kit, making it easier to deliver this part of postassault treatment. While the Department of Justice and several medical societies have issued rough guidelines about medical treatment, hospitals have the leeway to develop their own procedures that are influenced by concerns about time and money.

In 2001, Rebecca Campbell led a study about the experiences of rape survivors with service providers. The findings of the Campbell group, as reported in the *Journal of Interpersonal Violence* in 2001, indicate that a majority of rape survivors did not receive necessary services from police and hospital personnel. However, they did benefit from contact with the mental health system, rape crisis centers, and religious organizations. Campbell concluded that the trauma of rape extended far beyond the assault, since rape victims were further distressed by the immediate responders.

Researchers at the John H. Stroger, Jr. Hospital in Chicago identified 10 critical services that should be provided to rape victims after an attack. In a study published in June 2008 in the journal *Contraception*, the researchers discovered that fewer than 1 in 10 hospitals in Illinois provided such help as rape crisis counseling and preventive treatment of sexually transmitted diseases. The Stroger group found that all emergency rooms provided medical care but only two-thirds offered rape crisis counseling. Only 40 percent of emergency rooms provided emergency contraception, specifically the Plan B morning-after pill. This medication is a hormone, levonorgestral, which can reduce the chance of pregnancy when taken as directed up to 72 hours after unprotected sex. The hospitals did better with treating sexually transmitted diseases, with two-thirds testing for such infections. However, less than one-third provided precautionary HIV treatment.

The Stroger findings reinforced conclusions reached in earlier studies. A study published in 2007 in the *American Journal of Health–System Pharmacy* reviewed the treatment provided to almost 180,000 victims of sexual attacks across the nation. Fewer than 10 percent of patients received the antibiotics that are necessary to protect against sexually transmitted infections. (Antibiotics have been used to treat both gonorrhea and syphilis since penicillin became widely available in 1943). A 2004 study of Pennsylvania emergency rooms, published in the *International Journal of Fertility and Women's Medicine*, revealed that less than half of hospitals routinely offered emergency contraception counseling. New Mexico enacted a law in 2003 requiring that hospital emergency departments offer emergency contraception to survivors of sexual assault. However, a subsequent study of New Mexico hospitals revealed that most were not fully complying with the law and that some medical personnel had not even heard of the law.

The reluctance to offer emergency contraception may be tied to ethical concerns. Plan B, which has been available in the

United States since 2006, works by preventing a fertilized egg from implanting in the uterus. Some people liken this process to abortion. Hospitals, especially Catholic ones, may not offer Plan B because of religious objections to both abortion and artificial means of birth control. In New Mexico, some physicians are reportedly reluctant to offer Plan B to minors without the consent of parents, although the law does not require such consent. The physicians may be confusing one law with another since New Mexico abortion law requires parental consent for a minor seeking to end a pregnancy.

Providing Help for Raped and Battered Wives

Women who are raped by their husbands have long had trouble obtaining assistance from battered women's shelters. Many, if not most, of the frontline workers at shelters make a distinction between rape and battering that does not exist in the lives of these women. Victims of marital rape are sometimes attacked after being beaten, as their husbands try to use forced sex to apologize for the beating. Other women are raped during the course of being battered.

Yet Raquel Kennedy Bergen in *Wife Rape* quotes a number of workers at battered women's shelters who do not believe that their shelters should treated raped wives. One worker saw wife rape to be a qualitatively different type of problem than wife abuse. She stated that, "I think they should go to a rape crisis center. Let them deal with it—they have counselors." Another agreed: "I feel [that] a woman who has been raped has different needs; she needs a rape kit and to get some counseling, and there are a series of things I'm sure that should be provided for them that we may not be able to provide here because we deal with victims of domestic violence." Bergen quotes a woman named Wanda who felt neglected because she had been raped but not physically battered by her husband prior to coming to a women's shelter. Wanda recalled, "I don't know if they looked at me as if my problems weren't as significant as some women who come in beat up. Maybe they thought my problem wasn't serious because I didn't come in with bruises all over me. Now [the director] said to me, 'We look at abuse as abuse,' but the rest of the staff I didn't know about." Cory told Bergen that she felt less comfortable sharing her experiences of sexual abuse with the staff because "it's easier to talk about the physical because it's more accepted and they [the staff] understand that" (Bergen, 1996, p. 84).

Mental Health

The mental health aspects of a rape are often overlooked but they can have as much of an effect upon a survivor as more visible wounds. In 1974, Ann Burgess and Larry Holmstrom coined the term "rape trauma syndrome" to describe a type of posttraumatic stress disorder that affected female survivors of sexual assault. The syndrome is divided into acute and long-term stages. In the acute period, a rape victim suffers extreme disorganization, skeletal muscle tension, gastrointestinal irritability, disturbances in the urinary tract, and a wide range of emotional reactions. The long-term phase consists of efforts by survivors to rearrange their lives. The reactions noted in this stage are increased motor activity, such as changing residences or traveling for support; disturbing dreams and nightmares, and "traumatophobia." This last ailment includes fear of the indoors if the victim was raped in her bed, fear of the outdoors if the victim was attacked outside, fear of being alone, fear of crowds, fear of people walking behind her, and/or a fear of engaging in consensual sexual activity. (There has been some criticism of characterizing the reactions of women who have been raped as a syndrome, or an aberration. Such a designation allegedly shifts the focus from the prevalence of violence against women to women's reactions to it while simultaneously implying that such fears are somehow irrational.)

The stigma that some women feel after being sexually attacked influences how they heal from a rape. Bletzer and Koss, in their 2006 *Violence Against Women* article on after-rape, found that few of the low-income Southwestern American Indian, Mexican American, and Anglo women that they interviewed reported receiving mental health services. Several of the women had never told anyone about being attacked before the researchers asked them. Some had told a friend rather than a family member within a few hours of the incident. Some had waited years, occasionally after the end of adolescence, before they notified family members. Several victims from all three groups sought to hide the rape from their family, particularly if they were teenagers and still living at home. Some of the women were ingenious in hiding soiled clothes or washing them on returning home, participating in routine activities of family life (such as watching television), or making an excuse to stay in their room. They described parental reactions on arriving home, particularly mothers, whom they avoided. This was difficult when they came home disheveled, bruised, and bleeding.

Cultural factors clearly have an impact on how women respond to a rape. The Mexican American women interviewed by Bletzer and Koss had all been born in Mexico and spent many years of their lives south of the border. They may not have been representative of all Latina women. In 2007, Heather Littleton, Carmen Radecki Breitkopf, and Abbey B. Berenson spoke with 393 low-income European American and Latina women regarding their ideas about a typical rape. The Latinas said that they would feel less stigma than the Anglo women expected that they would experience. The difference in findings emphasize that more research is needed into cultural effects upon the responses of rape victims. It also needs to be highlighted that less stigma does not necessarily mean less trauma.

Television shows frequently portray rape victims who are so traumatized by a stranger rape that they have double-bolt locks lining their front doors. Apart from their emphasis on middle-class, young, white women to the near-total neglect of minority women, these television programs significantly depart from reality with respect to posttraumatic stress.

Locks on the door do little to make women feel safer from rape since the danger comes from inside the home. The women who suffer the most trauma from rapes are the ones who are attacked by their partners. In a 2007 *Violence Against Women* essay, "Differing Effects of Partner and Nonpartner Sexual Assault on Women's Mental Health," Jeff R. Temple and a team of researchers found that sexual assault by a current partner was the strongest predictor of posttraumatic stress disorder, stress, and dissociation. Non-intimate partner sexual assault was only a significant predictor of posttraumatic stress disorder for African American women. When considering the impact of sexual assault upon a victim, it is critically important to take into account the perpetrator of the crime.

Failure to do so can mightily contribute to the misery of the victim, who is more likely to abuse alcohol or attempt suicide, as Judith McFarlane discovered. McFarlane led a team of nurses who spoke with 148 African American, Anglo and Latina women who had been abused. In the November 2005 journal of *Issue in Mental Health Nursing*, the nurses revealed that women who reported more than one sexual assault were 3.5 times more likely to report beginning or increasing substance use compared to women who reported only one sexual assault. Sexually assaulted women reported significantly more risk factors for suicide compared to women who experienced only physical abuse. Women reporting sexual assault were 5.3 times more likely to report threatening or attempted suicide within a 90-day period as compared to women who were only physically abused.

The women who experience the worst levels of trauma are the ones who had some mental health issues before the attack. Libby O. Ruch and Joseph J. Leon, in a 1983 essay for the journal *Women and Health*, found that the severity of preexisting emotional problems significantly predicted the level of trauma experienced by rape survivors. Women with depression are likely to become more depressed or attempt suicide while those with drinking problems are likely to consume greater amounts of alcohol.

Despite the clear need for mental health services, less than half of female rape victims reportedly accept mental health help. It is not enough to treat only the physical injuries of a rape victim. Health providers must consider the mental health situation of victims and emphasize the importance of treatment to those in need.

Treating Male Victims of Sexual Assault

Men experience rape as an aggressive attack on their sexuality as well as a violation of their physical and psychological boundaries. Like most women, most men cope with a rape without developing major psychological problems. However, the experience shatters basic assumptions about personal vulnerability as well as the popular idea that disasters happen only to other people. While women are taught from childhood to guard against rape, most men are not. The outright surprise and shock of being raped is likely far higher for men than women.

Rape treatment plans have generally been developed under the notion that men were aggressors and never victims. This major gap in service provision is likely to reinforce the sense of isolation and stigmatization experienced by many men who have been the victims of sexual assault. Men have also, by and large, internalized the idea that they should be the aggressive leaders in sexual matters.

Some men never even consider going to rape crisis centers because such places are women-only spaces. In his book *Male on Male Rape: The Hidden Toll of Stigma and Shame,* Michael Scarce relates the case of Marcus, a rape survivor who happened to be friends with a rape counselor but who never even considered the local rape crisis center. Upon reflection, Marcus concluded that he never picked up the phone because the center was called Bay Area Women Against Rape.

As a result of male socialization, men also are less likely than women to accept that they need help, with the result that many rape victims are reluctant to receive psychological aid. Rape treatment programs report high rates of male drop out. Personnel throughout the entire medical and legal system need to be trained to respond sensitively to incidents of male rape.

Law Enforcement

Arrests for Rape

The violent crime rate, including the numbers of forcible rapes, has decreased significantly over the last few decades, for reasons that remain murky. It is clear, however, that law enforcement agencies are still struggling to formulate effective responses to rape. A person who reports a rape has a 50 percent chance that an arrest will be made in the attack, according to a 1999 report by the National Center for Policy Analysis. However, only 16.3 percent of rapists went to prison for their crimes at the turn of the century. Many organizations, including the National Center for Policy Analysis, have blamed poor law enforcement procedures for the discrepancy between the arrests and the imprisonment of rapists.

Human Rights Watch recommends that police departments take several steps to combat rape. They recommend the creation of formal system to send rape kits to crime labs for testing as well as the establishment of a police unit tasked with investigating all sex crimes. The differences between a police department that does not follow these recommendations and one that is viewed as a model of sex crimes policing can be seen in two of the largest cities in the United States: Los Angeles and New York City.

Partly because of issues with rape kits, a person who reports to the Los Angeles Police Department that she has been raped has about a one in four chance of seeing someone arrested for the crime, as Human Rights Watch notes in its 2009 report. In 1999, Los Angeles had a rape arrest rate of 30 percent. New York City also had a backlog of rape kits but it solved this problem in 2003. New York City crime labs now process rape kits within 30 to 60 days with the results provided to a special team of investigators who focus on rape kit DNA matches. New York City has seen an increase in arrests and prosecutions for rape since it changed its procedures.

Mistrust of Law Enforcement

Rape law reforms, along with improvements in the treatment of victims of sexual assault, are widely credited with elevating reports of rapes in the decades since the 1960s. Stripping gender from the law ended the requirement that victims be female and perpetrators male. The kinds of people subject to and protected by the law dramatically increased.

The police officers of the 21st century are not the same men who once were chosen for their jobs because of their willingness to crack heads. The modern police force is filled with men with degrees in criminology who spend much of their time acting as social workers. Jack, a police officer for 25 years and a sex crime investigator for 6 years, spoke with Timothy Beneke in an interview that appeared in Patricia Searles's and Ronald J. Berger's *Rape and Society: Readings on the Problem of Sexual Assault.* Jack said that, "Most rape victims are very honest and frightened. . . . I have one now that I'm working with who can't understand why the rapist isn't instantly caught. . . . Generally speaking, I believe something happened. I believe what the lady is saying happened to her. But I'm also aware that someone else looking at the incident may see it a little differently, and that's what the jury's going to be doing—examining the whole picture"(Searles and Berger, 1995, p. 53).

Law enforcement reforms have made it easier to report rapes. Yet legal reforms have not been followed by significant increases in either the reporting of rape cases or the likelihood of arrests and convictions for rape. The reasons are puzzling.

In some cultures, low reporting seems to be linked to mistrust of law enforcement. Native Americans, like other racial minority groups, have had a complicated relationship with law enforcement. In recent years, American Indian women have begun to loudly express their rage at their disproportionate victimization in crimes of sexual assault, most often committed by non-Indians. Much of this anger is directed at law enforcement agencies.

A Cherokee woman, Jami Rozell, is one of the women complaining. Raped by a non-Indian, first-grade teacher Rozell could not go to the tribal court since it is only permitted to handle crimes against Indians in Indian country. After five months of worrying about testifying in front of her family and the people that she had grown up with, Rozell spoke at a preliminary hearing in Tahlequah, Oklahoma, in 2005. Then Rozell received the news that the police had cleaned up the evidence room by throwing away her rape kit and, with it, all chance of prosecution. Kendra Hunter, another American Indian woman from Oklahoma, told the *New York Times* that she had been raped by three white men who held her captive for three days in 2001. Hunter said that she did report the gang rape, but that the police officers dismissed her. They claimed that, despite the cigarette burns on her body, the sex had been consensual and the three men would testify to that point. It is perhaps not surprising that Rozell and Hunter now have negative opinions of the police.

Sherry Hamby, in an essay for the 2008 *Journal of Prevention and Intervention in the Community,* addressed perceptions of law enforcement among Native American victims of sexual assault. American Indian women are sexually victimized at a much greater rate than women from U.S. racial groups, but they often receive very limited police services. Hamby's analysis of National Violence Against Women Survey data led her to conclude that Native American women did not report rape because of their suspicion of law enforcement. American Indian women, compared to women from other racial groups, more often said law enforcement would not believe or would blame them.

American Indians are also more likely to deal directly with the perpetrator, as the Indian women in Hamby's study acknowledged. Hamby identified other barriers that prevent American Indian women from seeking help, including prejudice, conflict between Western and native values, language barriers, and poverty. American Indians, fearing humiliation, are often reluctant to press a rape complaint. Some see the rape as a test of faith and prefer to let God handle the perpetrator.

Tribal police departments are the predominant means of providing public safety on most Indian reservations outside of Alaska and California. The quality and size of tribal law enforcement agencies varies widely. The largest police department, with over 300 officers, is operated by the Navajo Nation. Much smaller tribes may have 10 or fewer officers to cover vast tracts of territory. While some tribal police departments may be well-equipped, others may struggle to provide even minimal levels of service. Accordingly, Larry Cox of Amnesty International has identified another reason why Native American women are less likely to report rape. American Indian women who report rape may not get a police response for hours or days, especially in rural areas. It is possible that many Indian women simply do not trust the police to show up in a timely manner.

Police Sexual Misconduct

Some of the mistrust toward police can probably be linked to widely reported cases of sexual misconduct by police officers. The *New York Times* identified one particular case in 2009. Two New York City police officers were accused of raping an intoxicated woman after helping her to her home. The officers attacked the woman as she lay physically helpless upon her bed. The woman had already vomited several times, an indication that she was far too intoxicated to consent to sexual intercourse. Manhattan district attorney Robert M. Morgenthau charged the men with rape and official misconduct.

Such conduct as rape is apparently rare, though, with most cases of sexual misconduct involving lesser offenses. Timothy Maher looked at the views of police chiefs on police sexual misconduct in 2008 for the journal *Police Practice & Research*. Twenty police chiefs in a major metropolitan area were interviewed about their perceptions of the nature, extent, and causes of sexual misconduct by police. Maher's results suggested that chiefs believe that police sexual misconduct is a problem. The chiefs generally report that the serious/criminal forms of sexual misconduct (e.g., rape, sexual assault, and sex with a juvenile) are rare. They believe that the less serious, noncriminal incidents (e.g., flirting on duty, consensual sex on duty, and pulling over a driver to get a closer look) are more common. Maher concluded that four factors influence this behavior: lack of knowledge about police sexual misconduct, police departments' complaint systems, opportunity for sexual misconduct, and the police culture.

Rape Kits

A rape kit, also known as a sexual assault evidence kit (SAEK), is a collection of biological evidence taken from a rape or sexual abuse victim after an assault. Marty Goddard, an antirape activist in Chicago, invented the kit in the 1970s to aid in the prosecutions of rapists. The kit, which varies by state and situation, contains the forensic evidence necessary to obtain an arrest and conviction. It should be collected within 72 hours of the attack, with retrieval often taking up to four hours. The victim's informal consent is necessary for a rape kit to be used. Ideally, rape kits are completed by a Sexual Assault Nurse Examiner (SANE), a registered nurse who has received specific training to care for sexual assault victims, competently collect evidence, and provide effective courtroom testimony.

Processing a rape kit cost about $1,500 in 2009. This heavy expense is one that many cities and states struggled to pay, especially during economic downturns. To solve their financial headaches, some local and state governments decided to pass along the costs of rape kits to the victims. Most people were unaware of this policy change until 2008 when it became public knowledge that Republican Vice Presidential candidate Sarah Palin had supported such billings when she served as a mayor of Wasilla, Alaska. The charges created a small scandal as Palin faced condemnation for seeking to charge rape victims for processing evidence to prove their truthfulness. The fees seemed to be fundamentally unfair.

The Federal Violence Against Women Act prohibits states from charging victims for processing rape kits or risk losing federal funding. While all states have complied with the legislation, some have found creative ways to sidestep some of the costs. When a kit is collected, the rape victim may receive the hospital bill and then have to pursue payment from the government. In Oklahoma, legislators capped the compensation for rape victims at $450. Maine proved slightly more generous by enacting a $500 cap, still only one-third of the costs of processing a rape kit. Texas pays $700 and then forces the victim to apply to the victim compensation fund for the remainder of the bill. North Dakota, Oregon, and the District of Columbia pay all costs but only after the rape victim has paid the bill and sought compensation. Rape victims in Montana receive money from the crime victims' compensation fund as long as they cooperate with the prosecution of the attacker.

Not all rape victims are informed that they can seek compensation from the state or a crime victims' fund. Since low-income women are more likely to be raped than high-income women, such fees may be outside the financial wherewithal of victims. The result could be rapists who remain free to prey again.

There is one fee for collecting a rape kit and another expense for testing the material in the kit. In 2009, Human Rights Watch reported that Los Angeles County allowed 12,669 rape kits to collect dust in police storage rooms. Nearly 500 of the kits had been ignored for at least 10 years while the California statute of limitations expired. At least 1,218 kits were from unsolved cases in which the attacker was a stranger. Human Rights Watch claimed that thousands of rape kits had been destroyed without being tested. Sarah Tofte, the author of the report, "Testing Justice: The Rape Kit Backlog in Los Angeles City and County" (2009), emphasized that completing a rape kit is an ordeal for a victim and the failure to process the kits had denied justice to the victims. The county government claimed that it had lacked the funds to hire the personnel to test the kits. After a few weeks of very bad publicity, Los Angeles County found the money to hire up to 26 additional employees. The county also planned to outsource a number of kits to private labs, a step that it presumably could have taken some years earlier.

Human Rights Watch identified several disturbing results of the failure of Los Angeles to process the rape kits. A sexual assault nurse examiner treated a child who had been kidnapped near a bus stop and raped. She recalled the case of another child who had been taken from the same bus stop and raped. The details of both attacks seemed to match, leading the nurse to suspect that the same man had committed both crimes. The nurse contacted the police officer in charge of the case to inquire about the first child's rape kit. She was told that the kit had not yet been processed and that it might remain unprocessed for another six months. Meanwhile, the rapist presumably remained on the loose where he could commit further crimes against children. In another case, a Los Angeles detective was dissuaded by crime lab personnel from submitting a rape kit for testing. Told that testing could take eight months or more, the detective tried to solve the crime by other means. He failed and a man who attacked a woman following a party remains unknown. In a third case, a woman named Catherine was attacked at home while her young son slept. The police officer who investigated the crime had a hunch that the man was a repeat offender. Informed by Los Angeles crime lab personnel that testing could take up to eight months, the detective personally delivered the rape kit to a state lab in the hopes of faster results. He still had to wait eight months before the state linked DNA from Catherine's rapist to a man in the offender database. The rapist had used the extra time to rape two more people, including a child.

Judicial System

Rape Shield Laws

Legal scholars typically underscore the failures of law reforms by stressing that there is a difference between making laws in a sterile chamber and practicing the law in messy reality. Feminist critics of the criminal justice system have long argued that women who file rape complaints with the police are often discredited by prosecutors and in court if they fail to conform to the stereotype of a "real rape" victim. The perfect victim resembles a nun. She is morally and sexually virtuous as well as cautious, unassertive, and consistent.

Rape shield laws limit the introduction of the victim's sexual history in trials. These laws came about after defense attorneys would use a victim's past to suggest that she wanted to have sex with her alleged rapist. Women with extensive sexual histories were thought to more frequently fabricate allegations of rape than other women. They were thought to have asked for it.

In 2007, three researchers tested this theory. Heather D. Flowe, Ebbe B. Ebbesen, and Anila Putcha-Bhagavatula interviewed female college students, topless dancers, prostitutes, and women living in a drug and rehabilitation center. In an essay subsequently published in the journal *Law and Human Behavior*, women were less likely to say that they would take legal action in response to a rape if they had extensive sexual histories or if they had consented to an extensive amount of foreplay before the rape. In cases of consensual sexual activity, women with extensive sexual records were not more likely to say that they would report rape, even when provided with a motive for seeking revenge against their partner. In essence, women who are supposedly likely to ask for it are not likely to go to court to complain when they get it.

It is possible that these women in this study were unaware of rape shield laws. They might hesitate to report a rape because they thought that they would not be believed. Despite rape shield laws, women still hesitate to go to court for fear that their sexual histories will be made public and they will be prosecuted instead of the defendant. Several highly publicized cases reportedly made women less likely to come forward.

Rape shields do not work in highly publicized cases. In the Kobe Bryant case in 2004, the accuser's name became public and she received death threats from the professional basketball player's fans before the case even went to court. The rape shield applied to the victim but her name quickly spread across the Internet as media outlets around the globe were eager to give every detail of the case to the public. (It should be noted that rape shield laws do little for the defendant, who has a legal presumption of innocence. Bryant claimed that the sex was consensual. The rape shield law denied him access to evidence that might have indicated that the woman had a tendency to sleep with celebrity athletes.) In the Mike Tyson case, the name of the former Miss Black Rhode Island who accused the boxer of rape in 1991 can now be found on Wikipedia. "Iron Mike" had such notoriety by the time of the accusation that the media could not resist digging up every bit of information about his accuser, including her name.

Prosecution Challenges

Case screening is the gateway to the criminal court system. Prosecutors, acting as gatekeepers, decide which cases of alleged victimization will be passed on to be judged in court. A 1990 Department of Justice study suggested that a significant percentage of felony cases, including rape, never get beyond this point. Prosecutors prefer to prosecute cases that are solid or convictable, partly because they are judged at election time upon their conviction rates.

District attorneys do not like to prosecute rapes. Such cases are viewed as murky and ambiguous. Many, like the Kobe Bryant case, seem to come down to he said/she said. A number of studies on sexual assault have found that victim credibility is crucial in persuading a prosecutor to pursue a case. Prosecutors prefer victims who are virginal. When sex workers are the victims of assaults, prosecutors worry about the reaction of a jury to the victims. They typically simply refuse to prosecute such cases as a waste of time and resources. Lisa Frohmann, in her study of prosecutorial accounts of case rejections, concluded that when in doubt, prosecutors reject a case. The behavior of prosecutors is attuned more to avoiding the error of filing cases that are not likely to result in conviction than to avoiding the error of rejecting cases that will probably end in conviction.

Native Americans, who feature far more prominently as victims of rapes than they should as a percentage of the population, also have trouble getting rapes prosecuted. The link between victimization and inability to prosecute is probably not coincidental.

The roots of the difficulty date back several decades. In 1978, the U.S. Supreme Court removed the ability of Indian tribes to prosecute non-Indians for crimes committed on Indian reservations. The Court ruled in *Oliphant v. Suquamish Indian Tribe* that such prosecution violated the tribe's status as a "domestic dependent nation." The result is that tribal courts cannot try non-Indians charged with raping Native American women. Federal or state prosecutors must fill the jurisdictional void but law enforcement in such cases is haphazard at best.

The Department of Justice's own records show that in 2006, prosecutors filed only 606 criminal cases in all of Indian country. There are about four million American Indians and Alaska Natives. With more than 560 federally recognized tribes, this filing rate works out to a little more than one criminal prosecution for each tribe. Common sense indicates that something is peculiar in Indian country. In 2007, Amnesty International called upon Congress to extend tribal authority to all offenders on Indian land, not just Indians, and to expand federal spending on Indian law enforcement.

In 2007, Renee Brewer, a child welfare and family violence counselor at the Potawatomi Nation and a member of the Creek Muskogee tribe, spoke to the *New York Times* about American Indian concerns about rape prosecution. Brewer said she recently had four agencies arguing over jurisdiction after a woman from the Absentee Shawnee Nation had called 911 to say she had been raped. The victim eventually left Oklahoma while the accused rapist walked away scot-free.

Governments typically possess the authority to prosecute crimes committed within their borders. Tribal governments should be no exception. Many tribes have reported an increase in crimes committed by non-Indians against Indians, as the perpetrators know that the possibility of federal prosecution is slim. Even if outside prosecutors were willing to devote the time and resources necessary to handle crimes on Indian land more efficiently, it would still make better sense for tribal governments to have jurisdiction over all reservation-based crimes. Not every American Indian speaks English and does so fluently. European American cultural norms are not the norms that are found upon an Indian reservation. Distinct differences exist between tribal governments and U.S. governments. Tribal courts, as Native American activists like N. Bruce Duthu have argued, are simply in the best position to quickly and respectfully help victims of sexual assaults (*New York Times*, August 11, 2008).

Prohibiting Rape

Sexual offender laws were passed in two waves. The first batch, known as the sexual psychopath laws, passed between the late 1930s and the mid 1970s. They aimed to punish sexual offenders. A Minnesota law that allowed indefinite confinement for likely repeat offenders is typical. The states did not require treatment. The second batch, which became law after 1990, sought to manage sexual offenders through treatment as well as confinement. Both laws have had some significant implications for the correctional system. The idea of "lock 'em up and throw away the key" particularly appeals to a public frustrated by sexual offenders who seem resistant to cures.

Correctional System

Prison Rape

Prison rape has been well-known for many, many years. Many Americans have some difficulty summoning up sympathy for prisoners, so the issue has not received that much publicity. However, individuals who leave prison with psychological issues resulting from being the victims of rape are, perhaps, not the ideal sort of people to be walking around loose. They may victimize others out of anger. Most simply, rape is a crime. The law does not provide exemptions for people who supposedly deserve extra pain and misery. The United States has an obligation to protect the people that it locks up.

T. J. Parsell is a typical victim of prison rape. In 1978, as a 17-year-old, he robbed a store clerk with a toy gun on a lark. He received $50 and a sentence to be served in an adult jail. On his first night in prison, an older inmate spiked his drink with Thorazine and sexually abused and raped him. Other inmates then attacked him. As Parsell related to a Congressional committee considering legislation against prison rape, "While my friends prepared for our high school prom, I was being gang raped." He added, "What they took from me went beyond sex. They'd stolen my manhood, my identity and part of my soul." Parsell, as the *New York Times* reported, emerged from prison to become a successful New York City software executive.

As conditions in prison deteriorated from overcrowding, staff shortages and budget cuts, prison rape became more common. According to the National Prison Project of the American Civil Liberties Union, prison assaults rose 26 percent from 2000 to 2004. In 2003, Congress passed the Prison Rape Elimination Act (PREA) to try to address the issue.

Aviva N. Moster and Elizabeth L. Jeglic investigated the success of PREA in their essay, "Prison Warden Attitudes Toward Prison Rape and Sexual Assault: Findings Since the Prison Rape Elimination Act (PREA)" for the *Prison Journal* in 2009. PREA mandates a zero-tolerance policy for sexual assaults within correctional facilities and requires the collection of data on prison rape. Prison wardens play a key role in the implementation and enforcement of prison policies. For the most part, wardens were not impressed with PREA. Moster and Jeglic found that a majority of the wardens surveyed reported that their prison rape and sexual assault policies were considerably less effective than staff training and increased inmate supervision.

Sex Offender Residency Laws

No one wants to live next door to a sex offender. A spate of highly publicized sex crimes against children by individuals with past convictions for sexual crimes has badly frightened parents. In response to public demand, states and cities have forced sex offenders to register. A substantial number have also prohibited registered sex offenders from living within a number of feet from a school, day care center, or other place where children are likely to congregate. Some cities have tried to ban sex offenders from residing within city limits. Residency laws that prohibit sex offenders from residing in certain areas are clearly extremely popular with the general public and, therefore, politically risky for legislators to amend.

The effectiveness of such legislation, however, is not readily apparent. It is obviously difficult to measure the number of times that a crime does not occur, but much of the hysteria surrounding sex crimes against children seems to have been stirred up by the media. "There is no evidence that sexual molestation of children and incest is escalating," said Will Alexander, a research analyst for the Minnesota Department of Corrections, who studied the issue nationwide. Alexander spoke to the *New York Times* in 1996, as the first of the residency laws were being put into effect. Alexander added, "Over the past 20 years, there has been a large increase by newspapers [in reporting] these kinds of offenses. But the number of such offenses themselves have remained steady. In the case of rape and other violent sex offenses, trends are down."

Residency laws are based on the notion that sex offenders are likely to commit crimes where they live. In a 2003 study, the Minnesota Department of Corrections found that sex offenders seeking victims were likely to go a neighborhood where they would not be recognized. The neighborhood where they would not be recognized is obviously not the one in which they reside.

Children are not necessarily safer because sex offenders are not permitted to live where children play and go to school. Colorado's Department of Public Safety released a report in 2004 that concluded that convicted molesters who reoffended lived no closer to schools or child care centers than those molesters who did not commit additional crimes. Additionally, the Jacob Wetterling Foundation, which fights child exploitation, warns that residency laws provide a false sense of security, since the vast majority of sexually abused children are molested by people that they know. Problems with the various restrictions on sex offenders have become abundantly clear.

The residency laws have come under attack by everyone from civil libertarians to police officers. Oklahoma state legislator Lucky Lamons, retired from 22 years as a police officer, supported a revision of Oklahoma's laws that banned registered sex offenders from living within 2,000 feet of a school or day care center. Lamons, a Tulsa Democrat, argued that the legislation forced sex offenders to live in rural areas where they were difficult to monitor. Oklahoma law also did not differentiate between abusers of children and men who urinated in public, a sex offense in the state. Sergeant Gary Stansill, head of the Tulsa Police Department's sex crimes unit, complained to *USA Today* in 2007 that he spent far too much of time investigating cases of sex offenders who did not register. He stated that he investigated as many cases of sex offenders not registering as he did rape reports. Stansill considered less than 10 percent of Oklahoma's 8,000 convicted sex offenders to be high-risk. Both Stansill and Lamons support legislation that focuses more tightly on high-risk offenders.

Other states have also begun to consider revisions to sex offender residency laws for varying reasons. Some sex offenders, who complain that they are having trouble finding a place to legally live, stop registering with the police. They go underground, where they cannot be monitored. Additionally, laws that prevent sex offenders from living near schools do not prevent them from loitering in the area. John Walsh, who lost his son to murderous sex offender, argues that residency laws are worthwhile if they can be enforced. Walsh estimates that tens of thousands of nation's 600,000 sex offenders are giving false addresses to the police. Walsh persuaded Congress in 2006 to pass the Adam Walsh Child Protection and Safety Act, named after his son, which makes it a felony for serious sex offenders such as rapists to fail to register.

Sex Offender Registration

The Adam Walsh Act is particularly notable in that it has taken account of the high rate of sex crimes within Native American communities. It allows tribal governments to decide whether to establish and maintain registries of convicted sex offenders who reside, go to school, or are employed within their jurisdictions. Tribal sex offender registries must meet the same standards as state registries. The vast majority of eligible tribes have opted to run their own sex offender registries.

One of the problems with registering sex offenders is that teenagers are being punished for having consensual sex. Matthew Shettles had to register until Oregon legislators passed a bill in

2007 that ended registration for teenagers convicted of sex with someone underage if the younger person is at least 13 and the two teenagers are less than 5 years apart in age. Shettles had sex with his girlfriend on the night he graduated from high school. The girl, a few weeks shy of 15, told an adult, who reported the offense. Shettles, convicted of a misdemeanor, received probation and a fine plus community service. As a convicted sex offender, he had to register for life every time that he moved, got a new job, or made other life changes. Shettles could not find an apartment, while his college instructors were notified that they had a sex offender in class. The specifics of his crime were not identified on the register, leading some people to suspect the worst of the young man.

The case of Genarlow Wilson, a 17-year-old Georgia teen who received 10 years in jail for receiving oral sex at a party from his 15-year-old girlfriend, has also garnered considerable notoriety. The state termed such activity to be a felony, aggravated child molestation, and mandated a minimum 10-year sentence for the crime. The girl stated that she had consented, but the age of consent in Georgia is 16. The Georgia legislature eventually bowed to public pressure and changed the law to make such cases misdemeanors when they involved teenagers close in age. Wilson spent two years in prison before being released in 2007. As a sex offender, he must register for life. He is attempting to have his conviction overturned.

To stop sex offenders from reoffending, criminologists have recommended several steps other than residency and registration. David Finkelhor of the Crimes Against Children Research Center at the University of New Hampshire supports more checks by probation officers. Kim English of Colorado's Division of Criminal Justice advises psychological therapy in group residential centers for offenders. In the absence of further research, it is not clear whether these steps will be effective in stopping sex offenders from reoffending.

The case of David S. Kelley suggests that means other than residency restrictions and sex offender registration might be helpful in combating pedophiles. Kelley, a Boston area man, had twice committed sexual offenses against children. Kelley's Northborough neighbors knew where he lived and what he had done because he was in Massachusetts' registry of sexual offenders. The police had warned the neighbors about Kelley, as mandated by state law. Still, Kelley managed to rape a four-year-old boy in 1999. The boy was attacked at the home of a caregiver.

Stopping Repeat Sexual Offenders

Several states have created sexually violent predator laws to put these particular offenders in a mental health facility for an interdeterminate period of time. The laws require mental health professionals to evaluate sexual offenders who are in prison to determine whether they should be let loose or subjected to further confinement. The people who are locked up are those who are most likely to reoffend.

The U.S. Supreme Court declared such laws to be constitutional in *Kansas v. Hendricks* (1997), in which the Kansas Attorney General asked the Court to consider whether due process applied to the state's sexually violent predator law. The Court ruled that it is perfectly legal to confine those "who are unable to control their dangerousness" for as long as necessary. Freedom from bodily restraint does not always extend to those who have been convicted of committed sex crimes, even when they have completed their prison sentences.

Mitchell Gaff, a Washington state man, is one of the numerous sex offenders who remain jailed despite the expiration of their sentences. Not the most sympathetic of characters, Gaff completed a 10-year sentence in 1994 for brutally raping teenage sisters at knifepoint. Expecting to be released, he was surprised to discover that Washington prison officials had labeled him as too dangerous to be released. Gaff was transferred to indefinite confinement at a maximum-security prison used for pedophiles and rapists who are presumed to be likely to commit further crimes. "I was stunned," Gaff said to a reporter for the *New York Times* in 1995. He said, "I feel like I was being judged on who I used to be, not on who I've become" (*New York Times*, February 27, 1995). Since state legislatures establish maximum sentences for crimes, it is problematic for prison officials to effectively ignore the lawfully imposed sentences and impose indefinite ones.

Not all sex offenders go on to commit new crimes and those who do rarely announce their intentions to do so. Experts have had a notoriously difficult time in predicting sexual recidivism. Psychologists R. Karl Hanson and Monique T. Bussière have estimated that the accuracy of expert opinion in predicting sexual recidivism is only slightly above chance levels. Part of the problem lies in the fact that the factors that predict the likelihood that all convicted criminals will repeat their offenses are not the same factors that predict whether a sexual offender will repeat his crime.

Knowing that someone has committed a sexual offense does not provide evidence that the individual will commit another sex crime. Contrary to common opinion, the recidivism rate of sexual offenders is relatively low when compared with all offenders. In a 1993 article for the *Journal of Consulting and Clinical Psychology*, Hanson, Richard A. Steffy, and René Gauthier looked at the likelihood that child molesters would commit additional crimes after being released from prison. They concluded that sex offense recidivism rates can range as high as 30 to 40 percent within 20 years of the initial crime. This rate is less than the rate for nonsexual criminals.

Some assessment procedures may have the potential to provide reasonably good risk assessments of potential reoffenders. The strongest predictors of sexual offense recidivism are related to sexual deviancy, such as deviant sexual preferences, antisocial personality disorder, prior sexual offenses, early onset of criminal behavior, and committing a range of sex crimes. Sexual criminals who repeat all seem to have difficulties in forming long-term romantic relationships and poor social networks. They also tend to believe rape myths. Many have unstable lifestyles marked by frequent moves, unemployment, and substance abuse. Hanson and Bussière, in a 1998 essay on "Predicting Relapse: A Meta-Analysis of Sexual Offender Recidivism Studies" for the *Journal of Consulting and Clinical Psychology* reported that the criminals most likely to repeat were those with a sexual interest in children. The two psychologists used phallometric assessment to measure interest. This type of assessment involves the monitoring of changes in penile response when a man is presented with various types of erotic stimuli.

To predict the risk for sexual recidivism, psychologists may rely upon the Sex Offender Risk Appraisal Guide (SORAG), a variation of the Violence Risk Appraisal Guide (VRAG) that is among the most accurate means of predicting the likelihood that violent offenders will repeat. SORAG is moderately good at predicting recidivism but far from totally accurate. The Minnesota Sex Offender Screening Tool (MnSOST) tries to assess the risk of sexual recidivism among child molesters who do not target relatives. Like SORAG, MnSOST has had moderate success.

There is a debate among those who deal with sexual offenders as to the extent that treatment reduces recidivism rates. Not surprisingly, offenders who drop out of treatment are at higher risk for reoffending than offenders who complete their treatment programs.

Medical Treatment of Offenders

There is no magic pill to stop a sex criminal from doing it again. Over the years, authorities have employed various legal approaches to deal with the vexing problem of sexually violent offenders. Indefinite commitment to a mental health center, psychotherapy, and behavioral treatment have all been tried. No method has proven to be especially effective in stopping recidivism in sex criminals. These failures prompted some legal authorities to advise that sex offenders be given medications that reduce the intensity of sexual drives by lowering testosterone levels. This is apparently as close to a magic pill as those who seek to protect women and children believe that they can get.

The procedure is typically termed "chemical castration." This is actually a misnomer, since no castration in fact occurs when a drug is used. The drug most often employed, an Upjohn product called Depo-Provera, lowers the testosterone level in men and thus reduces sex drive. When use of the drug stops, the sex drive returns to a normal level.

The procedure has a fairly long history, though it only became widespread in the 1990s. R. M. Foote first administrated progesterone hormonal compounds to men in 1944 to reduce testosterone levels. The procedure stayed largely forgotten until John Money decided to try it with sex offenders in the late 1960s. Both Foote and Money had clinical goals in mind, not the control of criminals. The drug, medroxyprogesterone acetate (MPA), that Money used is not approved for rendering men impotent. It is supposed to be used to reduce abnormal levels of sex drive, to return sexual fantasies to normal levels, to permit patients to control their socially prohibited urges, and to allow them relief from the intrusive ideas and urges that they have great difficulty controlling.

The brand name Depo-Provera applies to depot medroxyprogesterone acetate (DMPA). It is a birth control drug that is normally prescribed to women. Depo-Provera gained national attention in 1983 when a Texas jury sentenced convicted rapist Joseph Frank Smith to 10 years of probation instead of prison after he volunteered to undergo Depo-Provera therapy. Smith, known as the "ski mask rapist," had been convicted for raping the same woman twice. Smith moved to the Richmond, Virginia, area after his conviction. He appeared on the television news magazine show *60 Minutes* as an example of the success of chemical castration. However, while on Depo-Provera and while promoting himself as the poster child for sex offender rehabilitation, Smith continued his career as rapist. In 1998, he pled guilty to committing two sex crimes. Virginia authorities suspected that he really committed 75. Smith received a 40-year sentence for breaking and entering, aggravated sexual battery, and two counts of attempted oral and anal sodomy in a June 1993 attack on a five-year-old girl.

Despite the heavily publicized Smith debacle, a number of states proceeded to pursue chemical castration. In 1996, California became the first state to mandate the procedure. The California legislature required any pedophile who had been convicted twice to be periodically injected, after release from prison, with a drug that inhibits sex drive. The particulars of drug delivery indicate that the legislators had the injectable Depo-Provera in mind. Sex offenders who voluntarily submitted to surgical castration were exempt. A first-time child molester convicted of a particularly heinous crime would have to undergo the same treatment. The bill's sponsor, Bill Hoge of Pasadena, defended the legislation to the *New York Times* by asking, "So why not give these people a shot to calm them down and bring them under control?" Hoges emphasized that U.S. law does permit the government to force individuals to take medicine. He said, "If you have smallpox in this country or some other kind of life-threatening epidemic disease, the law is clear on the fact that you can't refuse treatment."

Despite the wording that designates surgical castration as an equal to chemical castration, it is not nearly as popular because of the irreversible effect. Surgical castration, or orchiectomy, is the removal of the testes. It has a history in the United States dating to the period when proponents of eugenics in the early 20th century attempted to ensure that only the better sort of people would reproduce by sterilizing the mentally retarded and other "defectives." The laws at the time did not target sexual offenders because there was little scientific evidence that there was a genetic component to sexual behavior.

The American Civil Liberties Union (ACLU) objected to the California law as well as subsequent state ones that mandated castration for several reasons. As Valerie Small Navarro, an attorney with the American Civil Liberties Union, explained to a reporter for the *New York Times* in 1996, "This measure raises some very, very serious constitutional questions, not to mention medical questions." She elaborated, "There are problems regarding the right to privacy, the right to procreate, the right to control over one's body. There are questions about drug side effects and whether treatment will work in every case, especially if it isn't voluntary and isn't accompanied by therapy, which the bill doesn't mandate" (*New York Times*, August 27, 1996). The Eighth Amendment prohibits cruel and unusual punishment, which may cover the side effects of chemical castration drugs. The drugs have been linked to high blood pressure, shrinkage of the testicles, diabetes, heart problems, and irregular gallbladder functioning.

There is a debate among the medical profession as to whether chemical castration requirements have changed the physician from healer to agent of social control or agent of the state. As some medical professionals have complained, the duty to treat has apparently been changed to a duty to punish, or at best, control criminals. In 1998, the American Psychiatric Association decided to support the use of sex-drive reducing medications, but only after a thorough clinical evaluation and as part of a comprehensive medical plan. The Food and Drug Administration (FDA) has not approved chemical castration drugs, but for reasons that relate only to financial concerns. The drug companies, fearful of a lawsuit if a sex criminal on a chemical castration drug commits another sex crime, have not sought FDA approval for such drugs. Without FDA approval, physicians follow informal guidelines when prescribing chemical castration drugs.

Sex crimes result from many factors, including sexual urges. As the differences between the California state legislature and the ACLU indicate, there are strong differences of opinion over whether sexual predation is driven by sex urges or other causes. Some medical experts say a major drawback of castration, whether chemical or surgical, is that not all child molesters are driven solely by a sex urge. Other factors, like a violent nature or exhibitionism, can also be at work, and require psychiatric treatment. Additionally, some drugs simply do not work in some people. Drugs can have serious side effects and can be countered by other drugs. A sex offender might obtain steroids to increase his testosterone to counteract the Depo-Provera.

Conclusion

Sex crimes are not black-and-white issues despite the very human desire to simplify them into easily fixable parts. "There's no easy answer here," said Fred Berlin, the founder of the Sexual Disorders Clinic at Johns Hopkins University in Baltimore. Berlin, speaking to the *Times* of London in 1996 elaborated, "There are things that you can't punish away or legislate away. It's not enough just to say, 'Let's lock 'em up and castrate the bastards,' however horrible their misdeeds. Some people you just lock up. Some people you lock up and treat. Some people you treat. It's complicated" (Whittell, 1996, n.p.). The best method of treatment may include drugs and counseling, though further research is needed on this particular point.

Further Reading

Bachman, Ronet, and Lind Saltzman. *Violence Against Women.* Washington, DC: U.S. Department of Justice, 1994.

Bondurant, Barrie. "University Women's Acknowledgement of Rape: Individual, Situational, and Social Factors." *Violence Against Women* 7, no. 3 (March 2001): 294–331.

Boeringer, Scot B. "Associations of Rape-Supportive Attitudes With Fraternal and Athletic Participation." *Violence Against Women* 5, no. 1 (January 1999): 81–115.

Bergen, Raquel Kennedy. *Wife Rape: Understanding the Response of Survivors and Service Providers.* Thousand Oaks, CA: Sage, 1996.

Bletzer, Keith V., and Mary P. Koss. "After-Rape Among Three Populations in the Southwest." *Violence Against Women* 12, no. 1 (January 2006): 5–29.

Burgess, Ann, and Larry Holmstrom. "Rape Trauma Syndrome." *American Journal of Psychiatry* 131 (1974): 981–987.

Burt, Martha R. "Cultural Myths and Supports for Rape." *Journal of Personality and Social Psychology* 38 (1980): 217–230.

Campbell, Rebecca, and Sharon M. Wasco. "Understanding Rape and Sexual Assault: 20 Years of Progress and Future Directions" *Journal of Interpersonal Violence* 20 (2005): 127–131.

Finkelhor, David, and Kersti Yllo. *License to Rape: Sexual Abuse of Wives.* New York: Free Press, 1987.

Flowe, Heather D., Ebbe B. Ebbesen, and Anila Putcha-Bhagavatula. "Rape Shield Laws and Sexual Behavior Evidence: Effects of Consent Level and Women's Sexual History on Rape Allegations." *Law of Human Behavior,* 31, no. 2 (April 2007): 159–175.

Flynn, Kathryn A. *Sexual Abuse of Women by Members of the Clergy.* New York: McFarland, 2003.

Frohmann, Lisa. "Discrediting Victims' Allegations of Sexual Assault: Prosecutorial Accounts of Case Rejections." In Karen J. Maschke, ed. *The Legal Response to Violence Against Women.* New York: Taylor and Francis, 1997.

Gordon, Margaret T., and Stephanie Riger. *The Female Fear.* New York: Free Press, 1989.

Hamby, Sherry. "The Path of Helpseeking: Perceptions of Law Enforcement Among American Indian Victims of Sexual Assault. *Journal of Prevention & Intervention in the Community* 36, no. 1/2 (July 2008): 89–104.

Hanson, Richard, A. Steffy, and Rene Gauthier. "Long-term Recidivism of Child Molesters." *Journal of Consulting and Clinical Psychology* 61 (1993): 646–652.

Hinck, Shelly Schaefer, and Richard W. Thomas. "Rape Myth Acceptance in College Students: How Far Have We Come?" *Sex Roles* 40, no. 9/10 (May 1999), 815–832.

Leventhal, Beth, and Sandra E. Lundy, eds. *Same-Sex Domestic Violence: Strategies for Change.* Thousand Oaks, CA: Sage, 1999.

Littleton, Heather, Carmen Radecki Breitkopf, and Abbey B. Berenson. "Rape Scripts of Low-Income European American and Latina Women." *Sex Roles* 56, no. 7/8 (April 2007): 509–516.

Lonsway, Kimberly A., and Louise F. Fitzgerald. "Rape Myths." *Psychology of Women Quarterly* 18, no. 2 (June 1994): 133–157.

Maher, Timothy. "Police Chiefs' Views on Police Sexual Misconduct." *Police Practice & Research* 9, no. 3 (July 2008): 239–250.

McCauley, Jenna L., and Karen S. Calhoun. "Faulty Perceptions?: The Impact of Binge Drinking History on College Women's Perceived Rape Resistance Efficacy." *Addictive Behaviors* 33, no. 12 (December 2008): 1540–1545.

McMahon, Sarah. "Understanding Community-Specific Rape Myths." *Affilia: Journal of Women & Social Work* 22, no. 4 (December 2007): 357–370.

Messman-Moore, Terri L., Rose Marie Ward, and Amy L. Brown. "Substance Use and PTSD Symptoms Impact the Likelihood of Rape and Revictimization in College Women." *Journal of Interpersonal Violence* 24, no. 3 (March 2009): 499–521.

Moster, Aviva N., and Elizabeth L. Jeglic. "Prison Warden Attitudes Toward Prison Rape and Sexual Assault: Findings Since the Prison Rape Elimination Act (PREA)." *Prison Journal* 89, no. 1 (March 2009): 65–78.

Odem, Mary E., and Jody Clay-Warner, eds. *Confronting Rape and Sexual Assault.* Wilmington, DE: Scholarly Resources, 1998.

Ogilvie, Beverly A. *Mother-Daughter Incest: A Guide for Helping Professionals.* New York: Routledge, 2004.

Peterson, Zoë D., and C. L. Muehlenhard. "Was it Rape? The Function of Women's Rape Myth Acceptance and Definitions of Sex in Labeling Their Own Experiences." *Sex Roles* 51, no. 3/4 (2004): 129–144.

Ruch, Libby O., and Joseph J. Leon. "Sexual Assault Trauma and Trauma Change." *Women and Health* 8, no. 4 (December 1983): 5–21.

Russell, Diana. *Rape in Marriage.* Bloomington: Indiana University Press, 1990.

Rutman, Shira et al. "Urban American Indian and Alaska Native Youth: Youth Risk Behavior Survey 1997–2003." *Maternal and Child Health Journal,* 12, no. 1 (July 2008) 76–81.

Sanday, Peggy Reeves. *Fraternity Gang Rape: Sex, Brotherhood, and Privilege on Campus.* New York: New York University Press, 2007.

Scarce, Michael. *Male on Male Rape: The Hidden Toll of Stigma and Shame.* Cambridge, MA: Perseus Publishing, 1997.

Schwartz, Martin D., and Carol A. Nogrady. "Fraternity Membership, Rape Myths, and Sexual Aggression on a College Campus." *Violence Against Women* 2, no. 2 (June 1996): 148–174.

Searles, Patricia, and Ronald J. Berger, eds. *Rape and Society: Readings on the Problem of Sexual Assault.* Boulder: Westview Press, 1995.

Temple, Jeff R. et al. "Differing Effects of Partner and Nonpartner Sexual Assault on Women's Mental Health." *Violence Against Women* 13, no. 2 (March 2007): 285–297.

Tofte, Sarah. *Testing Justice: The Rape Kit Backlog in Los Angeles City and County.* New York: Human Rights Watch, 2009.

Warshaw, Robin. *I Never Called It Rape: The Ms. Report of Recognizing, Fighting, and Surviving Date and Acquaintance Rape.* New York: Harper and Row, 1988.

White, Sandy, and Niwako Yamawaki. "The Moderating Influence of Homophobia and Gender-Role Traditionality on Perceptions of Male Rape Victims." *Journal of Applied Social Psychology* 39, no. 5 (May 2009): 1116–1136.

Whittell, Giles. "Persistent Abusers May Face Statutory Castration." *Times* [London], August 28, 1996.

Yuan, Nicole P., Mary P. Koss, Mona Polacca, and David Goldman. "Risk Factors for Physical Assault and Rape Among Six Native American Tribes." *Journal of Interpersonal Violence* 21, no. 12 (December 2006): 1566–1590.

3

Worldwide Perspectives

One in five women around the world experience rape or an attempted rape. Sexual crime in Africa, Asia, Europe, and Latin America is not that much different from sexual crime in the United States. Rapists target women who ask for it. Women are too ashamed or frightened to report attacks. Laws often seem too lenient and many people, especially those in power, do not take such crimes seriously enough.

There are some notable differences among the continents, though. The low status of women in many cultures excuses the sexual abuse of females. Child sexual abuse is a major problem in some Asian countries, partly because of a tradition of selling daughters as prostitutes. Families who are struggling economically will sell their girls to earn income. Trafficking girls and women for sexual purposes has become a major source of income for criminals from Eastern Europe and Asia, with most of the largest criminal syndicates involved. Many of the trafficked women have been kidnapped and forced into sexual slavery. Rape as a part of war has bedeviled every country that has experienced political instability, with Africa suffering some of the most notorious atrocities.

The information that follows is not an exhaustive study of sexual crime around the world. The topic is far too large to be covered in a chapter. The material below is offered as an introduction to the problem.

Africa

Rape

Africa is widely reported to have the worst sexual violence in the world. Political instability in the region has combined with poverty and a lack of respect for women to create a crisis of staggering proportions. The AIDS virus that is ravaging the continent is exacerbating the problem as infected men spread the disease to their victims. A few countries have taken steps to reduce the incidence of sexual assaults, but such activism has come fairly late.

The United Nations labels the Democratic Republic of Congo as the place where a woman is most likely to be raped. It is the rape capital of the world. Tens of thousands of women, possibly hundreds of thousands, have been raped since the millennium. In the worst-hit region of South Kivu in the eastern part of the Congo, there were 4,066 reported cases of rape in the first three months of 2008. The Scottish Catholic International Aid Fund estimated that 70 percent of women in the Shabunda district of South Kivu had been raped. Victims ranged in age from 3 to 80 years old.

Many of the rapes were marked by a level of brutality that is shocking even in a place accustomed to violent warlords and drug-addled child soldiers. Guns and branches are sometimes shoved into women. About a fifth of victims are left with damage to their internal organs, sometimes leaving them unable to bear children, and many are left infected with the AIDS virus. Worse, a lot of women do not receive medical attention because there are only two hospitals in the eastern region with the ability to repair traumatic rape injuries.

Rapists in the Congo could long count on going free because of both official denial of the problem and reluctance by victims to endure the shame of coming forward. After horrendous worldwide publicity, the government of the Congo took a series of steps to stop rapes in 2008. It took this action partly in response to pressure brought to bear by international human rights organizations as well as such home-grown groups as the Network of Women for the Defense of Rights and Peace. The Women of Compassion Worldwide, as one example, publicly announced that it had recorded 1,128 cases of rape in the Nigerian state of Delta between January and July of 2008. News of the report prompted the Ministry of Women Affairs, Community, and Social Development to form a committee to lead a campaign against rape. Congolese state governments also decided to intensify efforts to enlighten their citizens about the dangers of rape. Dozens of activists traveled to villages to communicate the message that rape is wrong while women donned t-shirts reading in Kiswahili: "I refuse to be raped. What about you?"

Meanwhile, European aid agencies had already helped build courthouses and prisons across eastern Congo, in part to punish rapists who were notoriously active in this area of the country. Congolese crime scene investigators traveled to Europe to learn advanced forensic techniques. The American Bar Association opened a legal clinic in January 2008 specifically to help rape victims bring their cases to court. Mobile courts held rape trials in villages that were so remote that they reportedly had not seen a judge since the Belgians ruled the Congo.

The results of the government-supported antirape campaign were dramatic, for a brief moment. In the town of Bunia, rape prosecutions jumped 600 percent between 2003 and 2008. Yet the Congo penal code still does not penalize rapists who use a gun or an object instead of a penis as a means of penetration. Anti-rape activists complain that those in power still regard rape as a woman's problem, with low priority. A renewal of fighting in 2008 is jeopardizing the small gains made against rape. In 2009, human rights activists estimated that 1,500 were dying daily of war-related causes, including rape. All sides in the conflict are using rape as an instrument of war.

Other countries in Africa have taken various steps to address rape. At the behest of the Uganda Women Parliamentarians Association, Uganda increased the sentence for rape to include the death penalty. As of 2009, no rapists had been executed. Liberia, under the presidency of Ellen Johnson Sirleaf, sped up the prosecution of rape cases in 2008 by sending such cases to a special criminal court. It may not be coincidental that a woman understood the importance of such legislation.

In the Ivory Coast (Côte d'Ivoire), an education program may have led to more women reporting rape. It might also be possible that the number of rapes in the country has increased. Rapists in the Ivory Coast are rarely prosecuted, so the government is essentially encouraging such attacks by ignoring the problem. United Nations Secretary-General Ban Ki-moon said as much in a 2008 report, "The low level of prosecution . . . has heightened the pervading sense of impunity in the country" (IRIN, 2008, on-line). The International Rescue Committee has been informed by

Ivorians that government authorities harassed or ignored women who reported rape and, if a case is pursued, the attacker is generally released after a brief detainment. It is rare that an Ivory Coast man will be jailed for rape. To protect themselves, some communities have formed vigilante groups, but attitudes are difficult to change. Many Ivorians reportedly see rape as a sexual act rather than a crime.

Rape as a War Crime

As the situation in the Democratic Republic of Congo indicates, rape is often used as a tool of war in Africa to break up resistance and instill fear in the civilian population. The tactic is so common among warring groups that the Congolese have coined a new word: *reviolé* or "re-raped."

Mass rapes began in the Congo with the 1996 civil war, which spread to engulf neighboring countries. Mathilde Muhindo, head of one of Congo's oldest women's organization, Centre Olame, has categorized the systematic, collective rapes as a war within a war. Every single armed group in the country participated in mass rapes. Each group had its own signature style: some raped women with guns and fired the weapons as a finale while some forced sons to rape mothers. When a semi-peace descended on the Congo in 2003, the mineral-rich eastern area of the country continued to house 23 armed groups. The trouble in the east flared up in 2008 and brought a resurgence of rape.

Denis Mukwege, the only gynecologist at the Panzi Hospital in Congo, reported that he had treated 21,000 rape victims in a 12-year-span. He suspects that he is the world's leading expert on repairing injuries related to rape. The injured, who often arrive bleeding, typically leak feces and urine from torn vaginas. Many of the victims had been seen more than once. The Panzi medical staff had been demoralized by their inability to save women from repeated abuse.

In Zimbabwe, another African country torn by political conflict, rape is being used to intimidate political opponents. AIDS—Free World reported 53 cases of rape as a political weapon during contested elections in 2008. Betty Makoni, director of Girl Child Network, reported that youth militias raped about 800 girls on military bases. Other rape victims include female family members of opposing candidates as well as teachers, ward leaders, and clergy members. The attackers placed pesticides, sticks, and other objects in the vaginas of their victims. Makoni related that some women were raped in front of loved ones while some men were forced to rape their mothers-in-law. The victims were often forced to say that they would never support the opposition. Adding to the trauma, doctors at government hospitals refused treatment, even HIV drugs, to rape victims, for fear of reprisal from military forces.

Child Sexual Abuse

The United Nations (U.N) sends peacekeepers around the world to prevent violence. Accordingly, one might expect that peacekeepers would not participate in violence against women and girls. However, sexual abuses in the Democratic Republic of the Congo by U.N. forces became such a scandal that U.N. Secretary-General Kofi Annan banned all sexual contact between peacekeepers and local people in 2005. The peacekeepers would trade food and money for sex or just attack. Congo's Minister of Defense Jean Pierre Onde-kane reportedly had complained that the U.N. peacekeepers would only be remembered "for running after little girls" (Clayton, 2004, p. 9) The U.N. Security Council subsequently formally condemned acts of sexual exploitation by its troops

Thousands of U.N. peacekeepers had been sent to the Congo to help quell the various conflicts that were ripping the country apart and threatened to engulf the entire region. U.N. peacekeepers from Morocco who were based in Kisangani become notorious for impregnating 82 local girls and women. Uruguayan U.N. staffers impregnated another 59 girls in Kisangani. Meanwhile, two Russian pilots in Congo gave young girls mayonnaise and jam to have sex with them while a French logistics experts made videos of his sexual abuse of young girls. A French mechanic, later sentenced to nine years in prison by a French court, raped at least 20 African teenagers while posted in the Congo and the Central African Republic. Many other pornographic videos and photographs made by U.N. staffers were available for sale in Congo.

The steps taken by the U.N. in 2005 did not stop the problem. In 2007, Save the Children conducted a study in three countries with a strong U.N. presence—southern Sudan, Haiti, and Côte d'Ivoire. The charity found widespread sexual abuse of children, some as young as six, by peacekeepers. Many children are afraid to report such abuse because of intimidation. The U.N. has said that, with so many peacekeeping troops spread so widely, it is very difficult to police their actions. The peacekeepers reflect the values of their home countries.

Wife Rape

Domestic violence is a serious problem in Africa. The subordinate position of women is deeply entrenched in traditional, legal, social, and religious structures. Men are taught that women must submit to their demands, including demands for sex. Women are taught that violence in the home is normal. Women who complain about such matters as sexual violence within the home are blamed for "airing the family's dirty linen in public." Women who seek help from outside the family become outcasts, risk increased abuse, and suffer condemnation from their own relatives.

In Zimbabwe, family violence is not recognized as being as serious as stranger violence. There is no law preventing a husband from raping his wife. Additionally, HIV infection in Zimbabwe has reached endemic proportions, with infection estimates ranging from 25 to 33 percent. A woman who cannot say "no" to sex cannot refuse sex with her HIV-infected husband. The World Alliance of YMCAs has reported that 73 percent of Zimbabwean women report being forced to have sex with their partners with 69 percent of these women engaging in sexual relations with a man that they knew to be infected with a sexually transmitted disease.

Femicide

Femicide is the killing of a woman or a girl because of her gender. Examples of it can be found in war crimes when soldiers shoot women that they have just raped, but other examples are, unfortunately, common. In his memoir, *The Dressing Station*, South African surgeon Jonathan Kaplan recalled the horror that he felt when he saw a beautiful young black woman on an autopsy table during the days of apartheid. She had bled to death after being gang raped when her attackers kicked a bottle up her vagina and shattered the glass, slashing her pelvic arteries.

The violence against women in South Africa has accelerated since the end of apartheid, with about 150 women attacked daily and 33 percent of women reporting that they were raped within the past 12 months. Femicide is part of this epidemic. The human rights organization Action Aid has reported that gangs of South African men who rape lesbians to cure them of their sexual orientation have become common. This form of attack has been termed "corrective rape." The 2008 rape and murder of South African soccer player Eudy Simelane, a prominent lesbian activist, illuminated homophobic violence, particularly toward women. Simelane, one of only a few openly out lesbians in her home town of Kwa-Thema, was attacked by four men who then dumped her body in a KwaThema creek. One man pled guilty and the others were brought to trial. In most of South Africa, homosexuality is taboo and violence against lesbians is considered to be acceptable despite national laws offering protection to gays.

Asia

Rape

In Asia, as in much of the rest of the world, women are blamed for being raped if they dress provocatively. In the Islamic world, control is often seen as something imposed from the outside rather than an internal response. Instead of exercising self-control, many Muslims expect temptations to be unavailable. Debates about the freedoms accorded Muslim women often involve the women making themselves available to sexual assault. In northern Malaysia, a largely Muslim nation, a city council banned women in 2007 from wearing high heels or brightly colored lipstick with the aim of helping them preserve their dignity and avoid rape.

In 2007, Sheik Taj Din al-Hilali, the most senior Muslim cleric in Australia, delivered an infamous Ramadan sermon in which he likened women who did not wear the veil to uncovered meat that attracted predators. In the same speech, he said that women were weapons sent by Satan to entice men by swaying suggestively and wearing makeup. Other Australian Muslims were quick to condemn the cleric's speech, including Islamic Council of Victoria spokesman Waleed Ali who objected to comparing Muslim men to wild animals. However, the Sheik had also referenced a notorious gang rape and appeared to show sympathy for the attackers.

Australia had been rocked in 2000 by four brutal gang rapes of non-Muslim women by up to 14 Muslim Lebanese immigrant men led by Bilal Skaf. The attackers saw their teenage victims as asking for it because they did not cover themselves from head to toe and act like traditional Muslim women. During the hours-long attacks, the women were called "sluts" and "Aussie pigs." At the trial, the accused men smirked at testimony while their families threatened the victims and defense attorneys suggested that the women had enjoyed being raped. Skaf, who has never shown any remorse, spent some of his time in court drawing pictures of his ex-fiancé being gang-raped and murdered. (She had ended the relationship after his conviction, which he unsuccessfully appealed.) In the wake of the rapes, many Muslim leaders in Australia disavowed the rapists as disgraces to the Muslim community. Yet the idea that the victim is to blame remains common.

Wife Rape

Most countries in the world do not recognize rape within marriage as a crime. Two of the most prominent examples of countries that permit husbands to rape their wives with impunity are India and Malaysia. Thailand is one of the more progressive nations in this matter.

In 2007, the National Legislative Assembly of Thailand outlawed marital rape by amending its criminal laws. Under the legislation, a Thai who rapes a spouse could face up to 20 years in prison. The previous law defined a rapist as a person who raped a woman who was not his wife, meaning that a man could attack his wife with impunity. The new law contains the same penalties for anyone—male or female—who rapes.

Gang Rape

Many countries do not have specific legislation addressing gang rapes. Such attacks are prosecuted as routine sexual assaults despite the fact that victims suffer exponentially more trauma. Japan is an exception, however, having made gang rape into a specific crime in 2005. The legislation came in response to a series of gang rapes by 14 men who belonged to the Super Free social club at Waseda University. This attack followed a notorious 2003 gang rape by 15 football players at the elite Kokushikan University in Tokyo who attacked a 15-year-old girl at an apartment for seven hours.

Rape as a War Crime

In 2002, government soldiers from Myanmar, formerly known as Burma, were charged with raping at least 625 women and girls who belonged to the rebel Shan tribe. The Shans are one of seven main ethnic groups in Myanmar. They have been fighting for independence for decades. The Shan Human Rights Foundation charged that the military regime of Myanmar, which has a history of human rights abuses, was allowing its troops to systematically commit rape with impunity on a widespread scale in order to terrorize and subjugate the people of Shan State.

The 173 attacks were generally committed by commissioned officers in army camps in central Shan. In this region, over 300,000 villagers have been forcibly relocated since 1996. Many of the victims were detained while looking for food outside the relocation areas. Some were forced into becoming porters by the military and were raped while resting at army checkpoints. In one case, two students were arrested after they asked a politically sensitive question in class. They were detained for four days and raped repeatedly by soldiers. Many of the victims were tortured and killed. Since the bodies were dumped in the open, human rights activists suspect that the rapists had government approval for their actions. The activists also believe that many women have kept silent out of fear of reprisal and out of shame.

While it might be a bit of a stretch to categorize as war crimes the spate of rapes in the Japanese island of Okinawa by U.S. servicemen, the attacks do have a clear military connection. The U.S. occupied Okinawa as World War II wound to a close. U.S. military bases remained on the island after the end of hostilities because of its strategic location. With the end of the Cold War, there have been increasing demands by the Japanese to remove the 40,000 U.S. troops stationed on the island. Criminal acts by Americans, especially rapes of schoolgirls, have further fueled these calls for an end to the U.S. occupation.

As the Okinawa situation indicates, sexual crime can have serious diplomatic results. Major protests occurred on Okinawa in 1995 when three American soldiers were accused of gang-raping a 12-year-old girl. The men were court-martialed and convicted. The numbers of U.S. soldiers housed on the island were then reduced by a few thousand at the request of the Japanese. In the next few years, U.S. soldiers committed 14 more rapes, with the Japanese complaining because U.S. often took days to turn over suspects to Japanese police. In 2008, a staff sergeant faced charges that he had raped a 14-year-old girl, reigniting the protests. In the wake of this attack, the Okinawa legislature adopted a resolution urging the U.S. military to improve ethical training for its forces, while the U.S. ambassador flew to the island to express sorrow over the incident. Meanwhile, many Okinawans insisted that they would not feel safe until all U.S. troops had been withdrawn, since resolutions had little effect in the past.

Child Sexual Abuse

The numbers of sexual crimes against children are increasing throughout Asia for reasons that are not clear. In South Korea, the government estimated that 5,460 youths were the victims of sex crimes in 2007. Most attacks went unreported. Rape counted for the highest percentage of the 965 reported sex crimes against children in that year. With respect to child molestation, more than 70 percent of victims were under 13. The age of victims of molestation is dropping. The younger the victim, the more likely that the attack was committed by an acquaintance. Most offenders are men in their 30s who attack in the afternoon when schools have ended classes. Motels were commonly used for rapes while public bathhouses, or *jjimjilbang*, were used for molestation. The bathhouses, which are gender-segregated and feature saunas, are extremely popular among Koreans. To combat child sexual abuse, the Korean government posted information about sex offenders online in 2008.

In Cambodia, many men believe that raping a virgin will be keep you strong and imbue you with fresh strength. It is also held that raping a virgin will also cure you of AIDS. The AIDS epidemic arrived in Cambodia about 1994 and the county now has among the highest rates of infection in Asia. The brothels sell virgins, often aged five or six so that the man can be sure that she is truly a virgin, for a week. After the week is over, the brothel owners sew up the girl's internal injuries—without an anesthetic—and quickly sell her again. A virgin is supposed to scream and bleed and the girl will scream and bleed again and again. The girl is sold three or four times.

Selling women into prostitution apparently has a long history in Cambodia. By working in a brothel where a moneylender has an arrangement, a daughter acts as collateral and repays the loan. In other cases, the parents sell the daughter outright to the brothel. A 12-year-old girl might bring in $50 or $100, depending on the lightness of her skin. The brothel has the right to sell her to another establishment. The family goes to the brothel every month to pick up her earnings. Daughters have a duty to obey their parents and provide for them, so the arrangement is not challenged by the child. Somaly Mam, founder of a Cambodian organization against sex slavery, suggests that parents do not view their daughters emotionally but rather as a type of domestic livestock.

In 2005, the Future Group, a Canadian non-governmental organization, declared that at least 1 in 40 girls born in Cambodia will be sold into sex slavery. It estimates that the lowest number of prostitutes and sex slaves in Cambodia is between 40,000 and 50,000. Somaly Mam notes that there are virgins for sale in every large town in Cambodia.

There are two distinct modes of sexual trafficking in India: coercive trafficking and family-based trafficking. The latter form is done in collusion with parents or caregivers who may have been deceived into letting the child go or who may have knowledge of where the child is being taken. Practices that involve dedicating a daughter to a life of traditionally sanctioned prostitution as a *devadasi* continue in India despite the enactment of laws banning the custom. Victims of this practice are estimated to account for 20 percent of the children in prostitution.

Some families send daughters into prostitution as a matter of economic survival. The growth of slums in India has contributed to the rise in prostitution. The development of large dams, mines, and power projects has led to the eviction of large numbers of people from areas that they have traditionally farmed. Forced to move to find a new means of survival, these displaced people migrate to slums in the cities where the whole family must work to survive. Migrant child labor is treated as another commodity that can be bought and sold.

A government-sponsored survey in India in 1992 found that 40 percent of the sex workers stated that they had entered the sex trade when they were under the age of 18. Another study estimated that 300,000 to 400,000 children in India are victims of sex trafficking. About 60 percent of the children are believed to be from the lower castes. These castes are at the bottom of the economic ladder. Additionally, Nepali girls are being trafficked into India, with the Human Rights Watch—Asia reporting in 1995 that the average age of the girls dropped from 14–16 years to 10–14 years. Of the 200,000 or so Nepalese sex workers in India, children constitute 20 percent. The girls are trafficked from economically depressed areas to the major prostitution centers of Delhi, Mumbai, and Calcutta. Laws introduced to stop trafficking have had little noticeable effect.

The process of initiating children into prostitution, whether in India, Cambodia, or Thailand, is typically brutal. Various researchers have reported that new girls are subjected to torture in the form of electric shocks, cigarette burns, and beatings to break them in. Children are often drugged into submission and starved to destroy their wills and ensure their cooperation. Newly kidnapped girls, who can be difficult to control, are told stories about the plight of the maimed children to frighten them into submitting. Psychological abuse, threats, and intimidation are used with girls who are purchased as virgins and can therefore be sold for higher prices if their training does not include rape. The child may be told that she is dirty by one member of the staff while another staffer tries to befriend her and convince her that she is among family.

The vast majority of literature on prostitution focuses on girls but boys also participate in this practice. In India, young male prostitutes can be found in the major cities. The boys are often street children who have run away from home and need a source of income. In Bangalore, boys have been reported to hang around railroad stations to trade sexual services for gifts, food, money, and drugs. While the boys apparently enter into prostitution voluntarily, minors cannot legally give sexual consent so the practice is viewed as the sexual abuse of children.

Sex Trafficking

The subject of trafficking women and girls for purposes of prostitution is getting an increasing amount of attention. Such activity can often result in multimillion dollar profits for organized crime groups, with the money untaxed. In 1999, an international symposium on migration prompted representatives from the following countries to issue the Bangkok Declaration on Irregular Migration: Australia, Bangladesh, Brunei Darussalam, Cambodia, China, Indonesia, Japan, Republic of Korea, Lao PDR, Malaysia, Myanmar, New Zealand, Papua New Guinea, the Philippines, Singapore, Sri Lanka, Thailand, and Vietnam, as well as Hong Kong. The declaration expresses grave concern over the increasing trafficking activities by organized crime syndicates. The signatory countries agree to cooperate in the prosecution and punishment of anyone who sold human beings for any purpose, including sexual slavery.

As the Bangkok Declaration indicates, increased globalization has a dark side. Australia has seen a rise in women trafficked into the country, while Malaysian authorities believe that ethnic

Chinese crime syndicates are behind most of the trafficking in their country. Trafficked women and girls are usually fed into an extensive system of Chinese-owned lounges, nightclubs, and brothels that exist throughout most of Asia.

Many, if not most, of these girls and women are unwilling participants in prostitution. In China, criminal organizations are known as Triads. The Triads have been abducting and selling women and girls within Chinese borders. As one example, the Song clan group set up a business to hire people to go to Shanghai to purchase apparel or to Anhui to purchase traditional Chinese medicines. Lured under false pretenses, the young women who applied for the jobs were then kidnapped and delivered to buyers.

In Japan, the Yakuza are involved in trafficking women. The Yakuza are members of traditional organized crime syndicates. They are relative newcomers to the trafficking line of work. When the Japanese economy collapsed in 1992, the Yakuza had to find new sources of income. They found forced prostitution. Local brokers approach women in their home countries, mostly in Asia, Latin America, or Russia. These are the women who are the most vulnerable, often from areas that have suffered a disaster such as a typhoon. The Yakuza have also been known to traffic American women to Japan. The brokers promise well-paying jobs in legitimate professions in Japan. For their efforts, they are paid $6,000 to $10,000 per woman.

Once in Japan, the women are funneled to brothels by intermediaries, primarily Yakuza, who have purchased the rights to these women from the brokers. All of the women's earnings go to the traffickers. The Yakuza protect their financial investment by hiring a bodyguard for each woman, to prevent her escape. If a woman escapes, the Yakuza will post her picture and encourage members or affiliates to turn her in if spotted. The Japanese police are reportedly often the ones who turn in escapees to the Yakuza. Some Filipinas who tried to escape were reportedly put to death while shelters that house escapees have been severely vandalized.

In Thailand, there are at least seven crime families in Bangkok that recruit, sell, and smuggle Asian women throughout the world, including the United States, to serve as prostitutes. These families obtain travel documents for the women, arrange travel itineraries, and then sell the women to agents representing brothels. Escorts, known as jockeys, transport the women to their destinations. The women are charged $40,000 for the smuggling services. They pay back this debt through prostitution. Until the money is paid, the prostitute is under the control of her handler. She is frequently sold, exchanged, and battered. Meanwhile, the false passports that the women used to illegally enter a country are sent back to Thailand and recycled with other prostitutes.

The issue of forced prostitution has worldwide implications. Researchers estimated in 1999 that 40,000 to 50,000 women were trafficked into the United States each year by crime rings. Most of these women come from Asia and Mexico, with the majority apparently trafficked for sexual purposes. Few of the cases come to court because of the difficulties in identifying women who have been trafficked. Many victims fear testifying against individuals that have terrorized them and/or threatened their families. Several brutal Asian-American gangs, including the Flying Dragons, the Black Dragons, and the Koolboyz, are known to provide protection to brothels where trafficking is thought to have occurred. In China, major Asian organized crime syndicates, such as the Sun Yee On, 14 K, Big Circle Boys, and Wo on Lok, have all repeatedly been linked to smuggling illegal immigrants and to prostitution.

Legal authorities expect that trafficking has continued to increase but it is impossible to get an accurate count of victims of trafficking. The poor economic situation in many countries has forced women to look abroad for jobs. Improved international transportation has made it much easier and cheaper for people to move around the world. If women are lured into forced prostitution, it is very challenging for authorities to prosecute the responsible individuals. The enormous profit potential of prostitution has attracted the criminal syndicates with their long and wide reach.

Nevertheless, there have been several notable legal cases involving women who were trafficked from Asia to the United States and forced to serve as prostitutes. The cases are representative of sexual trafficking in that the women were tricked into prostitution, held captive, and forced to work as prostitutes until the costs of their transportation, housing, and other essentials were repaid. There have been no reports of women ever being freed after repaying what they allegedly owed. Women are kept in perpetual debt.

The *U.S. v. Kwon* (1998) is typical of the cases that have been prosecuted. The defendants recruited and transported Chinese-Korean women from China to the Northern Mariana Islands in the North Pacific from June 1995 to January 1998 for sexual purposes. (The Mariana Islands are a U.S. possession, thus giving the U.S. legal jurisdiction.) The women, who were promised legitimate jobs as waitresses, were forced to work at a karaoke club and to provide sexual services to customers. Some of the women also alleged that they suffered physical and sexual abuse at the hands of their employers. The defendants, who housed the women in barracks, took their passports, visas, and airline tickets, thereby blocking them from fleeing. The women could only leave the barracks with permission. They were threatened with violence, including death, if they left without permission. In November, 1998, the traffickers were indicted for conspiracy against rights, involuntary servitude, extortion, transportation for illegal sexual activity, and the use of a firearm in the commission of a crime of violence. The defendants pled guilty to conspiracy to violate the Thirteenth Amendment, which bans slavery throughout the United States, as well as to several other charges. They received sentences of two to eight years. The women who had been forced into prostitution moved to Guam, another island in the Mariana chain, and worked at jobs that the U.S. Department of Justice helped them to acquire.

The case of *U.S. v. Wattanasiri* (1995) shows how sex trafficking in Thailand has created a crime problem within the United States. Ludwig Janak, a German citizen worked in conjunction with Thai traffickers to recruit Thai women to come to the United States to work at legitimate jobs in restaurants. Once in the United States, the traffickers joined with a Korean madam to force the women into prostitution. As is typical, the women were held against their will in a brothel and forced to work until their smuggling debt—about $35,000—had been paid. The traffickers estimated that each woman would need to have sex with 400 to 500 customers to pay off the debt. The brothel had bars on its windows to keep the women captive as well as 24-hour surveillance. The U.S. government charged 18 defendants with kidnapping, alien smuggling, extortion, and white slavery. Twelve defendants were convicted and given sentences of four to nine years. Of the six defendants who fled to Thailand, two were extradited and jailed for several years. The remaining traffickers are still being sought by police.

The U.S. State Department has argued that it is probably impossible to stop trafficking. However, the practice might be reduced by improving prevention in the source countries. Microcredit, or assistance to small businesses that are operated by women, has the potential to reduce the economic incentive to look for work in other nations. The State Department also advises that the United States should strengthen the penalties against trafficking while providing more assistance and protection for the victims.

Anecdotal evidence suggests that some victims do not go to the police for fear of being deported back to the country that they were so desperate to leave.

Prostitution is also linked to AIDS, with Asia hit especially hard by the virus. In 1991, the infection rate of women in the sex industry began to explode, with the infection crossing national boundaries. AIDS in Myanmar seems to be spreading because of the high number of local women who return infected after working in Thai sex establishments. When the United Nations sent peacekeepers to monitor national elections in Cambodia in 1993, young men with money and little safe-sex knowledge arrived in a desperately poor country with little knowledge of AIDS. Infections by HIV virus that leads to AIDS suddenly jumped in Cambodia. HIV has since been spread by the clients of sex workers to wives and children. Sex tourism has also spread a version of HIV, known as subtype E, which is not common to the West. Tourists take subtype E back to their home countries.

To combat HIV, Asian governments have taken various steps. The drug cocktails to treat AIDS are not an option in most Asian countries because of the cost. A prostitute in Myanmar might have to serve more than 20 customers just to pay for two AZT pills. Accordingly, governments have focused on prevention rather than treatment. Myanmar, which had outlawed condoms until 1993, legalized them, but condoms remain too expensive for most people to afford. The Thai government began a national safe-sex campaign, "No condom, no service, no refund." It also distributed free condoms to prostitutes. However, girls and women who have been forced into prostitution are essentially being serially raped. Asking them to learn how to apply a condom to a client is essentially forcing them to confront something nightmarish. While many Thai men have been convinced by the same-sex campaign to request condoms, Thai sex workers operating near the Malaysian border report that Malaysian men do not want to use condoms. Malaysia has focused on abstinence rather than sex-safe to combat AIDS.

Europe

Rape

The prosecution of sexual crimes in Europe has been affected by age-old attitudes about women who "ask for it" as well as intimidation, physical violence, and psychological abuse. In Ireland, the Dublin Rape Crisis Center reported in 2008 that only 1 rape victim in 10 reported the crime to police. Scotland, with a 2.9 conviction rate in 2008, has one of the lowest rape conviction rates in Europe. Only 1 in 14 reported rapes in Scotland is even brought to court.

The Dublin antirape activists believe that women are afraid that they will not get justice since they have no advocates within the judicial system. They also do not have many advocates among the general public. A 2008 survey found that almost 40 percent of Irish adults believed that rape victims themselves bore some responsibility for being attacked. Such responsibility could include flirting or wearing sexy clothing. The antirape activists are calling for an amendment to the Constitution to establish strict liability for rape, so that rapists will not be able to evade punishment.

Italian antirape activists have had some of the same problems facing their Irish counterparts, namely a refusal by government authorities and the public to regard rape as a serious matter. In a notorious 1999 decision that directly influenced countless prosecutions, judges quashed the conviction of an Italian man who was accused of raping a young woman during a driving lesson. He argued that he could not have committed the rape since the victim wore jeans that were too tight for him to get into by himself. The accused rapist claimed that the sex had been consensual. The appellate judges found the man's argument convincing and released him. Other accused rapists then successfully used the same defense. After nearly a decade of protests by feminists, judges at the Italian Court of Cassation in 2008 reversed the ruling.

People in power in other parts of Europe displayed similar troubling attitudes toward rape. In 2008, a Polish legislator proposed legislation that would outlaw miniskirts and other enticements as a way of stopping rape. Sir Ken Macdonald, who as the Director of Public Prosecutions headed the Crown Prosecution Service and supervised all criminal prosecutions in the United Kingdom from 2003 to 2008, blamed young women for encouraging rape through promiscuity and heavy drinking. Donald Findlay, a prominent defense attorney in Scotland, has argued that his brethren should be able to refer in court to how an alleged victim was dressed. Perhaps not surprisingly, Rape Crisis—Scotland used funding from the government to launch a campaign in 2008 to challenge the notion that women are somehow to blame for being raped if they have been drinking, wearing revealing clothing, or have been sexually active.

Sex Trafficking

The end of the Cold War in 1989 had many unintended consequences, including a dramatic rise in the trafficking of women. The collapse of the Iron Curtain made it easier to cross international boundaries, while the collapse of Eastern European economies created a pool of women who were desperate for work and a group of people who were willing to sell others for cash. Interpol has collected data since the early 1990s that shows most sex-trafficked women in Europe come from Central Europe (39 percent), Eastern Europe (22 percent) and the Balkans (17 percent). The remainder of trafficking victims come from Asia and Africa.

The situation in Moldova is typical. Moldova, formerly a part of the Soviet Union, is now the poorest nation in Europe. In Moldova, it is not uncommon for an acquaintance, close friend, or relative to sell a woman or girl into prostitution. The girls, typically unaware of the scheme and under the belief that they will be working legitimate jobs, are taken to a destination such as Italy, Germany, or the United Kingdom. The traffickers confiscate passports and force the young women to work to repay the debt. Although they are supposed to be freed after repayment, traffickers typically sell them to other pimps.

Each Natasha—the nickname given to Eastern European prostitutes and one that is hated by sex-trafficked women—can generate considerable amounts of money for a network of pimps. There are no benefits for the victims, who receive none of the money that they make. The women are beaten and a majority contract sexually transmitted diseases, including hepatitis and AIDS. Many become addicted to the drugs and alcohol provided by pimps or psychologically impaired from repeated trauma from beatings and rapes. The International Organization of Migration, which operates a shelter in Moldova for trafficked women who have returned home, reports that many of the former prostitutes have contracted such trauma-caused ailments disorders as advanced schizophrenia and dissociative identity disorder.

The International Organization of Migration and the Global Survival Network both report that Russian organized crime groups control the European prostitution industry. Israel's Women's Network discovered that Russian organized crime controls the sex industry throughout Israel. These Russian organized crime syndicates include the Izmailovskaya, Dagestantsy, Kazanskaya, and Solntsenskaya, which are involved in the prostitution industry throughout the United States.

The Russian syndicates have moved Russian, Ukrainian, Georgian, and Chechen women throughout the world. One route goes through Bulgaria to Turkey, Greece, and elsewhere in Western Europe. The Mogilevich criminal syndicate owns nightclubs in Prague, Riga, and Kiev, where it traffics women for forced prostitution. Prostitutes in the United Arab Emirates are women imported by the Russian gangs and forced into sexual slavery. Russian organized crime has imported prostitutes to Canada. In one example, a Russian gang brought 11 women from the former Soviet Union to Canada in 1991. The women came to work as models but they were compelled to turn over their travel documents and work as stripper/prostitutes. They turned over their earnings to their Russian handlers after their loved ones back in Europe were threatened with bodily harm and death.

Given the way these gangs operate overseas and the brutality of their organizations, it is likely their prostitution operations in the United States routinely include trafficking in women through the use of deception, threats, and violence. *U.S. v. Milan Lejhanec and Ladislav Ruc* (1998) may be typical. In this case, the defendants recruited Czech women to work in legitimate jobs in the United States Upon arriving in the United States, the women found out that the legitimate jobs did not exist. They were forced to work in New York City strip clubs where customers fondled them for a fee. The defendants, who had taken the passports of the women, did not permit the women to leave until they had paid off the costs of smuggling them into the country. Both of the defendants received five years in jail for trafficking women for purposes of prostitution. Two other men were charged with witness tampering for trying to intimidate the Czech victims.

Gang Rape

In France, gang rape has been on the rise among teenagers since the millennium. Such crimes represent 10 to 20 percent of all serious cases in French juvenile courts. In a 2001 case in Versailles, seven youths were charged with gang-raping a 15-year-old girl repeatedly over a period of eight weeks. Fearful of reprisals against her family, she hesitated to tell police. A French antirape activist reported that the girl is typically seen as more *bourgeois*, or more materialistic, than the norm or better-educated. The gang who attacks her believes since she is supposedly having sex with her boyfriend, then she is fair game. The light penalties routinely given to attackers, including 11 young men who ganged raped a girl and received suspended sentences in 2001, do little to deter such crime.

Latin America

Rape

In Latin America, the land of *machismo,* many cultures have antiquated views of rape that block prosecution of sex criminals. Many Latin America societies teach men to believe that they are superior to and own women, with the act of deflowering regarded as proof of manhood. Although one of the most common violent crimes, rape is one of the least denounced, prosecuted, or punished. Rape and other sexual crimes are still not treated as serious matters. A few observers have even argued that rape has become virtually an institution in societies where bosses, landlords, union leaders, doctors, shopkeepers, and even teachers routinely solicit sex for favors.

Statistics from several countries show the prevalence of rape in Latin America as well as the difficulties of prosecution. Mexico is suspected to have the highest rate for rape in the region, with one Mexican woman raped every nine minutes. Women's groups estimate that only about one percent of rapes in Mexico are ever punished. The number is lower in rural areas. A United Nations study found that 9 out of 10 sexual assaults are not reported while 18 percent of Mexican victims do not even realize that rape is a crime. In many parts of Mexico, the penalty for stealing a cow is harsher than the punishment for rape. In Bogota, Colombia, women's rights advocates estimate that 10 rapes occur daily. In Costa Rica, the smallest Latin American country, antirape activists have concluded that for every 100 rapes reported there are 14 successful prosecutions. In Peru, those accused of rape are acquitted in 99 percent of the cases that make it to trial.

Prosecuting a crime in most of Latin America remains a very time-consuming process, with the result of deterring a victim from pursuing the matter. Peruvian rape victims have asserted that authorities in their country greet allegations of rape with indifference or ridicule. There is little interest in making the process easier for victims. A woman who has been sexually assaulted must make endless visits to police stations, followed by a long series of preliminary court hearings stretching over months. Since most rape victims are poor, often working jobs that pay by the hour, time away from the workplace is costly and could result in being fired. The decision to prosecute is wrapped up in economics.

A Mexican woman who seeks to file criminal charges must submit to a medical exam by a physician that is conducted in the prosecutor's office. There is typically little privacy or sensitivity, doubly victimizing the woman. The doctor looks for evidence of copulation, even though a bottle may have been used as the instrument of assault. Investigators sometimes ask women to prove that they were virgins before the attack. Once in court, women are often asked if they enjoyed the rape. Rapists' families and friends threaten victims who try to prosecute. Judges are more sympathetic to a woman who has suffered injury. A woman who complied without a struggle, perhaps because she was threatened with a gun, has difficulty proving her case. After the case has become public knowledge, victims face harassment from other men who think that because they have already lost their virginity, they have nothing left to lose.

The case of two deaf sisters, Antonia and Isabel Francisco Melendez, is representative of attitudes toward rape in Mexico. The Melendez girls, aged 13 and 16, were attacked in their central Mexican hometown of Reyeshogpan in 2001. Both became pregnant as a result of the rapes. Neither girl named her attacker. The girls' mother refused to pursue the matter because she did not want any trouble. Police have not investigated the crimes.

As the Melendez case indicates, although Mexican states punish rape with up to 20 years in prison, few people are convicted because few rapes are investigated. Official complaints of rape by women in poor urban barrios or isolated rural communities are virtually unknown. For girls such as the Melendez sisters, rape is just another of the many burdens of life that they have to bear. The few rape victims who go to the police are nearly always from the middle or upper classes.

Mexico's criminal code, most of which was written in 1931, offers little protection to women who are the victims of violence.

Women who charge rape have the burden of proving their innocence rather than the assailant's guilt. The criminal code specifics protection only for women who are honest and *casta*, or "of quality." In many of Mexico's 31 states, a minor child who accuses an adult man of statutory rape must first prove that she is "chaste and pure." Nineteen of the states require that statutory rape charges be dropped if the rapist agrees to marry his victim.

Marriage is seen as a way to restore honor to the victim and her family. There is also a common belief that a raped woman has been so soiled that no other man would want her. In 1997, Peru's Congress raised the issue of excusing rapists who married their victims. The Peruvian penal code, written in 1924, exonerated a rapist if he offered to marry his victim and she accepted. The 1996 case of a young woman named Maria Elena illustrates the workings of this pardon. Maria Elena, a 17-year-old who lived in the crime-ridden Villa El Salvador district of Lima, was gang-raped by a group of drunken men in their 20s while she walked home from work. Maria Elena's father and brother tracked down the rapists, who lived in the neighborhood. One of the men offered to marry Maria Elena. She declined the offer but the other two attackers threatened to slash her face. Meanwhile, her family pressured her to accept the proposal. Maria Elena, who had wanted to press charges, married her attacker under duress. Three months after the wedding, he abandoned her.

The Peruvian Congress removed the offer of marriage exemption in 1997. However, many other Latin American countries still exonerate rapists who marry victims. The list includes Argentina, Brazil, Chile, Colombia, Ecuador, Guatemala, Honduras, Nicaragua, Panama, Paraguay, the Dominican Republic, and Venezuela. In Costa Rica, a rapist is freed if he expresses an intention to marry his victim, even if she does not accept.

Wife Rape

If a rapist marries his wife, in most Latin American countries he is free to rape her again under the shield of marriage. Antirape activists have had comparatively little impact in Latin America. Mexico has seen the most improvement but with considerable room left for bettering the lives of rape victims.

In 1988, the first rape center opened in Mexico. The Center for Orientation and Support of Rape Victims in Mexico City may also have been the first rape center in Latin America. The center opened with significant financial support from the ruling Institutional Revolutionary Party (PRI), which dominated Mexican politics for most of the 20th century. The ability of feminists to obtain political support reflected growing political clout as well as a slow shift in attitudes toward rape. A subsequent landmark court decision showed that some men in government were hearing women's voices.

In 2005, the Mexican Supreme Court unanimously ruled that rape within marriage is a crime. The decision overturned a 1994 ruling by the Court that found forced sexual relations by a spouse did not constitute rape because the purpose of marriage is procreation. The 1994 opinion stated that marital rape was "an undue exercise of conjugal rights." In the 11 years between the rulings, Mexican women made many strides for equal rights. In 1997, Congress passed a law criminalizing wife rape. The Court decision reflected a gradually changing attitude toward women. In written comments, Justice Jose de Jesus Gudino Pelayo defined marriage as a relationship of equality in which the woman does not lose her sexual freedom.

However, Mexican women's rights organizations expected that few women would charge their husbands with rape. They advised that long-standing attitudes about the subservient place of women and machismo would make it difficult for women to go to the police. As the Melendez case indicates, it is also doubtful that the police would regard rape as a serious matter.

Religion and Sexual Assault

Roman Catholicism is the dominant faith throughout Latin America. The Roman Catholic Church holds that abortion is a sin. This viewpoint has clashed with the interests of rape victims who become pregnant as the result of an assault.

Mexico is one of the largest Catholic countries in the world. Its federal laws ban abortion on demand except in cases of rape, serious medical problems, and potential birth defects. However, states have objected to the federal policy and have established their own regulations regarding abortion. In 2000, the state of Guanajuato proposed to jail rape victims who had abortions. The legislation set off a firestorm of debate, with Bishop Juan Sandoval Iniguez of Guadalajara blaming rape victims for encouraging sexual attacks by dressing provocatively. Surveys of ordinary

Mexicans, however, have consistently shown that most favor allowing abortion in rape cases despite the teachings of the church.

Rape as a War Crime

Rape as a form of torture has commonly been used on Latin American political prisoners, especially during the days of the dictators in Argentina, Chile, and Uruguay. During a period of intense repression in 1979, rape or the threat of it was also used on political detainees in Colombia. An incident that occurred in Peru during its long war in the 1990s against the Shining Path guerillas is representative. Although Peru's security forces officially prohibited rape, in practice sexual attacks were common and sanctioned. In 1993, in the jungle town of Aucayacu, soldiers broke into nine homes and, in each home, raped a woman or girl. Americas Watch, a human rights group that publicized 40 similar attacks, reported that it was aware of no case in which an active member of Peru's security forces was ever punished for rape. The group suggested that for some security personnel in remote rural areas, the violence of rape served as a part of routine interrogation of suspected rebel troops. Robin Kirk, an Americas Watch researcher, speculated that women who serve as rebel guerillas break gender stereotypes, thus triggering intense fear and anger among government soldiers. Rape is the result.

Amnesty International has suggested another reason for the number of rapes by soldiers. In rural areas, many soldiers apparently see rape and pillage as informal compensation for loneliness and the low salaries of military life. Rape is essentially a bonus.

Many researchers have long held that the stigma that surrounds victims of rape has the side effect of removing rapes by soldiers from the historical record. Some recent research in Guatemala challenges that belief. Julie A. Hastings, author of a 2002 article "Silencing State-Sponsored Rape in and Beyond a Transnational Guatemalan Community" in the journal *Violence Against Women,* argues that such rape is underreported because of collusion between national and international forces to depoliticize rape and silence rape victims.

Guatemala has the unpleasant distinction of having one of the longest civil wars on record, from 1960 to 1996. As rape often accompanies political unrest, it not surprising that many Guatemalan women were attacked by soldiers. Although rapes occurred frequently, the accounts of rape survivors were excluded from public testimonials about the violence in Guatemala. The women were willing to speak out but the government refused to hear them.

Rape as a Hate Crime

Rape rarely receives much attention in the press. Yet a series of killings and rapes in Ciudad Juárez, Mexico, proved so disturbing that media outlets around the world picked up the story. More than 400 women and girls were murdered in the Chihuahua city between 1993 and 2009. Approximately one in three of the killings involved some form of sexual attack. The victims were all young, slim, pretty, and with long dark hair. Human rights groups categorized the abductions as rapes, and murders as "feminicide" or hate crimes. They suggested that the women were being killed because they were female and poor. Very few perpetrators were held to account, and for several years there was a lack of commitment by both federal and state authorities to investigate the crimes.

Ciudad Juárez, Mexico, sits on the other side of the Rio Grande River from El Paso, Texas. It is Mexico's fourth largest city and an industrial center that draws thousands of poor people from all around Mexico who take assembly-line jobs in factories, known as maquiladoras. Most of the maquiladora workers are women, some as young as 13 or 14. While some young women go missing or are found dead, more young women are always pouring into the city.

Human rights groups have charged that the police of Ciudad Juárez do not value the lives of the poor women who work in the maquiladoras. The factories, which are linked to such multinational corporations as General Electric and Alcoa, have not provided security for their workers even though some bodies have literally turned up at their doors. The killings led to the formation of women's rights groups, many of which counted the female family members of the victims among their ranks. In 2004, pressure from these groups forced the federal government to appoint a special federal prosecutor. The prosecutor, who had no power to order fresh investigations, charged 103 officials with negligence for failing to conduct proper investigation before she was replaced by Mexico's President Vicente Fox. In 2005, an Interior Ministry official argued that, since 97 percent of murders in Mexico went unpunished, the situation in Ciudad Juárez qualified as normal and did not warrant special attention.

Sex Trafficking

The trafficking of women for sexual purposes in Latin America is essentially the same as trafficking in women in Europe or Asia. The victims are desperate for employment and tricked into trusting members of criminal syndicates. These criminals force the women and girls into prostitution. Many of the victims wind up in American brothels, as the case described below indicates.

In *U.S. v. Cadena* (1998), about 25 to 40 Mexican women and girls were trafficked between February 1996 and March 1998 from the state of Veracruz in Mexico to Florida and the Carolinas. The victims thought that they had obtained legitimate jobs, albeit as illegal immigrants, in waitressing, housekeeping, landscaping, childcare, and elder care. Upon their arrival, the women and girls were informed that they had to work as prostitutes in brothels that catered to migrant workers or they would be harmed. The women who attempted to escape were beaten, with one locked in closet for 15 days as punishment for trying to flee. Guards used force to keep them in the brothels in order that they pay off their smuggling debts that ranged from $2,000 to $3,000. Women who became pregnant suffered forced abortions.

In March 1998, 16 men were indicted in Florida for enslaving the Mexicans. They were charged with importing aliens for immoral purposes, transporting women and minors for prostitution, involuntary servitude, visa fraud, conspiracy, and violation of civil rights. The defendants received sentences of 2 to 6 years with a ringleader getting 15 years behind bars. Several of the other ringleaders escaped to Mexico, where they are still being sought. The judge ordered the criminal syndicate behind the trafficking to pay $1 million in restitution to the victims. The government seized the assets of the traffickers and used the money to assist the victims, who currently reside in Florida.

Conclusion

As the accounts above indicate, sexual crime involves so many aspects that it is enormously difficult to combat. Human rights groups are working to bring soldiers who rape to justice while women's rights groups focus on persuading government officials to take rape seriously. Western countries, including the United States, are clearly more enlightened about sexual assault than less developed nations. However, there is room for considerable improvement in every country.

Further Reading

Batstone, David. *Not for Sale: The Return of the Global Slave Trade—and How We Can Fight It.* New York: HarperOne, 2007.

Burns, Catherine. *Sexual Violence and the Law in Japan.* London: Routledge Curzon, 2005.

Clayton, Jonathan, and James Bone. "UN Officials in Sex Scandal." *The Australian.* December 24, 2004, p. 9.

Curran, Bronwyn. *Into the Mirror: The Untold Story of Mukhtar Mai.* New Delhi, India: UBS, 2008.

Farr, Kathryn. *Sex Trafficking: The Global Market in Women and Children.* New York: Worth, 2004.

Frederick, Sharon, and The Aware Committee on Rape. *Rape: Weapon of Terror.* River Edge, NJ: Global Publishing, 2001.

Hastings, Julie A. "State-Sponsored Rape: In and Beyond a Transnational Guatemalan Community." *Violence Against Women* 8, no. 10 (October 2002): 1153–1174.

Human Rights Watch. *The War Within the War: Sexual Violence Against Women and Girls in Eastern Congo.* New York: Human Rights Watch, 2002.

IRIN. "Cote d'Ivoire: Rapes Are Encouraged." October 21, 2008. http://www.irinnews.org/report.aspx?ReportId=81038.

Jordan, Mary. "Machismo's Dark Side: Rape Often Goes Unpunished in Mexico." *Washington Post.* July 6, 2002, p. B3.

Kaplan, Jonathan. *The Dressing Station: A Surgeon's Chronicle of War and Medicine.* New York: Grove Press, 2003.

King, Gilbert. *Woman, Child for Sale: The New Slave Trade in the 21st Century.* New York: Chamberlain Bros., 2004.

Malarek, Victor. *The Natashas: Inside the New Global Sex Trade.* New York: Arcade, 2005.

Mam, Somaly. *The Road of Lost Innocence.* London: Virago, 2007.

Parrot, Andrea, and Nina Cummings. *Sexual Enslavement of Girls and Women Worldwide.* Westport, CT: Praeger, 2008.

Stiglmayer, Alexandra, ed. *Mass Rape: The War Against Women in Bosnia-Herzegovina.* Lincoln: University of Nebraska Press, 1994.

Williams, Phil, ed. *Illegal Immigration and Commercial Sex: The New Slave Trade.* London: Frank Cass, 1999.

4

Chronology

c. 2000 B.C.E.	The Babylonian Code of Hammurabi declares that a man is to be seized and slain if he kills a betrothed virgin, with the victim considered blameless. A married woman who is raped is considered to be guilty of adultery. She and her attacker are bound and thrown into the river.
c. 1600 B.C.E.	The Hittite Code of the Nesilim is written. It declares that a woman who is raped within her own home could be executed.
c. 1000 B.C.E.	The Assyrian Code of Assura is written. It permits a husband to kill or punish his wife if she is raped.
c. 1000 B.C.E.	Ancient Hebrews mandate that a married woman who is raped shall be stoned to death along with her attacker at the gates to the city. If a man rapes a virgin within the walls of the city, both victim and attacker are stoned under the reasoning that the girl would have been heard had she screamed. For an act of rape that takes place outside of the city where neighbors might not hear an assault, the rapist must pay the fifty silver shekels to the girl's father to compensate him for her bride price. If the girl is engaged to be married, the rapist shall be stoned to death.

429 B.C.E.   The Hippocratic Oath, which establishes ethical principles for physicians, bans sexual encounters within the doctor-patient relationship.

c. 930 C.E.   During the reign of King Athelstan of England, a man who attempts to rape a virgin forfeits all of his possessions while the successful rapist of a virgin loses his life as well as his possessions. A raped virgin is permitted to save her attacker's life by marrying him.

c. 1066   William the Conqueror of England punishes rapists of virgins by castrating and blinding them. The trial of a rapist is by combat, with the virgins defended by their kinsmen. It is unclear how many cases went to trial.

c. 1154   King Henry II of England ends trial by combat in favor of trial by jury. While raped virgins can go to court, there is apparently no provision for married women to do so. A virgin must make a complaint immediately following the attack and must show blood and torn garments.

c. 1300   In the Statutes of Westminster, King Edward I of England establishes the principle of statutory rape as the state begins to take an interest in the protection of children. The statutes made no distinction between the rape of a married or unmarried woman. The option of redeeming a rapist through marriage to the victim is eliminated. If a raped woman or her kin fails to begin prosecution within 40 days, the right to prosecute automatically passes to the state, thereby defining rape as an issue of public safety and government interest.

1385   In one of the earliest surviving Articles of War, Richard I of England decrees that none of his soldiers shall rape a woman on pain of death.

1736   In a posthumously published work, Sir Matthew Hale, Lord Chief Justice of England, argues in

History of the Pleas of the Crown that while rape is a detestable crime that is rightly punished with death, it is also an accusation that is easily made, hard to be proved, and harder to be defended. Hale's thinking dominates courtrooms for the next 250 years, as the man in a sexual assault case is viewed as a potential victim of a vengeful woman.

1736   In the same work, Hale comments on the impossibility of marital rape when he declares that a wife has agreed to sex by agreeing to marriage. For almost the next 250 years, men who attack their wives argue successfully that the marriage contract gave them the right to rape.

1746   When English forces put down a rebellion by Scottish Highlanders at the Battle of Culloden, the English then proceed to rape and sexually mutilate Scottish women throughout the Highlands in an effort to humiliate the Scottish men.

1765–1769   In his landmark, *Commentaries on the Laws of England*, legal scholar William Blackstone writes that "by marriage the husband and wife are one person in law; that is, the very being or legal existence of the woman is suspended in marriage." Since the wife has no legal existence, she also has no legal remedy against a sexual assault by her husband, who cannot be charged with essentially attacking himself.

1780   Revolutionary War soldier Thomas Brown of the Seventh Pennsylvania Regiment is sentenced to death for a rape at Paramus, New Jersey, while serving with George Washington's forces. The offense is Brown's second conviction.

1838   In *People v. Abbott* in New York State, a married minister is acquitted of rape because his accuser did not meet the conditions required for a charge. She had to be of good reputation, show evidence of physical resistance, and try to call for help.

1854   In *People v. Morrison* in New York State, the court declares that a rape did not occur if a woman did not resist using all of her natural abilities.

1892   African American journalist Ida B. Wells challenges the notion that black men are lynched primarily to avenge southern white women from rape. Her pamphlet *Southern Horrors,* titled to play on the justification of southern honor, argues that black men are lynched as a means to intimidate the entire African American community. She reports that only a third of the 728 lynching victims between 1884 and 1892 were even accused of rape. Earlier in 1892, Wells had published an editorial that revealed that most "rapes" were in fact often consensual liaisons between black men and white women. In response to the article, an angry mob of whites demolished Wells's newspaper office and she fled Memphis, Tennessee for good. She published *Southern Horrors* in the North.

1915   D. W. Griffith's silent film, *Birth of a Nation,* becomes a blockbuster hit. It depicts an animal-like black man intent on raping a white heroine, who leaps to her death rather than succumb. The film contributes to the myth of the black rapist and sparks the creation of the Second Ku Klux Klan.

1931   In a celebrated case, Thalia Fortescue Massie, the troubled wife of a Navy lieutenant, claims that a group of Hawaiian men raped her at Ala Moana, a lonely beach road leading from Waikiki to Honolulu, Hawaii. Five young men of Asian ancestry (two Hawaiian, two Japanese, and one Chinese) are arrested for the sexual assault. After evidence is presented at trial showing that none of the defendants had the opportunity to commit the crime, the jury deadlocks and all of the men are released on bail. Outraged white sailors beat one defendant so badly that he almost dies. Another defendant, native Hawaiian Joseph Kahahawai is found dead as the apparent victim of an honor slaying in the back seat of Massie's mother's car. Grace Fortescue had been deeply disturbed by the refusal of the jury to convict her daughter's alleged attackers. She is eventually tried and convicted of manslaughter but her sentence is commuted by the governor to one hour. Native Hawaiians view the case as an example of a miscarriage of justice and extreme racism.

1931   The trial of the Scottsboro Boys begins in Tennessee. Nine black young men aged between 13 and 20 years are arrested and charged with the rape of white women. They narrowly miss being lynched. At the trial, the judge does not accept evidence indicating that the white women were prostitutes who had semen in their bodies as a result of their line of work. The boys deny knowing the prostitutes. (DNA tests were not in existence in 1931 so the ownership of the semen could be proved.) The boys are convicted, with some sentenced to death and others given long terms in prison. The case gains notoriety around the world as racially based miscarriage of justice. Appeals block the executions and the last Scottsboro boy leaves prison in 1944.

1937   In the Rape of Nanking, Japan invades China's capital city and Japanese soldiers engage in the mass rapes of civilians. The Nanking International Relief Committee estimated that there were hundreds of rapes each night.

1938   The *Kristallnacht* attacks by Nazis against Jews in Germany include the rapes of Jewish girls and women by German soldiers although sexual intercourse between such individuals was prohibited by the Nuremberg race laws of 1935 as "race defilement."

1942   Papal envoy Archbishop Giuseppe Burzio in Bratislava, Czechoslovakia, informs Pope Pius XII that Germany is forcing young Jewish women to become prostitutes for German soldiers on the eastern front.

1942 The Soviet Union complains to Allied countries during World War II that German soldiers are conducting mass rapes of girls and women in occupied areas of the U.S.S.R.

1944 In a surprise raid on the village of St. Donat, a center for the French resistance, German soldiers rape 54 women ranging from ages 13 to 50.

1945 Russian soldiers who participate in the fall of Berlin rape masses of German women. The front-line soldiers are disciplined and well-behaved but the second wave of troops take revenge for World War II on the women of Berlin.

1945 Helene Deutsch's *Psychology of Women* is published. Deutsch argues that women are masochists who fantasize about being raped.

1946 Captured German documents presented at the Nuremberg war crimes tribunal indicate that Germany used rape as a weapon of terror during World War II.

1957 In what is apparently the first study of date rape, Eugene J. Kanin of Purdue University in West Lafayette, Indiana, shows that 30 percent of women surveyed had suffered an attempted or completed rape while on a high school date.

1962 The American Law Institute approves a Model Penal Code (MPI) for rape that prompts several states to revise their statutes to give more credence to women alleging rape. The common law definition of rape required that the woman prove that she had not consented to sexual intercourse, usually in the form of evidence that she had resisted such as bruises. While the common law definition gradually abandoned the standard of resistance to allow prosecutors to use evidence of force, such as a gun, many jurisdictions still required corroboration of a victim's testimony to prove that a crime had indeed been committed. A woman's word was not considered proof enough. Evidence of a victim's previous sexual history was admitted in the belief that if she had said "yes" in the past that she would always say "yes" to anyone. The MPI classifies the crime of rape as a felony in the first degree if the victim is a stranger to the attacker or if serious bodily harm in inflicted. Second degree rape occurs if a no such injury is inflicted or if the perpetrator was known, such as in date rape. The MPC, reflecting the thinking of 1962, maintains an exemption for marital rape, a corroboration requirement, a requirement that a complaint be made promptly, and a cautionary-instruction (from judge to jury) requirement. The revisions are not pro-victim but also do not overwhelmingly favor criminal defendants.

1967   Albert DeSalvo, the Boston Strangler, goes to prison. He confesses to 11 of 13 rape-murders that took place in the Boston area between June 14, 1962 and January 4, 1964. Most of the victims fall between the ages of 55 and 87, with the youngest aged 19. DeSalvo also admits to being the Green Man, responsible for raping women in four states while wearing green work pants.

1967   Eugene J. Kanin of Purdue University in West Lafayette, Indiana completes a study in which more than 25 percent of male college students admit having attempted to force sexual intercourse on a woman to the point where she cried or fought back.

1968   In the notorious My Lai massacre during the Vietnam War, men under the command of Lieutenant William L. Calley engage in rape, attempted rape, and rape with murder. Although the Army confirms that systematic rapes had taken place, the charges against the accused men are dropped.

1971   Rape had been viewed as a shameful secret before the women's movement. Conventional wisdom argued that women had "asked for it." As the

1971 (*contd.*)	movement begins to form, women begin to analyze and politicize the physical aspects of being female. Accordingly, feminists begin to focus upon rape reform as part of consciousness-raising about the various issues affecting women. To publicize the high incidence of rape, New York Radical Feminists (NYRF), a short-lived organization of young women, holds the first speak-out on rape at St. Clement's Episcopal Church in New York City to raise awareness about the issue. About 300 hundred women attend and 40 give rape testimonies. The event emphasizes that rape is not uncommon but that few women report it.
1971	Feminist Susan Griffin writes a pathbreaking article. "Rape—The All-American Crime" for *Ramparts* magazine in which she declares that she has never been free of the fear of rape. She is the first to make clear that only one rapist could keep women off the streets at night, frighten them away from taking night classes, and prevent them from taking night jobs. Griffin argues that power, not lust, is at the heart of rape.
1972	The first rape crisis hot line is established in Washington, D.C., in 1972 and rape centers began to spread across the country. Many are operated by women's liberation groups such as the National Organization for Women.
1973	New York City forms the first police Rape Investigation Unit, led by Lieutenant Julia Tucker.
1973	Senator Charles Mathias of Maryland proposes the formation of the National Center for the Prevention of Rape within the National Institute of Mental Health. Congress approves the bill but President Gerald Ford vetoes it. The bill subsequently passes in 1975 and creates the National Center for the Prevention and Control of Rape.
1973	The Women's Anti-Rape Coalition (WARC) forms in New York City to seek the repeal of the

corroboration requirement in legal statutes and to raise public awareness of rape issues. It declares August to be Rape Prevention Month.

1974 New York becomes the first state to repeal the corroboration requirement.

1974 Inez Garcia, a 30-year-old fruit picker, is raped by two men in Soledad, California. Married at 15, Garcia had lived in Miami until her husband was sent to a California prison. She lived near the prison with her 11-year-old son. Garcia responded to the rape by grabbing a rifle and searching for her attackers. She found them. When one drew a knife, she shot him dead. He had been the attacker who held her down during the rape. Charged with homicide, Garcia became a cause célèbre among feminists and political radicals. Observers debated whether a woman had a right to self-defense hours after being sexually assaulted. Garcia's attorney argued that she had a right to protect her integrity when violated. The jury convicted Garcia but she won an appeal and her release from prison two years later.

1974 Pop singer Connie Francis, famous for such 1950s and 1960s hits as "Who's Sorry Now" and "Where the Boys Are," is raped in a motel room at a New York Howard Johnson's after performing at the Westbury Music Fair. The rapist, who has never been caught, entered the room because the motel management did not repair a broken lock and torn screen. Francis becomes the first prominent woman to come forward as a rape victim when she sued the motel chain and subsequently won a substantial settlement. Francis does not perform again for seven years because of trauma from the attack.

1975 The National Organization for Women begins to hold nationwide events to reclaim the night from sexual predators. The event eventually turns into Take Back the Night, an annual event that aims to make public streets safer for women.

1975   Joanne Little, an African American prisoner in a
            Beaufort, North Carolina jail, stabs white county
            guard Clarence Alligood to death. Little claims
            that Alligood had attempted to rape her. The trial
            becomes another cause célèbre. Both feminists and
            black activists argue that white men had always and
            would always be acquitted for raping black women.
            A jury of six blacks and six whites takes 78 minutes
            to acquit Little.

1975   Susan Brownmiller publishes *Against Our Will,* which
            reveals the universality of rape upon men, women,
            and children in every era and in every place. Her
            pathbreaking book puts rape onto the political
            agenda. Partly as a result of Brownmiller's book,
            rape victims are viewed by police, legal authorities,
            and medical personnel as traumatized and innocent
            victims of a crime instead of sinners with a case of
            regret. The changes encourage more women to
            report rapes.

1975   In *Cox Broadcasting Corporation v. Cohn,* the U.S.
            Supreme Court nullifies a Georgia statute that
            banned news organizations from publishing the
            names of rape victims. The Court rules that such
            a prohibition violates the First and Fourteenth
            Amendments to the Constitution.

1976   Nebraska becomes the first state to expand rape law
            to prohibit rapes within marriage.

1977   Judge Archie Simonson is recalled from the bench
            for excusing a rapist. Simonson, from Madison,
            Wisconsin, justified the actions of a 15-year-old
            boy convicted of rape by blaming his actions upon
            women's revealing clothing and a "normal" reac-
            tion to relaxed cultural attitudes about sex. A female
            judge replaces him.

1977   In his final study on date rape, Professor Eugene
            J. Kanin of Purdue University finds that 26 percent
            of surveyed men had tried to force intercourse on

a woman while 25 percent of surveyed women reported experiencing an attempted or completed rape.

1977   Film director Roman Polanski flees the country after admitting to having sexual intercourse with a 13-year-old girl at the home of actor Jack Nicholson. Polanski faced up to 50 years in prison for statutory rape.

1977   The U.S. Supreme Court bans the death penalty for rape cases on grounds that it is unconstitutional in *Coker v. Georgia.* The decision has been credited with increasing both reporting of rapes and successful prosecutions of rapists.

1978   Sandra Butler publishes *The Conspiracy of Silence: The Trauma of Incest.* The book helps force a public discussion of incest by bringing it into the open. Few Americans had realized how many relatives sexually violated young girls. (Young male victims of incest remain hidden.)

1978   Congress passes the federal Privacy Protection for Rape Victims Act, which prohibits the sexual history of a rape victim from being brought out in court. Many rape victims had refused to prosecute for fear of being cross-examined over their sexual history.

1978   A jury in Salem, Oregon, acquits John Rideout of beating and raping his wife, Greta. The trial received considerable national attention. For the first, many Americans learn about marital rape in a context that criminalizes it. At the time, Oregon is one of three states that classify marital rape as a crime. Many Americans begin to debate whether a wife can legally withhold sex from her husband.

1979   The first article on marital rape to gain nationwide attention is titled "Legal Rape" and appears in *Family Circle*, a magazine sold in supermarkets and aimed at housewives.

1979   Laura X organizes the National Clearinghouse on Marital Rape in Berkeley, California. After learning that several foreign countries had outlawed the marital exemption for rape, Laura X pushes for the United States to also ban marriage as a justification for sexual assault. She spends the next two decades speaking at college campuses and at professional associations while lobbying state legislatures to reclassify marital rape as a crime.

1981   The New Jersey Supreme Court reinstates the rape conviction of a legally separated husband.

1981   The U.S. Supreme Court upholds California's statutory rape law, which applies only to male offenders in *Michael M. v. Superior Court.*

1981   Congress passes the Sexual Abuse Act, which modernizes federal rape legislation. The bill defines sex crimes in gender-neutral terms, focuses the trial on the conduct of the accused rather than the conduct of the victim, ends spousal immunity, and expands federal jurisdiction to include all federal prisons.

1982   Auburn University psychology professor and acquaintance rape specialist Barry R. Burkhart finds that 61 percent of surveyed men admit to sexually touching a woman against her will.

1982   Professor Mary P. Koss of Kent State University in Ohio completes a scientific survey of sexual aggression and victimization. The subsequent report in a national magazine, *Ms.,* brings widespread notice of the date rape problem.

1982   The New York State legislature eliminates the requirement that rape victim prove physical resistance.

1982   The Kansas Supreme Court rules that the existence of Rape Trauma Syndrome is relevant and admissible as evidence of rape.

1983   Reports of a gang rape that took place in a barroom in
            New Bedford, Massachusetts, appear in the national
            media. A 21-year-old woman, new to the neighbor-
            hood, stopped at Big Dan's Tavern for cigarettes and
            a drink on a Sunday evening. Three hours later, she
            emerged battered, partially nude, and screaming for
            help. She said that a group of men had hoisted her
            on to the bar's pool table and raped her repeatedly
            while the rest of the men in the bar watched and
            taunted her while occasionally cheering the attack-
            ers. The rapists were ultimately convicted when the
            jury refused to consider the victim's past sexual
            history as a justification for her rape.

1983   About 4,500 men and women, some carrying plac-
            ards stating "Rape is Not a Spectator Sport," march
            outside of New Bedford city hall eight days after
            the Big Dan's Tavern attack. The protest receives
            extensive national coverage.

1984   A 12-year-old boy who watched the Big Dan's Tav-
            ern trial on television reportedly throws a 10-year-
            old girl onto a pool table in his home and sexually
            assaults her as other children watch. The incident
            becomes part of the testimony about the impact of
            "rape publicity" before a Senate Hearing Commit-
            tee. The hearing examined the impact of the Big
            Dan's rape case as well as the effect of such highly
            publicized trials on rape victims and the right of the
            press to have access to rape trials.

1984   In a random sample of 930 women in the San
            Francisco area, researcher Diana Russell finds that
            44 percent of the women surveyed had been victims
            of rape or attempted rape and that 88 percent of the
            rape victims knew their attackers.

1984   In *Weishaupt v. Commonwealth*, Virginia ends the
            spousal rape exemption. The couple in question
            had been separated for about a year but had not
            filed the paperwork either to legally separate or to
            divorce. The husband is convicted and sentenced

1984 (*contd.*)	to two years on the grounds that the couple had intended to divorce so the spousal exemption does not apply.
1984	In *People v. Liberta,* the New York Court of Appeals rules that the marital exemption for rape does not apply when a defendant is under a court order to stay away from his wife, and also abolishes the marital exemption for rape.
1985	The *Ms.* Magazine Campus Project on Sexual Assault, funded by the Center for Antisocial and Violent Behavior of the National Institute of Mental Health is completed. It famously finds that one in four college women reports having been the subject of an attempted or completed rape.
1985	Paul Price teaches at a North Carolina Bureau of Indian Affairs school from 1971 to 1985 despite complaints from parents. He is arrested for sexually assaulting boys under his care.
1986	The Massachusetts Department of Public Health releases a study showing that two-thirds of the rapes reported to rape crisis centers were committed by acquaintances.
1986	Jill Saward, also known as the Ealing Vicarage Rape Victim, is brutally gang-raped in the vicarage by two men who have broken into her home. She becomes one of the first rape victims in Great Britain to talk publicly about her experience.
1987	The FBI finds that John Boone, a teacher at a Bureau of Indian Affairs Hopi day school in Arizona, had sexually abused at least 142 boys but the school's principal had never investigated any allegations of abuse.
1987	The Bureau of Indian Affairs issues a policy requiring sexual abuse at boarding schools to be reported.

1987   Law professor Susan Estrich introduces the terms "date rape" and "acquaintance rape" in her book *Real Rape*. The book prompts colleges all over the country to hold debates on date rape to teach young women to be clear about their intentions and young men to seek consent.

1987   North Dakota becomes the first state to pass a date rape bill. Prior to this passage, a man who raped a female acquaintance could escape being charged with a felony if the victim was a "voluntary companion" or if the couple had a previous sexual relationship.

1989   The Wisconsin state legislature passes a bill requiring the University of Wisconsin system to include information on sexual assault and sexual harassment in student orientation programs. The act also requires the dean of students of each campus to compile statistics on such incidents on campus and to publicly release those statistics. The legislation helps inspire the Clery Act.

1989   The U.S. Supreme Court upholds the right of the media to repeat public information, including the names of rape victims, in *Florida Star v. B.J.F.* Nevertheless, most news organizations refuse to name victims without their express consent.

1989   The Central Park jogger case makes national headlines when a female jogger is raped and nearly beaten to death. Some observers blame the woman for being out in a public park by herself but most Americans are deeply shocked by the attack.

1989   The Glen Ridge rape case raises questions about the "boys will be boys" attitude and the leniency shown toward popular athletes who sexually misbehave. The case begins when a mentally challenged 17-year-old girl in Glen Ridge, New Jersey, is sexually assaulted in a gang rape by a group of high school baseball players at the home of two of the players.

1989
(*contd.*)

Fifteen of the boys had gathered in the basement but six left when they realized that a sexual assault was in process. Of the remaining seven boys, several watched while the others sexually assaulted the girl by fondling her breasts, coercing acts of oral sex, and penetrating her vagina with a broom and baseball bat. The victim, described as having the intellectual and emotional maturity of a second-grader, told no one about the encounter, as she had been instructed. She had hoped to become part of the popular crowd by associating with the popular athletes who had attacked her. However, some of the boys bragged and planned a repeat attack to be videotaped. News of the assault soon spread and became a national story. Four boys ultimately faced trial for first-degree rape. The heavily publicized six-month trial in 1992 led to four convictions. Bryant Grober received probation and community service. Christopher Archer and twins Kevin and Kyle Scherzer received sentences of up to 15 years. The boys appealed but lost and finally entered jail in 1997. All the young men were free by 2002.

1990

Washington becomes the first state to require public notification when violent sexual offenders are released into a community.

1990

The Student Right to Know and Campus Security Act, also known as the Clery Act after rape victim Jeanne Clery, is passed.

1990

The Indian Child Protection Act is passed by Congress. It creates a registry for sexual offenders in Indian country, mandates a reporting system, provides the Bureau of Indian Affairs and the Indian Health Services with guidelines for doing background checks on prospective employees, and provides education to parents, school officials, and law enforcement personnel on how to recognize sexual abuse. Native Americans argue that the law is not sufficiently funded and, as a result, child sexual abuse rates have been dramatically increasing in Indian country.

1991   The Navy's Tailhook scandal shines a light on the sexual abuse of women, including female officers, by male naval personnel.

1991   The U.S. Supreme Court upholds the rape shield laws of states in *Michigan v. Lucas*. A rape shield law prevents a victim's sexual history from being used in court in an attempt to discredit her testimony.

1991   William Kennedy Smith, nephew of President John F. Kennedy and Massachusetts Senator Edward Kennedy, is charged with rape in Palm Beach, Florida. The case, which ends with Smith's acquittal, becomes a media circus.

1992   Antioch College adopts a sexual assault policy requiring students to obtain their partner's consent at every stage of a sexual encounter. The policy is aimed at stopping date rape. The college, in Yellow Springs, Ohio, has long been known as a bastion of liberal activism and the new policy is heavily mocked, especially by political conservatives. Many of the students, however, support it and regard it as seductive.

1992   Heavyweight boxer Mike Tyson is accused of date rape. Tyson is sent to prison for three years before being paroled.

1992   In a celebrated South Carolina court case, Trish Crawford claimed that her husband, Dale, tied her to her bed, terrorized her with a knife, and raped her. Dale Crawford had videotaped the event. He is acquitted by a jury who apparently believed that his wife enjoyed sadomasochistic sex, a conclusion supported by the testimony of Trish Crawford's first husband. Police reports in which Dale Crawford's first wife charged physical and sexual abuse are not admitted into court by the judge. Both Trish and

1992 (*contd.*)	Dale Crawford discuss the case on national television programs.
1992–1995	Bosnian women are gang raped by Serbian soldiers during the Bosnian War in the former Yugoslavia. The victims number in the thousands.
1993	The Spur Posse scandal in Lakewood, California, attracts national attention. A group of high school boys, many of whom were popular athletes, used a point system to compare their sexual activities with underage girls. The Los Angeles County Sheriff's Department arrests a number of the players for various sexual offenses. Prosecutors later drop most of the charges on the grounds that they were consensual. Some of the Spur Posse members then go on a number of television talk shows to brag about and defend their exploits.
1993	Katie Roiphe publishes *The Morning After: Sex, Fear, and Feminism on Campus*. A graduate student at Princeton University, Roiphe attacks "rape crisis feminism," arguing that she and her Princeton classmates had never felt in danger of being raped. Roiphe blames women who charge date rape with failing to accept responsibility for their own choices.
1994	New Jersey passed the first Megan's Law, requiring the registration of sexually violent predators. The law comes in response to the kidnap, rape, and murder of seven-year-old Megan Kanka by her neighbor, Jesse Timmendequas, in the state.
1994	The Sexual Offender Act, also known as the Jacob Wetterling Law, is passed by Congress. A result of public furor over the Megan Kanka case, the law requires that individuals convicted of sexual crimes against children register their places of residence and employment with local law enforcement.
1994	The Violent Crime Control and Law Enforcement Act, an outgrowth of Megan's Law, requires states

to register sexually violent predators for 10 years after their release from prison and establish criminal penalties for those individuals who fail to register. It also allows victims of sex crimes tried at the federal level to speak at the sentencing of their attackers and strengthens the requirements for sexual offenders to pay restitution to their victims.

1995   The Beijing [China] World Conference on Women passes a resolution recognizing marital rape as a violation of women's rights.

1996   Mass rapes begin during the civil war in the Democratic Republic of the Congo in Africa.

1995   Three American soldiers are accused of gang-raping a 12-year-old Japanese girl in Okinawa, Japan. The men are subsequently convicted.

1996   Congress passes the Drug-Induced Rape Prevention and Punishment Act, which provides up to 20 years imprisonment for any person who uses a date rape drug, such as Rohypnol, to commit a violent crime.

1997   Army Staff Sergeant Delmar Simpson is sentenced to 25 years in prison for raping female trainees.

1997   *United States v. Lanier* involves a case in which a state judge is accused of sexually abusing five women who appeared in his court. The U.S. Supreme Court rules that the defendant had violated the right to liberty provisions of the Fourteenth Amendment, which includes the right to be free from sexually motivated physical assaults and coerced sexual battery.

1997   Mary Kay Le Tourneau, a 35-year-old school teacher and married mother, is convicted of child rape after engaging in sexual relations with a 13-year-old student. After being released from prison on probation, Le Tourneau promptly violates parole by

1997 *(contd.)*	resuming a sexual relationship with the boy and is returned to prison. The couple produce two children.
1998	In a trial of Rwandan authorities accused of war crimes, a United Nations tribunal declares rape to be a crime of genocide. The declaration is the first to make such a designation.
1998	Playwright Eve Ensler's *The Vagina Monologues* opens. The play, which is an effort at consciousness-raising, features interviews with a variety of women about the experiences of having a vagina. Rape is part of this experience. The play becomes an enormous hit, playing to massive sold-out crowds for the next few years.
2000	Muslim Lebanese immigrant men under the leadership of Bilal Skaf brutally gang rape four non-Muslim women in Australia. Skaf and the other men are convicted and jailed for long terms. The rapes inflame tensions between Muslims and non-Muslims.
2002	Government soldiers from Myanmar, formerly known as Burma, are charged by human rights workers with raping at least 625 women and girls who belong to the rebel Shan tribe
2002	The Catholic Church is rocked by several sexual scandals involving priests who abused boys under their care. In many of the cases, the abuse continued for years, with the Church hierarchy protecting the offenders.
2002	Mukhtar Mai is gang raped in her Pakistan hometown on the orders of the village council. The episode becomes an international cause célèbre.
2003	The Prison Rape Elimination Act becomes law. It protects federal, state, and local prisoners from sexual assault. The problem of male rape in prisons

had previously been treated as a joke with remarks about "don't drop the soap" often eliciting general merriment. The legislation helped change the perception of prison rape from a joke to a human rights concern.

2003   In *Lawrence v. Texas*, the U.S. Supreme Court rules that sodomy between consenting adults is not a criminal act. In *Bowers v. Hardwick* in 1986, the Court had found that states could prohibit sodomy on the grounds that there was no constitutional right to sexual privacy. The decision decriminalizes sex between gay men.

2003   University of North Dakota student Dru Sjodin is kidnapped, raped, and murdered by registered sex offender Alfonso Rodriquez, Jr. Six months earlier, Rodriquez had been released from prison after serving 23 years for attempting to kidnap and stabbing a woman. He is also a convicted rapist. Since Sjodin's body was found in Minnesota, Rodriquez crossed state lines. He is convicted of federal rape charges and sentenced to death.

2006   The Adam Walsh Child Protection and Safety Act, named after a murdered Florida boy, requires the Justice Department to establish a national sex offender database, subsequently named the Dru Sjodin National Sex Offender Public Website, that allows users to specify a search radius across state lines. The website includes data about all 50 states, the District of Columbia, and Guam. The Walsh Act also strengthens federal penalties for sex crimes against children and provides funding to combat the sexual exploitation of minors on the internet.

2007   Sheik Taj Din al-Hilali, the most senior Muslim cleric in Australia, delivers an infamous Ramadan sermon in which he likens women who do not wear the veil to uncovered meat that attracts predators.

5

Biographies

The rate of burnout among people who deal with the worst aspects of humanity is quite high. Activists who address sexual crimes are not an exception to this rule. The individuals listed below have played significant roles in the fight against sexual crime. A few have an international focus, while others are active only in their home countries. Some of the individuals are still working to stop sex crimes while others have moved on to other issues or have died.

Paul Martin Andrews (1960–)

Paul Martin Andrews, who was kidnapped and repeatedly raped as a 13-year-old by a man who had twice been convicted of sexual crimes against children, led Virginia's campaign to keep child molesters in prison past their scheduled release dates. In January 1973, Richard Alvin Ausley kidnapped Andrews in Virginia. Eight days later, when Ausley went for groceries, Andrews screamed for help. Hunters found the boy buried in a plywood box four feet underground in remote Nansemond County. The box was four feet wide, four feet deep, and eight feet long. Andrews, who had partially forced the box open to yell for help, had a broken nose and two black eyes. He was attached to the box by a chain around his ankle. Andrews had been raped two and three times a day for the eight days.

Ausley had an extensive criminal record that dated to at least 1961, when he was convicted of abduction and kidnapping in Suffolk Circuit Court. According to court records, Ausley went to a recreation center one afternoon and asked a 10-year-old boy to help him fix his car. Ausley drove the boy to a secluded area and sodomized him. For the attack on Andrews, Ausley received 48 years in prison.

Ausley had spent 30 years behind bars when he was scheduled to be released on parole in 2003. Andrews found out about the scheduled release two months before Ausley would supposedly see freedom. Andrews, a computer technician in North Miami, Florida, immediately began campaigning to keep Ausley in prison. Most of Andrews's friends knew nothing about this part of his past and he broke his secrecy somewhat reluctantly. He acted to persuade the Virginia legislature to provide the money to enforce the Sexually Violent Predators Act passed in 1999. This legislation, intended to keep violent sexual predators in civil custody at a treatment center past their parole date or prison sentence if medical and correctional officials believed that they presented a danger to others, had not been carried out because of a lack of money to provide the necessary housing and treatment.

Andrews's persistent lobbying persuaded lawmakers to fund the program. He also persuaded a man who had been molested by Ausley as a teenager in 1972 to come forward. In August, 2003, Ausley was convicted of molesting this victim and received an additional five years in prison. In January 2004, Ausley died at the age of 64 after being strangled and beaten in Sussex I Prison in Waverly, Virginia. Andrews admitted to being very conflicted about Ausley's death but added that nobody deserved to be murdered.

Joanne Archambault (n.d.)

Joanne Archambault, a retired San Diego police sergeant who headed the city's sexual assault unit for 17 years, is the founder of SATI (Sexual Abuse Training and Investigations) and a lecturer on sexual assault. Archambault focuses on providing victim-centered, multidisciplinary training, and expert consultation about sexual assault. She particularly seeks to raise awareness about rape that does not fit the image of "real rape."

Archambault has warned that even authorities with the best of intentions and best training still struggle to formulate effective policy to stop sexual assaults. The problem of sex crime is multifaceted, making it very challenging to address effectively. She advises individuals to take steps to protect themselves. While speaking at the International Domestic Violence and Sexual Assault Conference in Australia in 2003, Archambault reminded the audience that women who got drunk or took drugs were more likely to be attacked. Women who fear drink-spiking with date rape drugs do not realize that this is relatively uncommon. Archambault argues that hysteria about drink-spiking could help perpetuate beliefs that women were only raped or sexually assaulted by strangers.

Barbara Blaine (n.d.)

Barbara Blaine founded Survivors Network of those Abused by Priests (SNAP) in 1988 to advocate for people sexually abused by Catholic clergy. Blaine, a native of Toledo, Ohio, experienced repeated sexual abuse at the hands of her parish priest as a child. Overcome by guilt and shame, Blaine did not tell anyone about the abuse for several years, until the statute of limitations had passed. Meanwhile, the priest found other victims. Once made aware of the situation, church officials declined to take any action against the priest.

The entire experience left Blaine with a strong interest in advocating for children. She earned a BA from St. Louis University and an MS in social work from Washington University in St. Louis. She spent some time as a schoolteacher in Jamaica and working with homeless youths in Chicago. Blaine then received a divinity degree from Catholic Theological Seminary in Chicago and a law degree from DePaul University School of Law. As an attorney, Blaine specialized in children's rights as a public guardian for Cook County, Illinois.

SNAP is the oldest organization for victims of clergy sexual abuse. At the time that Blaine created it, few people were even aware of clergy sexual abuse. She formed the group because of the refusal of the Catholic Church to admit clergy abuse and the attempts by high-ranking clergy to cover up examples of such abuse. Blaine saw SNAP as a means of helping herself confront and heal the pain that she had suffered because of the actions of Catholic officials.

The first SNAP meetings were held in south Chicago in a Catholic Worker homeless shelter that Blaine had operated for 10 years. The organization gradually grew by word-of-mouth and small advertisements. Yet by 2002, it still remained quite small. In January of that year, the sexual abuse scandal began to shake the Catholic Church. SNAP suddenly received a lot of attention and its membership jumped. By 2009, it had more than 8,000 members and 60 chapters throughout the United States, Canada, and Mexico.

Nearly half of SNAP's members are women, yet males have received the vast amount of attention as victims of clergy abuse. It is likely that female victims have been undercounted. Blaine and SNAP have lobbied Roman Catholic leaders in the United States to request that state legislatures remove the statutes of limitations that often block the prosecution of abusive priests. Removal of the limitation on prosecution would likely prompt more victims, including women, to come forward. SNAP also seeks national legislation that would require clergy members to notify civil authorities when abuse has occurred. In 2002, *Ms.* magazine chose Blaine as one of its "women of the year" for her work on clergy sexual abuse.

Yosef Blau (n.d.)

Yosef Blau, an Orthodox Jewish rabbi, is the most prominent member of the Jewish religious community to speak out against sexual abuse by clergy members. Blau received a BA in 1959 from Yeshiva University, the largest and best-known school of higher education for Orthodox Jews, in New York City. He earned an MS from Yeshiva in 1960 before being ordained at Yeshiva's Rabbi Isaac Elchanan Theological Seminary (RIETS) in 1961. Blau spent several years working with children as an assistant principal and principal before returning to Yeshiva in 1977. He serves as the *mashgiach ruchai*, or spiritual guidance counselor, at the university. Very active in the Jewish religious community, Blau has served as national president of Yavneh, the National Religious Jewish Students Association, and as officer in the National Conference of Yeshiva Principals.

Blau, a member of the Rabbinical Council of America (RCA) who has lectured internationally on the meaning of the Torah, has also served on the Orthodox Caucus. The latter is a coalition of rabbis, professionals, and lay leaders who devise responses within Jewish law to challenges facing contemporary Orthodox Jews. In this capacity, Blau has addressed the sexual abuse of Orthodox girls by rabbis. The Jewish community has had the same problem as the Catholics and other religious groups with sexually abusive clergy. In 2002, the RCA passed a resolution to provide therapeutic support to misbehaving rabbis and to aid rabbis who are falsely accused of sexual abuse. Blau publicly commended the resolution and stated that, in some situations, one accusation would be enough to expel a rabbi from the RCA. Blau has also spoken for the Orthodox Jewish community in the cases of Baruch Lanner, Mordechai Gafni, Matis Weinberg, and Mordecai Tendler. All four men were rabbis who molested female students.

Carol Bohmer (n.d.)

Carol Bohmer is an academic who has brought considerable attention to the problem of sexual assault on campuses. A native of New Zealand, Bohmer earned a BA in 1965 from Victoria University in Wellington, New Zealand. After receiving a LLM from Victoria, she earned a diploma in criminology from Cambridge University in 1968 before picking up a PhD in sociology from the University of Pennsylvania in 1975.

Currently a Visiting Associate Professor at Dartmouth University, Bohmer teaches about the law and public policy as well as gender and the law. She coauthored *Sexual Assault on Campus: The Problem and the Solution* with Andrea Parrot in 1993. The book became a classic. After publishing on sexual exploitation by professionals, Bohmer shifted focus in 2004 to address the problems of would-be immigrants seeking asylum.

Stephen Donaldson (1946–1996)

Stephen Donaldson worked to stop prison rape. Born Robert A. Martin, Jr., he served in the U.S. Navy during the Vietnam War.

Soon after receiving his discharge and newly converted to the pacific Quaker faith, Donaldson took part in a Quaker pray-in on the White House lawn in August 1973 to protest the bombing of Cambodia. Arrested for trespassing, he refused on principle to post $10 in bail. Donaldson was sent to a Washington, DC jail for two days.

Placed in overcrowded wing of the jail with hardened criminals, Donaldson later described himself as "fresh meat." During the two days that he was jailed, the 26-year-old Donaldson was gang raped approximately 60 times. He stopped counted after 50. By that point, he was being sold to other convicts for a pack of cigarettes a time. He received no medical treatment, not even an aspirin from jail authorities. When he left the jail, he spent a week in the hospital and required surgery. Donaldson described the ordeal at a press conference and provided testimony before the DC Council.

Donaldson formed Stop Prison Rape in 1973. Nicknamed "Donny the Punk," Donaldson became the foremost spokesperson against prison rape. (In prison jargon, which comes from baseball, the aggressor in a rape is the Pitcher, and the victim is the Catcher, or the Punk.) A skilled writer as well as speaker, he appeared in the *New York Times, USA Today, Los Angeles Times, Boston Globe,* and the TV news magazine *60 Minutes.*

In 1994, he merged Stop Prison Rape into the newly founded Just Detention International (JDI). The organization helped prison rape survivors file lawsuits for damages, locate expert testimony, and participate in class action suits against negligent institutions. In that same year, Donaldson also coordinated JDI's friend of the court brief for the 1994 Supreme Court case on prisoner rape, *Farmer v. Brennan.* In this case, the Court ruled that prison officials could be held liable for failing to protect a prisoner from violence when they knew that there was a substantial risk of harm. In 1996, Donaldson became involved in a lawsuit against the Communications Decency Act (CDA). The legislation, created to ban pornography on the Internet, restricted access to the sometimes explicit accounts of rape posted on the JDI website. Donaldson used such accounts to garner empathy for prison rape victims and to illustrate the terrors of rape. He also used an audio tape of a prison rape as part of a JDI education and training package for prison administrators. The Supreme Court ruled the CDA to be unconstitutional in 1997. Donaldson had died a year earlier in New York City of AIDS at the age of 49.

Mark Dratch (1958–)

Rabbi Mark Dratch is the founder of JSAFE, the Jewish Institute Supporting an Abuse-Free Environment. Dratch, born in 1958, earned a BA from Yeshiva University. He then received an MS in Jewish Education from Yeshiva before being ordained in 1982 at the university's Rabbi Isaac Elchanan Theological Seminary. Dratch spent 22 years serving congregations in New York City, Boca Raton, Toronto, and Stamford, Connecticut. He left his last post at Stamford's Congregation Agudath Sholom, the largest Orthodox Jewish synagogue in New England, to lead JSAFE.

Dratch, a member of the Clergy Task Force on Abuse of Jewish Women International and chair of the Rabbinical Council of America's (RCA) Task Force on Rabbinic Improprieties, has a long history of acting to stop the abuse of women. While in Brooklyn in the late 1980s, Dratch had a conversation with a pediatrician who discussed her difficulties in helping victims of child abuse with the Orthodox community as well as the obstacles being placed in her way by rabbis. Dratch, angered by the response of the religious community, began trying to shift attitudes about child abuse and domestic violence. In 1990, Dratch wrote an article on child abuse for the RCA. In response to the essay, he faced condemnation for airing dirty laundry in public and for *hillul Hashem*, or desecrating God's name. He gradually moved into the area of sexual abuse.

Dratch, who felt that it was an affront to God not to address the issue, had to wait years for acceptance by the RCA. Most Jewish leaders denied that there was a problem until several scandals made the issue unavoidable. In 2002, Dratch developed a resolution on sexual abuse for the RCA that helped set guidelines for how the organization would respond to rabbis accused of sexual abuse. Jews are barred from *mesirah*, or informing on other Jews to outsiders, but the resolution written by Dratch stated that protecting someone from abuse does not qualify as *mesirah*. Dratch has no formal training in the topic of preventing abuse. His knowledge comes from reading, discussions with professionals, and from counseling women who were victims of abuse.

Dratch worked with The Awareness Center until a dispute with Vicki Polin over publicizing accusations of sexual abuse sparked his exit. With JSAFE, Dratch aims to create a national certification program that would train principals, teachers, and administrators to recognize signs of abuse in schools and synagogues. He aims to maintain the integrity of Judaic law while stopping sexual abuse within the Orthodox Jewish community.

Susan Estrich (1952–)

Susan Estrich is a professor of law, a political commentator, and a rape survivor who authored the classic book, *Real Rape*. Born in 1952 in Lynn, Massachusetts, Estrich grew up outside of Boston in Swampscott, Massachusetts. Her father had a one-man law practice in a nearby town while her mother worked as an assistant in a doctor's office. In 1974, she graduated from Wellesley College with a BA. While attending Harvard University Law School with the help of loans and scholarship money, Estrich became the first woman president of the prestigious *Harvard Law Review.*

Upon receiving her magna cum laude degree in 1977, she gained some fame as a clerk for Supreme Court Justice John Paul Stevens by wearing blue jeans to work. In 1984, Rep. Geraldine Ferraro appointed Estrich to serve as executive director of the Democratic National Platform Committee, where she got high marks for the skill she showed in juggling the competing interests of three campaigns and 200 committee members. When Vice President Walter Mondale became the Democratic nominee, Estrich became a senior policy adviser. In 1988, she became the first woman to serve as a national campaign manager with the Dukakis-Bentsen campaign. When Dukakis lost, Estrich returned to her tenured post at Harvard Law School and found a sideline as a political commentator for newspapers and television shows. Estrich is currently Robert Kingsley Professor of Law and Political Science at the University of Southern California.

During her senior year at Wellesley, Estrich was raped by an unknown assailant. She was attacked in an alley behind her apartment building in Boston as she was struggling out of a car carrying two bags of groceries. The man held an ice pick to her throat and threatened to kill her. It took Estrich a long time to recover. In 1986, she wrote about the attack in the *Yale Law Journal*, using it as an introduction to an article that called for reform of the criminal justice system's handling of rape, particularly so-called date rape. The article was the final piece in her bid for tenure at Harvard, and it was considered a risky choice because no one discussed rape. The article eventually became the book, *Real Rape*. Estrich has made a career out of rape in part because in law school she recalled spending a lot of time talking about larceny and assault but not rape. When she began teaching in 1981, she taught about rape.

Bakira Hasecic (n.d.)

Bakira Hasecic, a Bosnian victim of rape, is president of Women Victims of War. The Bosnian War of 1992–1995 grew out of the breakup of the former Yugoslavia. When the multiethnic Yugoslavian province of Bosnia-Hercegovina sought independence, some Bosnian Serbs objected. Ostensibly to protect the Bosnia Serb minority, Serbia sent them guns and the civil war began. Thousands of Bosnian women, including Hasecic, were raped as part of the war. Hasecic suffered rape in 1992 in her eastern Bosnian hometown of Vilina Vlas, Visegrad, by Bosnian Serb soldiers.

Hasecic responded to the attack by fighting back through Women Victims of War. For Hasecic, the Bosnia War is not over as long as the individuals who committed war crimes are still at large. She has publicly called for victims, witnesses, and families of victims to refuse to forgive and forget. She argues that the survival of Bosnia-Hercegovina requires fighting to have the truth of the civil war made known. The Association of Women Victims of War does not believe that Serbs and Croats should receive equal victim status with Bosnians, chiefly because Bosnians were the targets of an attempted genocide.

Hasecic and her group have clashed frequently with authorities in Bosnia-Hercegovina. When the War Crimes Department of Bosnia-Hercegovina Court sentenced Serbian Nedjo Samardzic to 12 years in prison for war crimes against humanity in 2006, Hasecic objected to the short sentence. Samardzic, the first individual to be sentenced for war crimes by the Bosnia-Hercegovina Court, was convicted of committing multiple rapes and holding women in sexual slavery. Hasecic declared that she no longer trusted the Bosnia-Hercegovina Court to try war crime suspects, while the Association of Women Victims of War demanded that the crime of rape be removed from the jurisdiction of the Bosnia-Hercegovina Court. The effort did not succeed.

In 2007, Women Victims of War joined the Bosnia-Hercegovina Association of Former POW Camp Inmates and the Movement of Mothers of the Srebrenica and Zepa Enclaves to file lawsuits against Serbia and Croatia for the abuse of women, the torture of prisoners, and the loss of loved ones. The case is still unresolved as of 2009. Meanwhile, in 2009, Hasecic and her organization were fined for placing a memorial on a bridge in Visegrad to the 3,000 citizens killed in the city during the war. Women Victims of War objected to the fines on the grounds that the Visegrad Municipal Court had never sentenced the perpetrators of crimes, but only the victims. The organization also suggested that the government was attempting to rewrite history to remove war crimes.

Mukhtar Mai (1972–)

Mukhtar Mai is the survivor of a gang rape in Pakistan who publicly demanded the prosecution of her attackers and, in the process, created an international scandal about Pakistan's treatment of women. Mai was born in 1972 in the village of Meerwala in the southern Punjab section of Pakistan. The province is known for being especially poor and rural.

On June 22, 2002, Salma Mastoi, a 20-year-old Meerwala girl from the Mastoi Baloch clan, encountered Mai's 15-year-old brother, Shakoor, a member of the Tatla Gujjar clan, in a field. It is not clear what happened between the two but Mastoi claimed rape. At nightfall, the Tatla clan delivered Shakoor's oldest sister, Mai, to the Mastoi men to atone for her brother's "disrespect." There are conflicting versions of Mai's role at this point. She was either brought to beg pardon for her brother or her family had agreed to give her away in marriage to Salma's brother to compensate for the rape. The practice, known as *vani,* of giving away a girl as a drudge bride to compensate for the crime of a male relative is aimed to save the relative from jail or a death sentence. Salma's relatives claim that they did not go to the police about the rape because the matter had been handled through *vani*. Mai was then sexually assaulted by at least one man in revenge. The attack had been authorized by a tribal council to restore the honor of the Mastoi clan.

Mai pursued charges against 14 men accused of cooperating in her sexual assault. On July 1, 2002, a local journalist reported that a woman had been gang-raped on the orders of an informal tribal court, as atonement for her teenage brother's behavior. The story initially met with disbelief from Western journalists but it also fit their perceptions that brutality against women was rampant in rural Pakistan. Facing international castigation, Pakistani President Musharraf took the unprecedented step of giving Mai 500,000 rupees (US$8,300) in compensation within three days of the first press report. The amount is more than 160 times the average monthly wage. The men accused of attacking Mai and abetting the crime were convicted and sent to death row in 2002. However, in 2005, Pakistan's High Court acquitted most of the men on appeal. They returned to a festive homecoming in the village where Mai still lives.

By this time, Mai had come under heavy attack in Pakistan. Critics condemned her for being a divorcee and, therefore, not sexually pure. She faced accusations that she had talked too much about something that should remain secret, that she had tarnished Pakistan's image, and that she had allowed herself to be used by people who were just seeking money. Doubts about Mai's truthfulness have become widespread in Pakistan. She has received death threats, and, at one point, was banned from leaving the country. Undeterred by the attacks and determined to save the next generation of girls, Mai has used her notoriety to raise funds to set up schools for girls and health clinics for women.

Betty Makoni (n.d.)

Betty Makoni is the founder of the Zimbabwe Rape Survivors Association and the Girl Child Network. As a six-year-old in 1977, Betty Hazviperi Makoni sold tomatoes and candles in Chitungwiza, near Zimbabwe's capital. One night, a neighbor lured her and three other girls, ages 10, 12 and 14, into his shop and raped them. The man held to the folk belief that if you take the blood of virgins and smear it over the walls of your business, then your fortunes will multiply. Zimbabwe, then known as Rhodesia, was under white rule and blacks like Makoni had no access to the police.

After attending college, Makoni returned to Chitungwiza to teach at a high school. One day, a 13-year-old girl told her she had been raped by her mother's boyfriend. Soon, other girls came forward, and Makoni started a club to counsel the group of 10. The next week, 50 girls showed up. There are now 35,000

Zimbabwean girls in such clubs, part of the Girl Child Network that Makoni founded in 1999. She aims to create a culture that prevents sexual abuse and to better the place of women in the world. As a result of the efforts of the Girl Child Network, Zimbabwean boys behave more cautiously, refraining from taunting girls at their first signs of puberty for fear of disciplinary action at school. Her efforts have also helped jail men for abuses.

The rapidly deteriorating economic and political conditions in Zimbabwe have affected Makoni's activism. In 2007, she was arrested for smuggling in foreigners to cover the country's crisis without accreditation. In reality, Makoni had helped two Americans to film a documentary on the Girl Child Network. A few months after this incident, Makoni won the World Children's Prize for the Rights of the Child.

Meanwhile, an increasing number of Zimbabwean women were being raped as a penalty for supporting the opposition political party in a hotly contested presidential election. In 2008, Makoni responded to these attacks by creating the Zimbabwe Rape Survivors Association (ZRPS). The organization records women's politically motivated rape cases, lobbies for legal justice, and rehabilitates rape survivors at a safe house in neighboring Botswana, as many women, out of fear of retribution, are too scared to testify in Zimbabwe. ZRPS works with a team of lawyers from the U.S.-based AIDS-Free World to gather evidence and seek legal recourse through international or regional courts. ZRPS does not trust the Zimbabwean courts because the country has no history of trying cases of human rights violations in a transparent manner. ZRPS has assisted some 150 rape survivors with 20 women providing affidavits against men, mostly army officers. No cases have come to court as of 2009. As another way of helping rape victims, Makoni has lobbied for passage of the International Violence Against Women Act, which aims to integrate U.S. efforts to end gender-based violence into U.S. foreign assistance programs.

Somaly Mam
(b. 1970 or 1971–)

Somaly Mam, a Cambodian sold into prostitution as a young girl, co-founded Acting for Women in Distressing Situations

(AFESIP) in 1997 to combat sexual slavery. Born about 1970 or 1971 in the village of Bou Sra in the Mondulkiri province of northeastern Cambodia near the Vietnam border, Mam has no memories of her parents, who left her with her maternal grandmother. Her father was Khmer but her mother was Phnong and lineage is determined through the mother. Mam is Phnong, part of a group of dark-skinned mountain people who are commonly viewed as ugly savages by the dominant Khmer of Cambodia. The stereotype made Mam into a target for physical and emotional abuse through the first part of her life.

Given a home by a village couple, the husband either gave or sold Mam at the age of about 10 to an older Cambodian man visiting the area. He took her to Thloc Chhroy to work as his domestic servant. He frequently beat Mam, who realized that she could expect no help from anyone. When she was just entering puberty, he sold her virginity to a Chinese merchant in exchange for the forgiveness of a debt. Mam never told anyone about the rape because, as she later explained, Cambodian people do not discuss such things. When she was about fourteen, her grandfather gave her to another man, to whom he owed money, in an arranged marriage. Mam's husband beat her frequently and then disappeared. In 1986, Mam's grandfather then sold her to a brothel in Phnom Penh, the Cambodian capital. Two girls in the brothel were killed by the owners for failing to obey. Others, including Mam, were tortured by electrodes hooked up to a battery, and frequently beaten. Mam, who had already learned to go numb, shut off all feeling.

About 1991, Mam managed to escape the brothel. Most girls do not. She lived with a French national, Pierre Legros, whom she married in 1993. The couple briefly lived in Paris where Mam worked as a house cleaner before returning to Cambodia. The couple worked in a Doctors Without Borders clinic where Mam worked as an assistant to the team that treated sexually transmitted diseases. She began distributing condoms to prostitutes to help stem the spread of diseases. Most of the girls were debt slaves, who had been sold by their parents to brothels to pay back a loan. The first girl that Mam rescued was a 16-year-old who had worked as a prostitute for a year. Mam took her to a tailor who had agreed to train girls as seamstresses.

Realizing that girls seeking to leave prostitution needed housing, Mam created Acting for Women in Distressing Situations in

1996. She picked a name that had no obvious connection with prostitution to avoid attracting attention. With funds from Save the Children UK, she opened a home for girls. As pimps threatened her life, Mam received increasing international notice as well as money from the United Nations and European Union. AFESIP expanded into Vietnam in 2002. While the organization is well-established, it still struggles mightily for funding, especially since the demand is so great. Cambodia is estimated by Mam to have at least 40,000 child prostitutes. In 2007, she founded the Somaly Mam Foundation to help raise funds for AFESIP. Mam, who is very active in the Asian women's movement, has received numerous international honors such as the World Children Award and being named as a CNN Hero.

Trisha Meili (1960–)

Trisha Meili went for a jog one night in 1989 and wound up as the poster child for random, violent sexual assault. Patricia Meili was born and raised in Paramus, New Jersey, and Pittsburgh, Pennsylvania. She attended Wellesley College in Massachusetts as an economics major. She then earned both an MBA. and an MA. from Yale University. Meili went to work as an associate at the Wall Street investment bank of Salomon Brothers. Her golden life nearly ended when she decided to run through Central Park in New York City after 9 P.M. on April 19, 1989.

About the same time that Meili began her jog, a group of 40 young black males had entered the park with the intent of mugging, robbing, scaring, and beating anyone who crossed their paths. Police records show that the men attacked and robbed a homeless man, accosted a couple on a tandem bicycle, and assaulted two male joggers. The attacks were so extensive and so vicious that the term "wilding" was coined to explain the behavior. Meili was found in the early morning hours, gagged, comatose, suffering from exposure, with her left eye torn from its socket and with 75 percent blood loss as well as severe brain damage. She was only identified by a distinctive ring that she wore. Doctors at Metropolitan Hospital believed that Meili would die. The story grabbed headlines around the world as people contemplated what the savagery of the attack said about American society.

The young men were blamed for the attacks. Police arrested five teenagers, all either black or Latino, and charged them with the attack. Four of the youths confessed on videotape, providing graphic descriptions of their actions. The Central Park Five served from 7 to 11 years in prison. In December 2002, serial rapist Matias Rayes confessed to the crime and DNA evidence connected him to the attack. The cases against Kharey Wise, Kevin Richardson, Antron McCray, Yusef Salaam, and Raymond Santana were overturned. The New York Police Department continues to maintain that the youths were involved in the attack in some way but prosecutors believe that Rayes acted alone.

Meili remained in coma for 14 days. She has since made a successful recovery, although she is unable to multitask, has continuing problems with balance and coordination, and has permanently lost her sense of smell. She still has no memory of the attack. In 1995, she ran in the New York City Marathon. She has returned to work and tours frequently as a motivational speaker.

Florence Mumba (1948–)

Florence Mumba, a judge from Zambia, became the first jurist to declare that rape qualified as a war crime. Florence Ndepele Mwachande Mumba was born on December 17, 1948, at Mufulira, Zambia. She worked as a trial attorney in Zambia before becoming the director of the Department of Legal Aid in 1978. Mumba became a trial court judge in 1980. In 1997, she joined the Supreme Court of Zambia. Meanwhile, she married Nevers Mumba, who became vice president of Zambia in 2003.

Mumba has had a long interest in the human rights, particularly the rights of women. She represented Zambia in 1985 at the Conference on Women in Nairobi and in 1994 at the African Regional Conference on Women. A member of the International Commission of Jurists since 1993, Mumba worked with other legal experts on the establishment of an African Court on Human Rights. She represented Zambia on the United Nations Commission on the Status of Women from 1992 to 1995.

Mumba won election as judge of the International Criminal Tribunal for the former Yugoslavia in 1997. In this capacity, Mumba heard testimony relating to war crimes committed during the Bosnia War of 1992–1995. In 2001, Mumba spoke for the tribunal when three Bosnian Serbs were convicted of rape and sexual enslavement. Mumba dismissed the excuse that the soldiers were only following orders. Calling the men "lawless opportunists," she advised them that they could expect no mercy, whatever their place in the chain of command. Mumba added, "In time of peace as much as in time of war, men of substance do not abuse women." For the first time, a war crimes tribunal ruled that rape was a crime against humanity and that rape did not have to be ordered from above to rise to that highest level of atrocity. Such an international judgment is significant because it has the potential to make it easier to prosecute soldiers accused of rape and it may make commanders less likely to approve of rape as an instrument of war.

Victoria Polin (n.d.)

Vicki Polin is the founder and executive director of The Awareness Center, a Baltimore, Maryland-based organization that addresses childhood sexual abuse in Jewish communities worldwide. An Illinois native, Polin earned a BA in Women's Studies from Roosevelt University in Chicago and then received an MA from the University of Illinois at Chicago. She completed her education at the Neve Yerushalayim School of General Jewish Studies in Jerusalem, Israel, and the Etz Chaim Center for Jewish Learning in Baltimore. She is a board certified art therapist as well as licensed clinical professional counselor.

Polin specializes in treating victims, both adults and children, of sexual violence through creative therapies. She also has worked with Holocaust survivors and their children as well as individuals, families, and groups that have survived political torture and violent crimes. She has presented seminars to community and educational groups about childhood sexual abuse and neglect. Polin has also qualified as expert witness and provided testimony in juvenile court. With respect to volunteerism, Polin has served as a rape victim advocate in Chicago and a volunteer speaker with a rape crisis center. She is a board member of Alternative Behavior Treatment Centers for juvenile sex offenders.

Polin came up with the idea for The Awareness Center in 2001 before incorporating the organization in Maryland in 2003. The center focuses on providing education and information to anyone concerned about sexual abuse in the Jewish community. It helps victims of such abuse network with each other to help the healing process. Much of its information is available online.

Kathy Redmond (n.d.)

Kathy Redmond, the victim of an acquaintance rape by a University of Nebraska football player, founded the National Coalition Against Violent Athletes (NCAVA) in 1998. In 1991, Katherine Redmond graduated from Columbine High School in Colorado. A Nebraska native, she became part of the fourth generation of her family to attend the University of Nebraska. It was the only college to which she had applied. She knew many of the athletic trainers from years of attending games and alumni events. Her great uncle wrote the Nebraska fight song, and her grandmother's Russian meat-and-cabbage sandwiches were sold in the football stadium. Redmond's parents had founded the alumni group, Coloradans for Nebraska, and helped endow an annual $10,000 scholarship.

Within two weeks of arriving on the Lincoln campus, the 18-year-old Redmond was raped by Christian Peter, a Nebraska football star now with the Giants. The 5-foot-2-inch, 120-pound Redmond had met the 6-foot-2-inch, 265-pound Peter, a nose tackle on the football team on campus. She says Peter, who could bench-press 450 pounds, lured her to his room and raped her. She recalls saying, "No." The next day, she says, Peter pushed his way past dorm security and into her room, where he raped her again, this time with two of his teammates keeping watch. She again said, "No."

The attack took away Redmond's bubbly personality. She focused on schoolwork and worked out her anger playing club lacrosse. It took two years before she could form a relationship with a man. She eventually told her sisters, who told her mother, who kept it from her father for months. Bill Redmond, who had played baseball for Nebraska and proudly boasted of being an alumnus, stopped wearing his varsity ring. The attack left the Redmond family reeling and feeling betrayed by an institution that it had cherished.

Redmond did not report the rapes for two years, until other women had come forward with accusations against Peter. Redmond reportedly did not go to the police until after she had met with Coach Tom Osborne, whom she knew, and had found him unresponsive. She later reported that she had feared that Nebraskans would turn her into the villain and that she would lose her home away from home. To an extent, her fears came true. Redmond received death threats and prank phone calls—with the callers playing the Nebraska fight song. Her car was vandalized. Peter was never charged with assaulting Redmond, but he was convicted of assaulting other women and received 18 months probation. He also picked up eight arrests with four convictions while at Nebraska. He was suspended for one game, a spring exhibition. Peter wound up playing six NFL seasons with the Giants, Colts, and Bears.

Redmond earned a BA in Journalism from Nebraska in only three years and found work in public relations in Denver. In July 1995, angered by the university's inaction and the assaults on other women, Redmond filed a federal Title IX sex discrimination lawsuit against the University of Nebraska. Her lawsuit was the first to specifically charge an institution with sexual discrimination caused by indifference. It sent shock waves through college administrations nationwide because it claimed they could be held financially liable for not protecting women on campus. Redmond received a $50,000 out-of-court settlement from Nebraska, along with an undisclosed settlement—but not an apology—from Peter. Redmond created NCAVA after the suicide of a 22-year-old woman who said she was assaulted by New York Giants defensive back Tito Wooten. She has since become a frequent media commentator on athlete violence.

Jill Saward (1965–)

Jill Saward, also known as the Ealing Vicarage Rape Victim, became one of the first rape victims in Great Britain to talk publicly about her experience. At lunchtime on a gray afternoon in March 1986, 21-year-old Saward was watching TV in her home, in west London, with her boyfriend, David Kerr. Meanwhile, her father, the Reverend Michael Saward, Vicar of Ealing, worked on a sermon in the study. Three armed men, high on vodka and Valium, broke into the vicarage looking for the cash box. They forced Saward and Kerr into the study with the vicar. When they discovered that the cash-box was empty, the men forced Saward upstairs. The ringleader of the break-in tried to protect Saward, but the two other men took turns raping her anally, vaginally, and orally. She was also sexually assaulted with the handle of a knife. During the attack, Saward could hear her father and boyfriend being beaten with cricket bats. She cut off emotionally and focused on detail to be able to identify the criminals later. Eventually, the rapists tied Saward up with a jump rope and dumped her on the bedroom floor. The vicar and Kerr were left near death with fractured skulls.

Since the attack took place in the Ealing Vicarage, the incident led to an international media storm of attention. It took three days for the attackers to be captured, further adding to the hysteria around the crime. As a rape victim, Saward had the legal right to remain anonymous. However, she knew that the notoriety of the attack would not make anonymity truly possible. Four days after the attack, a national newspaper named Saward. Encouraged by a female police officer to speak up on behalf of other rape victims, she went public.

When Saward's attackers went to trial a year later, the judge proclaimed that her ordeal had been "no great trauma." The rapists received the same sentence for the rape as they did for the burglary—three and five years, whereas the ringleader, had who tried to prevent the rape, was given 14 years. As Saward later stated, the judge's remark reflected enormous ignorance about the reality of rape and what she had gone through. She was angry because she expected a man with his authority to be better informed. (Upon his retirement some years later, the judge apologized for his blunder.)

Saward, who later described herself as "rather wishy-washy" and without a career focus, quickly developed laser-like focus. Saward's anger prompted her to become Britain's best known antirape activist. She appeared in a BBC documentary about rape, becoming the first rape victim to talk about her experiences. In 1990, Saward coauthored a book with Wendy Green about her experiences, *Rape: My Story*. Saward has spent much of her life demanding better treatment for rape victims and stronger deterrents for would-be perpetrators. She has helped to set up better training for police officers on issues of sexual violence, supported around 3,000 victims of domestic and sexual assault, and sat on various government bodies on rape and sexual assault. Some of Saward's views are a bit controversial. She has said that women who dress scantily should not be surprised if they are attacked.

In 2008, Saward narrowly lost a race to serve in Britain's Parliament. Saward ran against former Home Secretary David

Davis because he objected to a national DNA database, a tool that Saward regards as essential to the fight against crime, especially rape. As part of her campaign, dubbed "True Liberty," Saward called for the justice system to take more account of the needs of victims than the needs of wrongdoers. Saward, who now remembers the essence of the rape but not the specifics of it, married Gavin Drake in 1993 and lives in Liverpool with her husband and children.

Russell Dan Smith (1950–)

Smith, a former federal prisoner, founded the first organization dedicated to protecting prisoners from sexual abuse, People Organized to Stop the Rape of Imprisoned Persons (POSRIP). Little is known about Smith's life. Born in 1950, he was convicted of a juvenile offense and sent at the age of 13 to the Stonewall Jackson Training School in Concord, North Carolina, for two years. Upon his release, he promptly stole a car and was sent to a state prison in North Carolina. As a teenage inmate, Smith became prey for older and larger inmates. He suffered repeated rapes and became a sex slave for other prisoners. By 1973, Smith had moved up to federal prisons, where he found conditions to be worse than in the state prisons.

While in the U.S. Penitentiary in Terre Haute, Indiana, Smith began to advocate against prison rape. Perhaps not surprisingly considering his background, Smith advised a violent response. Smith founded the National Gay Prisoners Coalition while at Terre Haute. Sent to the federal prison at Marion, Illinois, in 1974, Smith was sent to the Control Unit, or long-term segregation from the rest of the prisoner population. Smith, who believed that administrators sent him to the Control Unit because of his efforts to organize prisoners, found allies among the other men in the unit. Upon his release from the unit in 1976, Smith returned to the general prisoner population and suffered yet another rape. He responded violently, as he had advised others to do, but prison officials charged him with assault. Prisoner advocates then formed the International Committee to Free Russell Smith (ICFRS) to aid his defense. Smith left prison in 1980.

Smith had spent most of his life in prison. Like other long-term prisoners, he struggled to live independently. He also suffered from posttraumatic stress disorder as a result of the repeated sexual assaults. Smith donated his personal papers to the University of Michigan and then disappeared. Other prisoner activists presume that he died sometime in the 1980s.

Shortly after his release, Smith founded POSRIP in 1980 to address the problems of rape, sexual assault, non-consensual sexual slavery, and forced prostitution within prisons in the United States. The group eventually merged into Stop Prisoner Rape, which changed its name in 2008 when it became part of Just Detention International.

Sandyawan Sumardi (1958–)

Father Sandyawan Sumardi, a Jesuit priest in Indonesia, is an antirape activist with Volunteers for Humanity and the operator of the Jakarta Social Institute for the urban poor. Born in 1958 as the youngest son of a police chief and nurse, Sumardi grew up in Janeponto, South Sulawesi, in middle-class comfort. He shared the view of many indigenous Indonesians that they were the victims of an economic system dominated by Chinese immigrants. After attending seminary school in Yogyakarta, Sumardi was ordained as a priest in 1988. He devoted himself to alleviating poverty, mostly on behalf of indigenous Indonesians.

Sumardi organized Volunteers for Humanity in 1996 when he was charged with hiding prodemocracy demonstrators. He set up an information gathering system, to keep track of those killed, missing, or injured in their attempts to bring political reform under the former dictator Suharto. When President Suharto resigned from office on May 21, 1998, as the result of a tumbling economy and increasing political opposition, violence broke out against Indonesia's ethnic Chinese minority. During the riots, ethnic Chinese showed up at Sumardi's Jakarta Social Institute office seeking help. Sumardi turned from seeing the Chinese as oppressors to seeing them as the victims of terrorism. Many of the Chinese were women and girls who had been raped in a systematic manner.

In 1998, Sumardi led a Volunteers for Humanity investigation that reported to the National Commission on Human Rights that they had 182 documented cases of gang rape committed by plainclothes Indonesian soldiers as part of the terror campaign against the ethnic Chinese. The Indonesian army and government tried to discredit and intimidate Sumardi. Three weeks after the riots, he found a live grenade in front of his office. In July 1999, a military minivan rammed into the back of his car. Sumardi persisted, and eventually the Indonesia government formed a Joint Fact-Finding Team in 1999. However, rape victims and their families were harassed to the point that very few were willing to testify. Sumardi reported to the press that even gynecologists were being targeted for intimidation. Many rape victims spoke only under condition of anonymity, throwing doubt upon their claims. Only one victim appeared in a 1999 closed session at a United Nations subcommission alongside Sumardi. She did not return home because her family had been harassed. None of the assailants were ever brought to justice. Despite the difficulties in prosecuting military rapists, Sumardi has persisted in his humanitarian efforts.

John Walsh (1945–)

John Walsh, who lost his son Adam to a serial killer, has played a pivotal role in protecting children from abduction and sexual assault by founding the National Center for Missing and Exploited Children. Born in 1945 in Auburn, New York, and educated at the University of Buffalo, Walsh moved to Florida with his wife, Revé. The couple had a son, Adam, and Walsh worked as a developer of luxury hotels. On July 27, 1981, Revé left Adam playing in the toy department at a Sears at a Hollywood, Florida, mall, but could not find him when she returned. Two hours after the disappearance, police were called. Two weeks later, Adam's head was found. His body remains missing. Serial killer and drifter Ottis Toole eventually became the prime suspect. The police closed the case in December 2008 after Toole's death while in prison for other crimes.

In the wake of Adam's death, Walsh and his wife agreed that a lack of information and a lack of coordination among law enforcement agencies contributed to the difficulty in finding missing children. They decided that leadership on behalf of children was urgently needed. Accordingly, they lobbied Congress to pass the Missing Children's Act. Signed into law in 1982, it required the FBI to enter data about missing children into a national crime database. Prior to the passage of this legislation, the FBI had databases on stolen cars and stolen guns but not stolen children.

Walsh's experiences taught him that the nation was in desperate need of leadership in the fight to protect children. Along with his wife, he decided to create something positive out of personal tragedy. From the ad hoc organization they put together to help with the search for Adam, John and Revé established the Adam Walsh Child Resource Center, which eventually merged with the National Center for Missing & Exploited Children (NCMEC), which they cofounded in 1984. The NCMEC, which is one of the most highly rated charities in the United States because it spends more than 90 cents of every dollar raised on programming, provides resources to parents, children, and law enforcement in the United States and internationally. Meanwhile, Walsh became the host of the TV show, *America's Most Wanted*, which profiles missing criminals.

It is largely due to Walsh's efforts that missing children now appear on milk cartons and flyers. He also played an instrumental role in persuading parents nationwide to fingerprint their children. Walsh also spurred the creation of missing persons units at every large police department. In 1990, police recovered 62 percent of missing kids, with the number jumping to about 96 percent nearly 20 years later. In 2006, on the 25th anniversary of Adam Walsh's kidnapping, Congress passed the Adam Walsh Child Protection and Safety Act, which expanded the national registry of sex offenders and stiffened penalties against such abusers.

While Walsh's work is generally lauded, he has also been criticized for creating a climate of fear. The Department of Justice estimates that 115 children are kidnapped annually in what are labeled "stereotypical" kidnappings—a stranger taking a child with intent to keep or harm or kill. Fewer than half of those cases end in deaths. By raising awareness of the threat to children in a somewhat hysterical way, Walsh has been faulted for creating enormous and perhaps unwarranted anxiety among parents and taking childhood away from children.

Laura X (n.d.)

Laura X, who uses this particular surname to protest the legal ownership of women that supports marital rape, is the director of the National Clearinghouse on Marital and Date Rape (NCMDR) in Berkeley, California. Born and raised in St. Louis, Missouri, Laura Murra graduated from Vassar College. She is one of the many women of her generation who moved from civil rights activism to support for women's rights, though she had long been uneasy with the place of women in society. At age 12, Laura recalled making a connection between her cousin being handed off in marriage and slave children being auctioned off. As a college student, Laura served as a Congress of Racial Equality (CORE) picket captain during the civil rights protests in Alabama in 1963. After arriving at the University of California at Berkeley to pursue a graduate degree, she participated in the famed Berkeley Free Speech Movement.

In 1968, Laura founded the Women's History Research Center in Berkeley, California. At the time, few recognized women's history as a subject worthy of study. The connection between the center and the women's liberation movement that had sparked its development led battered women and rape victims to the center's door. No other shelter or help for such women existed. Meanwhile, the library published the first interviews with rape survivors in its journal, *SPAZM*. In 1969, Laura officially adopted the pen name of Laura X.

In conversations with author Diana Russell, Laura became conscious of the problem of marital rape. She discovered that while marital rape was a crime in several other countries, the United States had never criminalized it. Laura, who identifies as a human rights activist rather than a women's rights activist and strongly dislikes being known as single issue advocate, argues that marital rape is connected with all other civil and human rights issues. Antirape activism became a logical extension of her other activism. She began work to criminalize the rape of a wife by her husband. In 1980, in the wake of the successful California campaign to criminalize marital rape, Laura founded the NCMDR. She then traveled across the United States to promote antirape legislation. When the last state criminalized marital rape in 1994, Laura shifted her attentions to the international effort to combat wife rape. She is also trying to improve U.S. legislation. Some states that have criminalized marital rape have included exemptions for husbands who rape their unconscious or intoxicated wives. Laura X and NCMDR oppose these exemptions.

Further Reading

Bohmer, Carol, and Andrea Parrot. *Sexual Assault on Campus: The Problem and the Solution*. New York: Lexington Books, 1993.

Curran, Bronwyn. *Into the Mirror: The Untold Story of Mukhtar Mai.* New Delhi, India: UBS, 2008.

Estrich, Susan. *Real Rape: How the Legal System Victimizes Women Who Say No.* Cambridge, MA: Harvard University Press, 1987.

Mam, Somaly. *The Road of Lost Innocence.* London: Virago, 2007.

Walsh, John. *Tears of Rage.* New York: Pocket Books, 2008.

6

Data and Documents

S exual crime has generally been a private concern through the ages, with government officials doing little to halt it. Only in the latter decades of the 20th century did it become such a great topic of public concern that several federal agencies, ranging from the Federal Bureau of Investigation (FBI) to the Centers for Disease Control, now study the problem. The information that they have gathered covers sexual crime as matter of public health as well as a legal offense.

Historical Data

Many women have refused to report sexual crimes out of doubt that they would be believed and for fear of further victimization by authorities. As a result, historical data about sexual crime is both hard to find and of questionable accuracy.

19th-Century Data

Ida B. Wells, an African American journalist who dedicated much of her life to stopping the lynching of blacks, published *A Red Record: Tabulated Statistics and Alleged Causes of Lynchings in the United States, 1892–1894* (Chicago: Donohue & Henneberry, 1895). This 1894 booklet served as Wells's attempt to recast lynching in the public eye so that it was no longer perceived as an understandable yet unpleasant response to criminal behavior but as a crime against American values. Wells pointed out that, contrary to widespread belief, most lynchings were not in response to rapes of white women by black men.

Record for the Year 1892

In 1892 there were 241 persons lynched. The entire number is divided among the following states:

Alabama, 22; Arkansas, 25; California, 3; Florida, 11; Georgia, 17; Idaho, 8; Illinois, 1; Kansas, 3; Kentucky, 9; Louisiana, 29; Maryland, 1; Mississippi, 16; Missouri, 6; Montana, 4; New York, 1; North Carolina, 5; North Dakota, 1; Ohio, 3; South Carolina, 5; Tennessee, 28; Texas, 15; Virginia, 7; West Virginia, 5; Wyoming, 9; Arizona Territory, 3; Oklahoma, 2.

Of this number 160 were of Negro descent. Four of them were lynched in New York, Ohio, and Kansas. The rest were murdered in the South. Five of this number were females. The charges for which they were lynched cover a wide range. They are as follows:

Rape, 46; murder, 58; rioting, 3; race prejudice, 6; no cause given, 4; incendiarism, 6; robbery, 6; assault and battery, 1; attempted rape, 11; suspected robbery, 4; larceny, 1; self defense, 1; insulting women, 2; desperadoes, 6; fraud, 1; attempted murder, 2; no offense stated, boy and girl, 2.

Wartime Rapes

Rape has long been a part of warfare. It is a way to punish the enemy without much fear of retribution as well as a method of celebrating the power of the victor. Susan Brownmiller broke a long public silence about rape by publishing the history of the crime in her best-selling *Against Our Will: Men, Women, and Rape* in 1975. Brownmiller devoted a chapter of the book to rape in wartime. She included official U.S. government figures from the office of the Judge Advocate General but warned that cases of rape often were reduced to lesser charges before trial. The Army Judiciary provided no statistics on the number of convictions for these lesser charges, or the number of reported rapes, arrests, and rape cases brought to trial to compare with the number of convictions. Brownmiller noted that more than two-thirds of the convictions took place in occupied areas. When the fighting had ceased and military officials were seeking cooperation with enemy civilians, military judges were more likely to convene over a case of a soldier raping an enemy woman. The

Clerk of the Court speculated that the increase in convictions represented an increase in overall troop strength while the increase in rapes indicated that soldiers had more time on their hands. Rape is a capital offense under military jurisprudence (Brownmiller, p. 76–77).

Brownmiller also obtained statistics relating to the conduct of U.S. Army and Air Force personnel during the Vietnam War. Court-martial statistics for the Navy and Marine Corps were not available. In Vietnam, the number of military convictions for rape by Army personnel was 58 percent of the number of cases tried, slightly higher than the civilian conviction rate at the time. American soldiers tended to participate more in gang rapes than individual rapes, perhaps as the result of being warned against the security dangers of individual fraternizing on operations. The overall personal conduct of the American troops proved far better than the other occupiers of French Indo-China: the French, their mercenaries, or the Japanese (Brownmiller, p. 101–103).

Current U.S. Military Policy on Rape

The Department of Defense has been formally investigating sexual harassment within the military since 1988, but it did not regard sexual assault as a major area of concern. In 1994, the Secretary of Defense ordered the development of a sexual harassment policy action plan. As part of the plan, military personnel were surveyed in 1995 about sexual harassment and the results were compared to the survey findings from 1988. Although men and women reported less sexual harassment, fewer sexually suggestive gestures, and less pressure for sexual favors, the *1995 Sexual Harassment Survey* found that the percentage of women reporting an attempted or actual rape remained statistically steady (see Table 6.1).

In 1998, Congress required the Department of Defense to improve the conduct of sex crime investigations. Members of Congress and members of the military both agreed that sex crimes occurred in the Armed Forces with unacceptable frequency. In 1997, the military conducted criminal investigations into over 3,700 attacks. Accordingly, in 1999, the Panel on Military Investigative Practices recommended in *Adapting Military Sex Crime Investigations to Changing Times* that changes be made to improve

TABLE 6.1
Any Type of Unwanted Sexual Attention

	Percent			
	Men		Women	
	1988	1995	1988	1995
Service				
Army	21	14	68	61
Navy	18	16	66	53
Marine Corps	14	15	75	64
Air Force	14	12	57	49
Coast Guard	16	13	62	59
Unwanted sexual attention				
Behavior				
Rape/assault, including attempts	—	—	5	4
Pressure for Sexual favors	2	1	15	11
Touching, cornering, pinching	9	6	38	29
Suggestive looks, gestures	10	7	44	37
Letters, telephone calls	3	2	14	12
Pressure for dates	3	2	26	22
Sexual teasing, jokes	13	10	52	44
Whistles, calls	5	3	38	23
Attempted sexual activities	2	2	7	7
Other	1	1	5	5

Source: U.S. Department of Defense 1995 Sexual Harassment Survey.

sex crime investigations and to better assist the victims of such crimes. The panel advised that

- more female and minority investigators be hired to help military criminal investigative organizations (MCIOs) to better reflect the population that they serve
- MCIOs develop on-call regional specialists who can provide expert advice on sex crime investigations and assistance on medical, psychological, and forensic issues
- each MCIO develop a center to monitor investigations and assist investigators
- sex crime and domestic violence units be developed which are familiar with family and psychological counseling as well as social services
- opportunities for civilian investigators be increased, especially in specialist positions, so that military agents are not pigeon-holed to the detriment of their careers

- the Secretary of Defense strengthen and vigorously enforce prohibitions against commanding officers interfering with investigations
- MCIOs continue to ban using wiretaps, electronic monitoring, and polygraphing
- MCIOs be given the authority to arrest civilians on military installations because of the increasing number of civilian employees on bases

In response to reports that victims of sexual crimes at U.S. military service academies were afraid to report such attacks because of possible retaliation or damage to their careers, Congress in 2003 mandated an investigation. In the defense budget bill, the Secretary of Defense was required to establish a Defense Task Force on Sexual Harassment and Violence at the Military Service Academies. Of the 12 members of the committee, 6 were senior military personnel while the remainder came from the private sector and the Department of Justice. The committee assessed the efforts and effectiveness of the academies at preventing and responding to sexual harassment and sexual violence on their campuses. The first report became public on September 22, 2004, and it is issued annually. According to the 2006–2007 report:

- 40 sexual assaults were reported by students
- 7 rapes were reported at the U.S. Air Force Academy in Colorado Springs, Colorado
- 7 rapes were reported at the U.S. Military Academy at West Point, New York
- 4 rapes were reported at the U.S. Naval Academy at Annapolis, Maryland
- Half of the 40 complaints were filed under a system that allows military personnel to report confidentially and to obtain care without triggering an official investigation or becoming involved in the criminal justice system
- Most students reported that they understood the definition of a sexual assault
- Most students regarded sexual assault as a serious matter
- Many had difficulty defining a "universally accepted definition" of appropriate sexual behavior
- Some female students said that they would not report assaults for fear of career repercussions.

Prostitution

Prostitution is often categorized as a victimless crime because it is assumed that no one is damaged by it. Although the definition of prostitution ranges from state to state, it is generally described in legal codes as: performing, offering, or agreeing to perform any act of sexual intercourse as defined by state statute or any touching of the sexual organs of one person by another person for any money, property, token, object, or article or anything of value, for the purpose of sexual arousal or gratification.

Accurate figures on prostitution have been difficult to obtain because of the often hidden aspect of the crime and definitional problems. The National Center for Missing and Exploited Children warns that there are no reliable estimates of the number of prostitutes because no one has defined the concept of prostitution in measurable terms.

Sexual services offered by prostitutes include every conceivable sexual act. However, most streetwalkers prefer to engage in fellatio or oral sex. Such an act is a favorite among customers, most practical for performing in a car, and quick, thereby enabling easier escape if police arrive on the scene.

Prostitution is the only sexual crime in which more female than male offenders are arrested. Most arrested prostitutes are women, with only 20 percent of prostitution arrests involving male prostitutes and 10 percent involving clients or "johns." A disproportionate number of arrested prostitutes are women of color, and women of color more often receive jail sentences. Streetwalkers are more visible than other types of prostitutes so it is no surprise that 85 to 90 percent of those arrested work on the streets, though street work is estimated to account for only about 20 percent of prostitution (Flowers, *Sex Crimes*, 2006, p. 158, 181).

Child Prostitution

It is impossible to get an accurate count of the number of child prostitutes. However, in 1996, according to the Department of Health and Human Services, there were as many as 300,000 prostitutes under the age of 18 in the United States. Estimates are that at least one in five streetwalkers is a teenage girl.

The median age of juvenile prostitutes has been estimated at between 15.5 years and 16.9 years. Most are white, with studies estimating that from 60 to 80 percent of prostitutes are white. African American girls make up the next biggest group, with Native Americans and Latinas representing less than 10 percent of prostitutes. Researchers disagree on the class background of prostitutes, with research involving larger groups of prostitutes indicating that most come from the middle and upper classes.

Many of these girls are homeless, missing, or runaway youths who have turned to prostitution as a means of survival in a type of prostitution known as survival sex. They have no other marketable skills. The National Center for Missing and Exploited Children estimates that up to 77 percent of youths involved in prostitution report running away from home at least once. One study indicated that more than half of youths involved with prostitution still lived at home while about 30 percent lived in shelters or on the streets. The remainder lived with friends or pimps.

Many juvenile prostitutes have come from unstable, dysfunctional homes in which they were subject to physical and sexual abuse as well as neglect. In studies, two out of every three female prostitutes reported being victims of childhood physical abuse. Anastasia Volkonsky, an expert on child sexual abuse, reported in 1996 that most runaway girls turned prostitutes have experienced a major childhood trauma such as incest, domestic violence, or rape prior to entering prostitution. Most have drug or alcohol problems. In one study, over 80 percent of teenage prostitutes reported that they were already using alcohol or drugs prior to joining the sex trade. Some prostitutes trade sex for drugs, such as methamphetamine or crack cocaine (Flowers, *Runaway*, 2001, p. 53–54)

The vast majority of prostitutes have been introduced to the sex trade by a pimp and work under the supervision of one. About 20 percent of juvenile prostitutes enter the trade through their acquaintance with other streetwalkers while about 10 percent became prostitutes through direct propositions by clients.

Male Prostitution

Most of the attention on prostitution has focused on women and girls who sell sexual favors. Females are more likely than males to be arrested for prostitution, but this may only reflect differences in law enforcement strategies and visibility. There may be as many as 500,000 male prostitutes in the country, but the numbers of such boys and men are impossible to determine accurately.

It is known that young male prostitutes match the demographic profile of teenage girl prostitutes. They are runaways or throwaways, victims of physical or sexual abuse, substance abusers, predominantly white, and from middle class backgrounds. Larger cities are more likely to have a higher proportion of boys involved in prostitution.

Male prostitutes are generally divided into categories. Hustlers find male customers on the streets or in bars. They may be heterosexual or bisexual. Drag queen hustlers are transgendered individuals who dress as women and specialize in oral sex. Call boys obtain clients from a call book and have a more upscale clientele, who are often regulars. Male escorts find customers through local advertising.

Violent Sexual Criminals

Sexual violence occurs when consent to sexual activity is not obtained or freely given. There are many types of sexual violence and just as many types of sexual offenders.

Sex Offender Data

Violent sexual criminals are overwhelmingly males who attack females. The Centers for Disease Control have determined that individuals who commit sexual violence are more likely to have sexually aggressive friends, abuse drugs or alcohol, experienced or witnessed violence as a child, and live in an environment that supports sexual violence.

The Bureau of Justice Statistics compiles data about crime and victimization. The Bureau, a branch of the Department of Justice, has gathered information about imprisoned sexual offenders. Many of its reports, like the one excerpted below, are only issued periodically.

Convicted Sex Offenders

- Over 234,000 convicted sex criminals were in some form of custody in 1994. The majority of these offenders were under conditional supervision in their communities.

- The victims of convicted sexual criminals are typically young. Victims of all sexual crimes averaged less than 13 years old, while rape victims averaged 22 years.
- Many sexual criminals are repeat offenders. About 24 percent of those imprisoned for rape and 19 percent of those imprisoned for sexual assault were been on probation or parole at the time that they committed the sexual crime for which they were jailed.
- Of the 9,691 male sex offenders released from prisons in 15 selected states in 1994, 5.3 percent were arrested for committing another sex crime within three years of release.
- Of released sex offenders who were convicted of committing another sexual crime, 40 percent attacked within a year or less from the date of their prison discharge.

Child Molesters

- Criminals who target children have the same recidivism rate as those who target adults. About 3.3 percent of child molesters were rearrested for another sex crime against a child within 3 years of release from prison.
- It is estimated that 16 percent of rape victims are under age 12. This is a conservative estimate, based only upon rapes reported to law enforcement officials. Many rapes are not reported, meaning that the number may be far higher.
- Most child molesters are relatives of their victims, with 46 percent of victims and 70 percent of convicted child rapists related in some manner to their victims.
- About 1 in 5 victims under age 12 is raped by his or her father.
- 60 percent of child molesters released from prison in 1994 had been jailed for molesting a child 13 years old or younger.
- Child molesters tend to be older than the rapists who target adults. Nearly 25 percent of child molesters were age 40 or older, but about 10 percent of the inmates with adult victims fell in that age range.

Victim Data

Sexual violence affects public health because of both the emotional and physical effects of the crime. Victims of sexual assault may have sexually transmitted diseases and long-lasting physical problems. They may suffer from depression, anxiety, and an inability to trust others. As a result of these emotional problems, victims may develop eating disorders, abuse drugs or alcohol, engage in risky sex, and contemplate suicide.

Two Federal statistical programs provide national measures of rape incidence: the FBI's Uniform Crime Reporting (UCR) program, which records rapes reported to law enforcement agencies, and the Bureau of Justice Statistics's National Crime Victimization Survey (NCVS), which records reported and unreported rapes based on Census Bureau interviews with the American public ages 12 years and older.

Relationship Between Victim and Attacker

Interviews conducted with rape victims and rapists in Alabama, South Carolina, and North Dakota in 1991 by Richard Florence of the Justice Research and Statistics Association give information about the age of victims and their relationship to their rapists. While there is some discrepancy among the data reported, the respondents generally agreed about the ages of victims. As shown in Table 6.2, all of the victims were female and all of the attackers were male.

Almost half of attackers of women over age 18 said that they picked targets who were strangers, according to this same study. However, 33 percent of victims over 18 years said their attackers were strangers. There may be definitional differences over the word "stranger" as well as a hesitance to report rapes.

TABLE 6.2
Percent of Female Rape Victims

	Total	Under 12	12–17	18 or Older
Victims	100%	14%	29%	57%
Imprisoned rapists	100	14	24	62

Source: Child rape victims, 1992. *Crime Data Brief.* U.S. Department of Justice, Office of Justice Programs, Bureau of Justice Statistics, June 1994. Available from http://www.ojp.usdoj.gov/bjs/pub/pdf/crv92.pdf.

Violent Sexual Crimes Against Persons Age 65 or Older, 1993–2002

The National Crime Victimization Survey (NCVS) and the Uniform Crime Reports (UCR) provide data that allow the comparison of rape/sexual assault crimes committed against individuals aged 65 or older against persons in younger age groups. Americans over the age of 65 are less likely to become the victims of violent crime than younger individuals. Between 1993 and 2002, the elderly experienced nonfatal violent crime at a rate 1/20th that of persons between the ages of 12 and 24 (4 per 1,000 age 65 or older versus 82 victimizations per 1,000 persons age 12–24). Violent crimes include rape, sexual assault, robbery, and aggravated and simple assaults.

Although the elderly are less likely to be victims of violent crime when compared to younger persons, persons age 65 or older were:

- equally likely to face offenders with weapons (30% versus 26%)
- more likely to offer no resistance (45% versus 29%)
- equally likely to receive serious injuries (3% for both groups)
- somewhat more likely to face offenders who were strangers to them (53% versus 46%)
- more likely to face offenders age 30 or older (48% versus 30%)
- equally likely to face male offenders (about 79% versus 76%)
- less likely to be attacked at night (25% versus 50%)
- more likely to make a report to the police (53% versus 44%)

Sexual Crime on Campus

One of the earliest surveys of date rape began in 1978 as a survey of sexual aggression and victimization among 4,000 students at Kent State University in Ohio. The researcher, Dr. Mary P. Koss, used the words "hidden rape" to describe her project since the term date rape had not yet been invented nor was there any convincing evidence that "normal" people would rape. Koss reported her results in 1982 and the study became the topic of a *Ms.* magazine article on date rape. *Ms.*, a feminist publication that has since folded, became the first national magazine to report about date rape. The magazine obtained funding from the National Institute for Mental Health to fund a national study to determine the extent of the problem.

The *Ms.* Project on Campus Sexual Assault is the report that famously declared that 25 percent of American women had been sexually assaulted in their lifetimes. It aimed to (1) learn how much sexual aggression and victimization, including acts of rape, were occurring among college students; (2) gather details about actual incidents; (3) study women who had been victimized; (4) identify characteristics of men who commit sexually aggressive acts; and (5) measure the psychological difficulties, if any, that result from sexual victimization. Men were not viewed as potential victims of sexual attacks and women were not considered as perpetrators of sexual crimes. The survey gathered 6,159 responses that included 3,187 women and 2,972 men. The average age of the female respondents was 21.4 with 85 percent single, 11 percent married, and 4 percent divorced. Of these women, 86 percent were white, 7 percent were black, 3 percent were Latina, 3 percent were Asian, and 1 percent were Native American. The characteristics of the male students were nearly identical (Warshaw, p. 197–209).

The *Ms.* Project on Campus Sexual Assault found that one in four college women had experienced rape or attempted rape (of the 3,187 women surveyed, 15 percent had been raped) and that 84 percent of the raped women knew their attacker. Fifty-seven percent of the rapes took place on dates. In one year, these 3,187 women reported suffering: 328 rapes (as defined by law), 534 attempted rapes (as defined by law), 837 episodes of sexual coercion (sexual intercourse obtained through the aggressor's continual arguments or pressure), 2,024 experiences of unwanted sexual contact (fondling, kissing, or petting committed against the woman's will). Of the male students surveyed, 1 in 12 admitted committing acts that met the legal definition of rape or attempted rape. For both men and women, the average age when a rape incident occurred (either as perpetrator or victim) was 18½ years old. Only 27 percent of the women whose sexual assault met the legal definition of rape thought of themselves as rape victims (Warshaw, p. 197–209).

Jeanne Clery Disclosure of Campus Security Policy and Campus Crime Statistics

The Clery Act, named after Lehigh University student Jeanne Clery, mandates that colleges and universities report crimes occurring on campus. Clery died at the age of 20 in 1986 in her Bethlehem, Pennsylvania, dorm room after being beaten, raped, sodomized, and strangled by a stranger who was also a fellow student. The crime was attributed to a lack of information about crime and breaches of security on campus. Despite this horrifying crime, campuses remain among the safest places in the nation.

Clery's parents aimed to make campuses even safer and they lobbied to pass a bill in tribute to their daughter. The 1990 Jeanne Clery Disclosure of Campus Security Policy and Campus Crime Statistics Act requires institutions of higher education that participate in federal financial aid to keep and disclose information about crime on and near campus. The full text follows:

(1) Each eligible institution participating in any program under this subchapter and part C of subchapter I of chapter 34 of Title 42 shall on August 1, 1991, begin to collect the following information with respect to campus crime statistics and campus security policies of that institution, and beginning September 1, 1992, and each year thereafter, prepare, publish, and distribute, through appropriate publications or mailings, to all current students and employees, and to any applicant for enrollment or employment upon request, an annual security report containing at least the following information with respect to the campus security policies and campus crime statistics of that institution:

(A) A statement of current campus policies regarding procedures and facilities for students and others to report criminal actions or other emergencies occurring on campus and policies concerning the institution's response to such reports.

(B) A statement of current policies concerning security and access to campus facilities, including campus residences, and security considerations used in the maintenance of campus facilities.

(C) A statement of current policies concerning campus law enforcement, including—

(i) the enforcement authority of security personnel, including their working relationship with State and local police agencies; and

(ii) policies which encourage accurate and prompt reporting of all crimes to the campus police and the appropriate police agencies.

(D) A description of the type and frequency of programs designed to inform students and employees about campus security procedures and practices and to encourage students and employees to be responsible for their own security and the security of others.

(E) A description of programs designed to inform students and employees about the prevention of crimes.

(F) Statistics concerning the occurrence on campus, in or on noncampus buildings or property, and on public property during the most recent calendar year, and during the 2 preceding calendar years for which data are available—

    (i) of the following criminal offenses reported to campus security authorities or local police agencies:

        (I) murder;

        (II) sex offenses, forcible or nonforcible;

        (III) robbery;

        (IV) aggravated assault;

        (V) burglary;

        (VI) motor vehicle theft;

        (VII) manslaughter;

        (VIII) arson; and

        (IX) arrests or persons referred for campus disciplinary action for liquor law violations, drug-related violations, and weapons possession; and

    (ii) of the crimes described in subclauses (I) through (VIII) of clause (i), and other crimes involving bodily injury to any person in which the victim is intentionally selected because of the actual or perceived race, gender, religion, sexual orientation, ethnicity, or disability of the victim that are reported to campus security authorities or local police agencies, which data shall be collected and reported according to category of prejudice.

(G) A statement of policy concerning the monitoring and recording through local police agencies of criminal activity at off-campus student organizations which are recognized by the institution and that are engaged in by students attending the institution, including those student organizations with off-campus housing facilities.

(H) A statement of policy regarding the possession, use, and sale of alcoholic beverages and enforcement of State underage drinking laws and a statement of policy regarding the possession, use, and sale of illegal drugs and enforcement of Federal and State drug laws and a description of any drug or alcohol abuse education programs as required under section 1011i of this title.

(I) A statement advising the campus community where law enforcement agency information provided by a State under section 14071(j) of Title 42, concerning registered sex offenders may be obtained, such as the law enforcement office of the institution, a local law enforcement agency with jurisdiction for the campus, or a computer network address.

(2) Nothing in this subsection shall be construed to authorize the Secretary to require particular policies, procedures, or practices by institutions of higher education with respect to campus crimes or campus security.

(3) Each institution participating in any program under this subchapter and part C of subchapter I of chapter 34 of Title 42 shall make timely reports to the campus community on crimes considered to be a threat to other students and employees described in paragraph (1)(F) that are reported to campus security or local law police agencies. Such reports shall be provided to students and employees in a manner that is timely and that will aid in the prevention of similar occurrences.

(4)(A) Each institution participating in any program under this subchapter [20 U.S.C. § 1070 et seq.] and part C of subchapter I of chapter 34 of Title 42 [42 U.S.C. § 2751 et seq.] that maintains a police or security department of any kind shall make, keep, and maintain a daily log, written in a form that can be easily understood, recording all crimes reported to such police or security department, including—

(i) the nature, date, time, and general location of each crime; and

(ii) the disposition of the complaint, if known.

(B) (i) All entries that are required pursuant to this paragraph shall, except where disclosure of such information is prohibited by law or such disclosure would jeopardize the confidentiality of the victim, be open to public inspection within two business days of the initial report being made to the department or a campus security authority.

(ii) If new information about an entry into a log becomes available to a police or security department, then the new information shall be recorded in the log not later than two business days after the information becomes available to the police or security department.

(iii) If there is clear and convincing evidence that the release of such information would jeopardize an ongoing criminal investigation or the safety of an individual, cause a suspect to flee or evade detection, or result in the destruction of evidence, such information may be withheld until that damage is no longer likely to occur from the release of such information.

(5) On an annual basis, each institution participating in any program under this subchapter and part C of subchapter I of chapter 34 of Title 42 [42 U.S.C. § 2751 et seq.] shall submit to the Secretary a copy of the statistics required to be made available under paragraph (1)(F). The Secretary shall—

(A) review such statistics and report to the Committee on Education and the Workforce of the House of Representatives and the Committee on Labor and Human Resources of the Senate on campus crime statistics by September 1, 2000;

(B) make copies of the statistics submitted to the Secretary available to the public; and

(C) in coordination with representatives of institutions of higher education, identify exemplary campus security policies, procedures, and practices and disseminate information concerning those policies, procedures, and practices that have proven effective in the reduction of campus crime.

(6)(A) In this subsection:

(i) The term "campus" means—

(I) any building or property owned or controlled by an institution of higher education within the same reasonably contiguous geographic area of the institution and used by the institution in direct support of, or in a manner related to, the institution's educational purposes, including residence halls; and

(II) property within the same reasonably contiguous geographic area of the institution that is owned by the institution but controlled by another person, is used by students, and supports institutional purposes (such as a food or other retail vendor).

(ii) The term "noncampus building or property" means—

(I) any building or property owned or controlled by a student organization recognized by the institution; and

(II) any building or property (other than a branch campus) owned or controlled by an institution of higher education that is used in direct support of, or in relation to, the institution's educational purposes, is used by students, and is not within the same reasonably contiguous geographic area of the institution.

(iii) The term "public property" means all public property that is within the same reasonably contiguous geographic area of the institution, such as a sidewalk, a street, other thoroughfare, or parking facility, and is adjacent to a facility owned or controlled by the institution if the facility is used by the institution in direct support of, or in a manner related to the institution's educational purposes.

(B) In cases where branch campuses of an institution of higher education, schools within an institution of higher education, or administrative divisions within an institution are not within a reasonably contiguous geographic area, such entities shall be considered separate campuses for purposes of the reporting requirements of this section.

(7) The statistics described in paragraph (1)(F) shall be compiled in accordance with the definitions used in the uniform crime reporting system of the Department of Justice, Federal Bureau of Investigation, and the modifications in such definitions as implemented pursuant to the Hate Crime Statistics Act. Such statistics shall not identify victims of crimes or persons accused of crimes.

(8)(A) Each institution of higher education participating in any program under this subchapter and part C of subchapter I of chapter 34 of Title 42 shall develop and distribute as part of the report described in paragraph (1) a statement of policy regarding—

    (i) such institution's campus sexual assault programs, which shall be aimed at prevention of sex offenses; and

    (ii) the procedures followed once a sex offense has occurred.

(B) The policy described in subparagraph (A) shall address the following areas:

    (i) Education programs to promote the awareness of rape, acquaintance rape, and other sex offenses.

    (ii) Possible sanctions to be imposed following the final determination of an on-campus disciplinary procedure regarding rape, acquaintance rape, or other sex offenses, forcible or nonforcible.

    (iii) Procedures students should follow if a sex offense occurs, including who should be contacted, the importance of preserving evidence as may be necessary to the proof of criminal sexual assault, and to whom the alleged offense should be reported.

    (iv) Procedures for on-campus disciplinary action in cases of alleged sexual assault, which shall include a clear statement that—

        (I) the accuser and the accused are entitled to the same opportunities to have others present during a campus disciplinary proceeding; and

(II) both the accuser and the accused shall be informed of the outcome of any campus disciplinary proceeding brought alleging a sexual assault.

(v) Informing students of their options to notify proper law enforcement authorities, including on-campus and local police, and the option to be assisted by campus authorities in notifying such authorities, if the student so chooses.

(vi) Notification of students of existing counseling, mental health or student services for victims of sexual assault, both on campus and in the community.

(vii) Notification of students of options for, and available assistance in, changing academic and living situations after an alleged sexual assault incident, if so requested by the victim and if such changes are reasonably available.

(C) Nothing in this paragraph shall be construed to confer a private right of action upon any person to enforce the provisions of this paragraph.

(9) The Secretary shall provide technical assistance in complying with the provisions of this section to an institution of higher education who requests such assistance.

(10) Nothing in this section shall be construed to require the reporting or disclosure of privileged information.

(11) The Secretary shall report to the appropriate committees of Congress each institution of higher education that the Secretary determines is not in compliance with the reporting requirements of this subsection.

(12) For purposes of reporting the statistics with respect to crimes described in paragraph (1)(F), an institution of higher education shall distinguish, by means of separate categories, any criminal offenses that occur—

(A) on campus;

(B) in or on a noncampus building or property;

(C) on public property; and

(D) in dormitories or other residential facilities for students on campus.

(13) Upon a determination pursuant to section 1094(c)(3)(B) of this title that an institution of higher education has substantially misrepresented the number, location, or nature of the crimes required to be reported under this subsection, the Secretary shall impose a civil penalty upon the institution in the same amount and pursuant to the same procedures as a civil penalty is imposed under section 1094(c)(3)(B) of this title.

(14)(A) Nothing in this subsection may be construed to—

(i) create a cause of action against any institution of higher education or any employee of such an institution for any civil liability; or

(ii) establish any standard of care.

(B) Notwithstanding any other provision of law, evidence regarding compliance or noncompliance with this subsection shall not be admissible as evidence in any proceeding of any court, agency, board, or other entity, except with respect to an action to enforce this subsection.

(15) This subsection may be cited as the "Jeanne Clery Disclosure of Campus Security Policy and Campus Crime Statistics Act".

Prison Rape

The sexual assault of prisoners by other prisoners has long been a problem. Estimates of the numbers of prisoners who are the victims of sexual crimes range from 10 to 25 percent. Prisoners have been attacked by other prisoners, male or female, and they have also been assaulted by prison staff. However, the problem attracted little public attention partly out of the belief that criminals deserved whatever they got. Convicted criminals simply do not tug at the heart strings of the public.

The Prison Rape Elimination Act of 2003 (PREA) passed Congress as the result of lobbying by the families and friends of prisoners as well as concerns about the public health impact of assaults upon prisoners who would eventually join the wider world. Human rights groups also joined in the effort to pass the legislation. PREA requires correctional systems at the federal, state, and local levels to implement a zero-tolerance policy against prison rape in all confinement facilities. It also established a National Prison Rape Commission to investigate the problem and propose solutions.

The text of the law follows:

Prison Rape Elimination Act of 2003

Sec. 2. Findings
Congress makes the following findings:

(1) 2,100,146 persons were incarcerated in the United States at the end of 2001: 1,324,465 in Federal and State prisons and

631,240 in county and local jails. In 1999, there were more than 10,000,000 separate admissions to and discharges from prisons and jails.

(2) Insufficient research has been conducted and insufficient data reported on the extent of prison rape. However, experts have conservatively estimated that at least 13 percent of the inmates in the United States have been sexually assaulted in prison. Many inmates have suffered repeated assaults. Under this estimate, nearly 200,000 inmates now incarcerated have been or will be the victims of prison rape. The total number of inmates who have been sexually assaulted in the past 20 years likely exceeds 1,000,000.

(3) Inmates with mental illness are at increased risk of sexual victimization. America's jails and prisons house more mentally ill individuals than all of the Nation's psychiatric hospitals combined. As many as 16 percent of inmates in State prisons and jails, and 7 percent of Federal inmates, suffer from mental illness.

(4) Young first-time offenders are at increased risk of sexual victimization. Juveniles are 5 times more likely to be sexually assaulted in adult rather than juvenile facilities—often within the first 48 hours of incarceration.

(5) Most prison staff are not adequately trained or prepared to prevent, report, or treat inmate sexual assaults.

(6) Prison rape often goes unreported, and inmate victims often receive inadequate treatment for the severe physical and psychological effects of sexual assault—if they receive treatment at all.

(7) HIV and AIDS are major public health problems within America's correctional facilities. In 2000, 25,088 inmates in Federal and State prisons were known to be infected with HIV/AIDS. In 2000, HIV/AIDS accounted for more than 6 percent of all deaths in Federal and State prisons. Infection rates for other sexually transmitted diseases, tuberculosis, and hepatitis B and C are also far greater for prisoners than for the American population as a whole. Prison rape undermines the public health by contributing to the spread of these diseases, and often giving a potential death sentence to its victims.

(8) Prison rape endangers the public safety by making brutalized inmates more likely to commit crimes when they are released—as 600,000 inmates are each year.

(9) The frequently interracial character of prison sexual assaults significantly exacerbates interracial tensions, both within prison and, upon release of perpetrators and victims from prison, in the community at large.

(10) Prison rape increases the level of homicides and other violence against inmates and staff, and the risk of insurrections and riots.

(11) Victims of prison rape suffer severe physical and psychological effects that hinder their ability to integrate into the community and maintain stable employment upon their release from prison. They are thus more likely to become homeless and/or require government assistance.

(12) Members of the public and government officials are largely unaware of the epidemic character of prison rape and the day-to-day horror experienced by victimized inmates.

(13) The high incidence of sexual assault within prisons involves actual and potential violations of the United States Constitution. In Farmer v. Brennan, 511 U.S. 825 (1994), the Supreme Court ruled that deliberate indifference to the substantial risk of sexual assault violates prisoners' rights under the Cruel and Unusual Punishments Clause of the Eighth Amendment. The Eighth Amendment rights of State and local prisoners are protected through the Due Process Clause of the Fourteenth Amendment. Pursuant to the power of Congress under Section Five of the Fourteenth Amendment, Congress may take action to enforce those rights in States where officials have demonstrated such indifference. States that do not take basic steps to abate prison rape by adopting standards that do not generate significant additional expenditures demonstrate such indifference. Therefore, such States are not entitled to the same level of Federal benefits as other States.

(14) The high incidence of prison rape undermines the effectiveness and efficiency of United States Government expenditures through grant programs such as those dealing with health care; mental health care; disease prevention; crime prevention, investigation, and prosecution; prison construction, maintenance, and operation; race relations; poverty; unemployment and homelessness. The effectiveness and efficiency of these federally funded grant programs are compromised by the failure of State officials to adopt policies and procedures that reduce the incidence of prison rape in that the high incidence of prison rape—

  (A) increases the costs incurred by Federal, State, and local jurisdictions to administer their prison systems;

  (B) increases the levels of violence, directed at inmates and at staff, within prisons;

  (C) increases health care expenditures, both inside and outside of prison systems, and reduces the effectiveness of disease prevention programs by substantially increasing the incidence and spread of HIV, AIDS, tuberculosis, hepatitis B and C, and other diseases;

(D) increases mental health care expenditures, both inside and outside of prison systems, by substantially increasing the rate of post-traumatic stress disorder, depression, suicide, and the exacerbation of existing mental illnesses among current and former inmates;

(E) increases the risks of recidivism, civil strife, and violent crime by individuals who have been brutalized by prison rape; and

(F) increases the level of interracial tensions and strife within prisons and, upon release of perpetrators and victims, in the community at large.

(15) The high incidence of prison rape has a significant effect on interstate commerce because it increases substantially—

(A) the costs incurred by Federal, State, and local jurisdictions to administer their prison systems;

(B) the incidence and spread of HIV, AIDS, tuberculosis, hepatitis B and C, and other diseases, contributing to increased health and medical expenditures throughout the Nation;

(C) the rate of post-traumatic stress disorder, depression, suicide, and the exacerbation of existing mental illnesses among current and former inmates, contributing to increased health and medical expenditures throughout the Nation; and

(D) the risk of recidivism, civil strife, and violent crime by individuals who have been brutalized by prison rape.

Sec. 3. Purposes
The purposes of this Act are to—

(1) establish a zero-tolerance standard for the incidence of prison rape in prisons in the United States;

(2) make the prevention of prison rape a top priority in each prison system;

(3) develop and implement national standards for the detection, prevention, reduction, and punishment of prison rape;

(4) increase the available data and information on the incidence of prison rape, consequently improving the management and administration of correctional facilities;

(5) standardize the definitions used for collecting data on the incidence of prison rape;

(6) increase the accountability of prison officials who fail to detect, prevent, reduce, and punish prison rape;

(7) protect the Eighth Amendment rights of Federal, State, and local prisoners;

(8) increase the efficiency and effectiveness of Federal expenditures through grant programs such as those dealing with health care; mental health care; disease prevention; crime prevention, investigation, and prosecution; prison construction, maintenance, and operation; race relations; poverty; unemployment; and homelessness; and

(9) reduce the costs that prison rape imposes on interstate commerce.

Sec. 4. National Prison RAPE Statistics, Data, and Research

(a) ANNUAL COMPREHENSIVE STATISTICAL REVIEW-

(1) IN GENERAL- The Bureau of Justice Statistics of the Department of Justice (in this section referred to as the 'Bureau') shall carry out, for each calendar year, a comprehensive statistical review and analysis of the incidence and effects of prison rape. The statistical review and analysis shall include, but not be limited to the identification of the common characteristics of—

(A) both victims and perpetrators of prison rape; and

(B) prisons and prison systems with a high incidence of prison rape.

(2) CONSIDERATIONS- In carrying out paragraph (1), the Bureau shall consider—

(A) how rape should be defined for the purposes of the statistical review and analysis;

(B) how the Bureau should collect information about staff-on-inmate sexual assault;

(C) how the Bureau should collect information beyond inmate self-reports of prison rape;

(D) how the Bureau should adjust the data in order to account for differences among prisons as required by subsection (c)(3);

(E) the categorization of prisons as required by subsection (c)(4); and

(F) whether a preliminary study of prison rape should be conducted to inform the methodology of the comprehensive statistical review.

(3) SOLICITATION OF VIEWS- The Bureau of Justice Statistics shall solicit views from representatives of the following: State departments of correction; county and municipal jails; juvenile correctional facilities; former inmates; victim advocates; researchers; and other experts in the area of sexual assault.

(4) SAMPLING TECHNIQUES- The review and analysis under paragraph (1) shall be based on a random sample, or other

scientifically appropriate sample, of not less than 10 percent of all Federal, State, and county prisons, and a representative sample of municipal prisons. The selection shall include at least one prison from each State. The selection of facilities for sampling shall be made at the latest practicable date prior to conducting the surveys and shall not be disclosed to any facility or prison system official prior to the time period studied in the survey. Selection of a facility for sampling during any year shall not preclude its selection for sampling in any subsequent year.

(5) SURVEYS- In carrying out the review and analysis under paragraph (1), the Bureau shall, in addition to such other methods as the Bureau considers appropriate, use surveys and other statistical studies of current and former inmates from a sample of Federal, State, county, and municipal prisons. The Bureau shall ensure the confidentiality of each survey participant.

(6) PARTICIPATION IN SURVEY- Federal, State, or local officials or facility administrators that receive a request from the Bureau under subsection (a)(4) or (5) will be required to participate in the national survey and provide access to any inmates under their legal custody.

(b) REVIEW PANEL ON PRISON RAPE-

(1) ESTABLISHMENT- To assist the Bureau in carrying out the review and analysis under subsection (a), there is established, within the Department of Justice, the Review Panel on Prison Rape (in this section referred to as the 'Panel').

(2) MEMBERSHIP-

(A) COMPOSITION- The Panel shall be composed of 3 members, each of whom shall be appointed by the Attorney General, in consultation with the Secretary of Health and Human Services.

(B) QUALIFICATIONS- Members of the Panel shall be selected from among individuals with knowledge or expertise in matters to be studied by the Panel.

(3) PUBLIC HEARINGS-

(A) IN GENERAL- The duty of the Panel shall be to carry out, for each calendar year, public hearings concerning the operation of the three prisons with the highest incidence of prison rape and the two prisons with the lowest incidence of prison rape in each category of facilities identified under subsection (c)(4). The Panel shall hold a separate hearing regarding the three Federal or State prisons with the highest incidence of prison rape. The purpose of these hearings shall be to collect evidence to aid in the identification of common characteristics of both victims and perpetrators of prison rape, and the identification of common characteristics of prisons and prison systems with a high incidence of prison rape, and the identification of common characteristics of prisons and prison systems that appear to have been successful in deterring prison rape.

(B) TESTIMONY AT HEARINGS-

    (i) PUBLIC OFFICIALS- In carrying out the hearings required under subparagraph (A), the Panel shall request the public testimony of Federal, State, and local officials (and organizations that represent such officials), including the warden or director of each prison, who bears responsibility for the prevention, detection, and punishment of prison rape at each entity, and the head of the prison system encompassing such prison.

    (ii) VICTIMS- The Panel may request the testimony of prison rape victims, organizations representing such victims, and other appropriate individuals and organizations.

(C) SUBPOENAS-

    (i) ISSUANCE- The Panel may issue subpoenas for the attendance of witnesses and the production of written or other matter.

    (ii) ENFORCEMENT- In the case of contumacy or refusal to obey a subpoena, the Attorney General may in a Federal court of appropriate jurisdiction obtain an appropriate order to enforce the subpoena.

(c) REPORTS-

  (1) IN GENERAL- Not later than June 30 of each year, the Attorney General shall submit a report on the activities of the Bureau and the Review Panel, with respect to prison rape, for the preceding calendar year to—

    (A) Congress; and

    (B) the Secretary of Health and Human Services.

  (2) CONTENTS- The report required under paragraph (1) shall include—

    (A) with respect to the effects of prison rape, statistical, sociological, and psychological data;

    (B) with respect to the incidence of prison rape—

      (i) statistical data aggregated at the Federal, State, prison system, and prison levels;

      (ii) a listing of those institutions in the representative sample, separated into each category identified under subsection (c)(4) and ranked according to the incidence of prison rape in each institution; and

(iii) an identification of those institutions in the representative sample that appear to have been successful in deterring prison rape; and

(C) a listing of any prisons in the representative sample that did not cooperate with the survey conducted pursuant to section 4.

(3) DATA ADJUSTMENTS- In preparing the information specified in paragraph (2), the Attorney General shall use established statistical methods to adjust the data as necessary to account for differences among institutions in the representative sample, which are not related to the detection, prevention, reduction and punishment of prison rape, or which are outside the control of the State, prison, or prison system, in order to provide an accurate comparison among prisons. Such differences may include the mission, security level, size, and jurisdiction under which the prison operates. For each such adjustment made, the Attorney General shall identify and explain such adjustment in the report.

(4) CATEGORIZATION OF PRISONS- The report shall divide the prisons surveyed into three categories. One category shall be composed of all Federal and State prisons. The other two categories shall be defined by the Attorney General in order to compare similar institutions.

(d) CONTRACTS AND GRANTS- In carrying out its duties under this section, the Attorney General may—

(1) provide grants for research through the National Institute of Justice; and

(2) contract with or provide grants to any other entity the Attorney General deems appropriate.

(e) AUTHORIZATION OF APPROPRIATIONS- There are authorized to be appropriated $15,000,000 for each of fiscal years 2004 through 2010 to carry out this section.

Sec. 5. Prison Rape Prevention and Prosecution

(a) INFORMATION AND ASSISTANCE-

(1) NATIONAL CLEARINGHOUSE- There is established within the National Institute of Corrections a national clearinghouse for the provision of information and assistance to Federal, State, and local authorities responsible for the prevention, investigation, and punishment of instances of prison rape.

(b) REPORTS-

(1) IN GENERAL- Not later than September 30 of each year, the National Institute of Corrections shall submit a report to

Congress and the Secretary of Health and Human Services. This report shall be available to the Director of the Bureau of Justice Statistics.

(2) CONTENTS- The report required under paragraph (1) shall summarize the activities of the Department of Justice regarding prison rape abatement for the preceding calendar year.

(c) AUTHORIZATION OF APPROPRIATIONS- There are authorized to be appropriated $5,000,000 for each of fiscal years 2004 through 2010 to carry out this section.

Sec. 6. Grants to Protect Inmates and Safeguard Communities

(a) GRANTS AUTHORIZED- From amounts made available for grants under this section, the Attorney General shall make grants to States to assist those States in ensuring that budgetary circumstances (such as reduced State and local spending on prisons) do not compromise efforts to protect inmates (particularly from prison rape) and to safeguard the communities to which inmates return. The purpose of grants under this section shall be to provide funds for personnel, training, technical assistance, data collection, and equipment to prevent and prosecute prisoner rape.

(b) USE OF GRANT AMOUNTS- Amounts received by a grantee under this section may be used by the grantee, directly or through subgrants, only for one or more of the following activities:

(1) PROTECTING INMATES- Protecting inmates by—

(A) undertaking efforts to more effectively prevent prison rape;

(B) investigating incidents of prison rape; or

(C) prosecuting incidents of prison rape.

(2) SAFEGUARDING COMMUNITIES- Safeguarding communities by—

(A) making available, to officials of State and local governments who are considering reductions to prison budgets, training and technical assistance in successful methods for moderating the growth of prison populations without compromising public safety, including successful methods used by other jurisdictions;

(B) developing and utilizing analyses of prison populations and risk assessment instruments that will improve State and local governments' understanding of risks to the community regarding release of inmates in the prison population;

(C) preparing maps demonstrating the concentration, on a community-by-community basis, of inmates who have been released, to facilitate the efficient and effective—

(i) deployment of law enforcement resources (including probation and parole resources); and

      (ii) delivery of services (such as job training and substance abuse treatment) to those released inmates;

  (D) promoting collaborative efforts, among officials of State and local governments and leaders of appropriate communities, to understand and address the effects on a community of the presence of a disproportionate number of released inmates in that community; or

  (E) developing policies and programs that reduce spending on prisons by effectively reducing rates of parole and probation revocation without compromising public safety.

(c) GRANT REQUIREMENTS-

  (1) PERIOD- A grant under this section shall be made for a period of not more than 2 years.

  (2) MAXIMUM- The amount of a grant under this section may not exceed $1,000,000.

  (3) MATCHING- The Federal share of a grant under this section may not exceed 50 percent of the total costs of the project described in the application submitted under subsection (d) for the fiscal year for which the grant was made under this section.

(d) APPLICATIONS-

  (1) IN GENERAL- To request a grant under this section, the chief executive of a State shall submit an application to the Attorney General at such time, in such manner, and accompanied by such information as the Attorney General may require.

  (2) CONTENTS- Each application required by paragraph (1) shall—

    (A) include the certification of the chief executive that the State receiving such grant—
      (i) has adopted all national prison rape standards that, as of the date on which the application was submitted, have been promulgated under this Act; and
      (ii) will consider adopting all national prison rape standards that are promulgated under this Act after such date;

    (B) specify with particularity the preventative, prosecutorial, or administrative activities to be undertaken by the State with the amounts received under the grant; and

    (C) in the case of an application for a grant for one or more activities specified in paragraph (2) of subsection (b)—
      (i) review the extent of the budgetary circumstances affecting the State generally and describe how those circumstances relate to the State's prisons;
      (ii) describe the rate of growth of the State's prison population over the preceding 10 years and explain

why the State may have difficulty sustaining that rate of growth; and

(iii) explain the extent to which officials (including law enforcement officials) of State and local governments and victims of crime will be consulted regarding decisions whether, or how, to moderate the growth of the State's prison population.

(e) REPORTS BY GRANTEE-

(1) IN GENERAL- The Attorney General shall require each grantee to submit, not later than 90 days after the end of the period for which the grant was made under this section, a report on the activities carried out under the grant. The report shall identify and describe those activities and shall contain an evaluation of the effect of those activities on—

(A) the number of incidents of prison rape, and the grantee's response to such incidents; and

(B) the safety of the prisons, and the safety of the communities in which released inmates are present.

(2) DISSEMINATION- The Attorney General shall ensure that each report submitted under paragraph (1) is made available under the national clearinghouse established under section 5.

(f) STATE DEFINED- In this section, the term 'State' includes the District of Columbia, the Commonwealth of Puerto Rico, and any other territory or possession of the United States.

(g) AUTHORIZATION OF APPROPRIATIONS-

(1) IN GENERAL- There are authorized to be appropriated for grants under this section $40,000,000 for each of fiscal years 2004 through 2010.

(2) LIMITATION- Of amounts made available for grants under this section, not less than 50 percent shall be available only for activities specified in paragraph (1) of subsection (b).

Sec. 7. National Prison Rape Reduction Commission

(a) ESTABLISHMENT- There is established a commission to be known as the National Prison Rape Reduction Commission (in this section referred to as the 'Commission').

(b) MEMBERS-

(1) IN GENERAL- The Commission shall be composed of 9 members, of whom—

(A) 3 shall be appointed by the President;

(B) 2 shall be appointed by the Speaker of the House of Representatives, unless the Speaker is of the same party as the President, in which case 1 shall be appointed by the Speaker of the House of Representatives and 1 shall be appointed by the minority leader of the House of Representatives;

(C) 1 shall be appointed by the minority leader of the House of Representatives (in addition to any appointment made under subparagraph (B));

(D) 2 shall be appointed by the majority leader of the Senate, unless the majority leader is of the same party as the President, in which case 1 shall be appointed by the majority leader of the Senate and 1 shall be appointed by the minority leader of the Senate; and

(E) 1 member appointed by the minority leader of the Senate (in addition to any appointment made under subparagraph (D)).

(2) PERSONS ELIGIBLE- Each member of the Commission shall be an individual who has knowledge or expertise in matters to be studied by the Commission.

(3) CONSULTATION REQUIRED- The President, the Speaker and minority leader of the House of Representatives, and the majority leader and minority leader of the Senate shall consult with one another prior to the appointment of the members of the Commission to achieve, to the maximum extent possible, fair and equitable representation of various points of view with respect to the matters to be studied by the Commission.

(4) TERM- Each member shall be appointed for the life of the Commission.

(5) TIME FOR INITIAL APPOINTMENTS- The appointment of the members shall be made not later than 60 days after the date of enactment of this Act.

(6) VACANCIES- A vacancy in the Commission shall be filled in the manner in which the original appointment was made, and shall be made not later than 60 days after the date on which the vacancy occurred.

(c) OPERATION-

(1) CHAIRPERSON- Not later than 15 days after appointments of all the members are made, the President shall appoint a chairperson for the Commission from among its members.

(2) MEETINGS- The Commission shall meet at the call of the chairperson. The initial meeting of the Commission shall take place not later than 30 days after the initial appointment of the members is completed.

(3) QUORUM- A majority of the members of the Commission shall constitute a quorum to conduct business, but the Commission may establish a lesser quorum for conducting hearings scheduled by the Commission.

(4) RULES- The Commission may establish by majority vote any other rules for the conduct of Commission business, if such rules are not inconsistent with this Act or other applicable law.

(d) COMPREHENSIVE STUDY OF THE IMPACTS OF PRISON RAPE-
(1) IN GENERAL- The Commission shall carry out a comprehensive legal and factual study of the penalogical, physical, mental, medical, social, and economic impacts of prison rape in the United States on—
(A) Federal, State, and local governments; and
(B) communities and social institutions generally, including individuals, families, and businesses within such communities and social institutions.

(2) MATTERS INCLUDED- The study under paragraph (1) shall include—

(A) a review of existing Federal, State, and local government policies and practices with respect to the prevention, detection, and punishment of prison rape;
(B) an assessment of the relationship between prison rape and prison conditions, and of existing monitoring, regulatory, and enforcement practices that are intended to address any such relationship;
(C) an assessment of pathological or social causes of prison rape;
(D) an assessment of the extent to which the incidence of prison rape contributes to the spread of sexually transmitted diseases and to the transmission of HIV;
(E) an assessment of the characteristics of inmates most likely to commit prison rape and the effectiveness of various types of treatment or programs to reduce such likelihood;
(F) an assessment of the characteristics of inmates most likely to be victims of prison rape and the effectiveness of various types of treatment or programs to reduce such likelihood;
(G) an assessment of the impacts of prison rape on individuals, families, social institutions and the economy generally, including an assessment of the extent to which the incidence of prison rape contributes to recidivism and to increased incidence of sexual assault;
(H) an examination of the feasibility and cost of conducting surveillance, undercover activities, or both, to reduce the incidence of prison rape;

(I) an assessment of the safety and security of prison facilities and the relationship of prison facility construction
and design to the incidence of prison rape;

(J) an assessment of the feasibility and cost of any particular proposals for prison reform;

(K) an identification of the need for additional scientific
and social science research on the prevalence of prison
rape in Federal, State, and local prisons;

(L) an assessment of the general relationship between
prison rape and prison violence;

(M) an assessment of the relationship between prison rape
and levels of training, supervision, and discipline of
prison staff; and

(N) an assessment of existing Federal and State systems for
reporting incidents of prison rape, including an assessment of whether existing systems provide an adequate
assurance of confidentiality, impartiality and the absence of reprisal.

(3) REPORT-

(A) DISTRIBUTION- Not later than 2 years after the date of
the initial meeting of the Commission, the Commission
shall submit a report on the study carried out under
this subsection to—
  (i) the President;
  (ii) the Congress;
  (iii) the Attorney General;
  (iv) the Secretary of Health and Human Services;
  (v) the Director of the Federal Bureau of Prisons;
  (vi) the chief executive of each State; and
  (vii) the head of the department of corrections of each
  State.

(B) CONTENTS- The report under subparagraph (A) shall
include—
  (i) the findings and conclusions of the Commission;
  (ii) recommended national standards for reducing
  prison rape;
  (iii) recommended protocols for preserving evidence
  and treating victims of prison rape; and
  (iv) a summary of the materials relied on by the Commission in the preparation of the report.

(e) RECOMMENDATIONS-

(1) IN GENERAL- In conjunction with the report submitted under
subsection (d)(3), the Commission shall provide the Attorney

General and the Secretary of Health and Human Services with recommended national standards for enhancing the detection, prevention, reduction, and punishment of prison rape.

(2) MATTERS INCLUDED- The information provided under paragraph (1) shall include recommended national standards relating to—

(A) the classification and assignment of prisoners, using proven standardized instruments and protocols, in a manner that limits the occurrence of prison rape;

(B) the investigation and resolution of rape complaints by responsible prison authorities, local and State police, and Federal and State prosecution authorities;

(C) the preservation of physical and testimonial evidence for use in an investigation of the circumstances relating to the rape;

(D) acute-term trauma care for rape victims, including standards relating to—

(i) the manner and extent of physical examination and treatment to be provided to any rape victim; and

(ii) the manner and extent of any psychological examination, psychiatric care, medication, and mental health counseling to be provided to any rape victim;

(E) referrals for long-term continuity of care for rape victims;

(F) educational and medical testing measures for reducing the incidence of HIV transmission due to prison rape;

(G) post-rape prophylactic medical measures for reducing the incidence of transmission of sexual diseases;

(H) the training of correctional staff sufficient to ensure that they understand and appreciate the significance of prison rape and the necessity of its eradication;

(I) the timely and comprehensive investigation of staff sexual misconduct involving rape or other sexual assault on inmates;

(J) ensuring the confidentiality of prison rape complaints and protecting inmates who make complaints of prison rape;

(K) creating a system for reporting incidents of prison rape that will ensure the confidentiality of prison rape complaints, protect inmates who make prison rape complaints from retaliation, and assure the impartial resolution of prison rape complaints;

(L) data collection and reporting of—

(i) prison rape;

(ii) prison staff sexual misconduct; and

(iii) the resolution of prison rape complaints by prison officials and Federal, State, and local investigation and prosecution authorities; and

(M) such other matters as may reasonably be related to the detection, prevention, reduction, and punishment of prison rape.

(3) LIMITATION- The Commission shall not propose a recommended standard that would impose substantial additional costs compared to the costs presently expended by Federal, State, and local prison authorities.

(f) CONSULTATION WITH ACCREDITATION ORGANIZATIONS- In developing recommended national standards for enhancing the detection, prevention, reduction, and punishment of prison rape, the Commission shall consider any standards that have already been developed, or are being developed simultaneously to the deliberations of the Commission. The Commission shall consult with accreditation organizations responsible for the accreditation of Federal, State, local or private prisons, that have developed or are currently developing standards related to prison rape. The Commission will also consult with national associations representing the corrections profession that have developed or are currently developing standards related to prison rape.

(1) IN GENERAL- The Commission shall hold public hearings. The Commission may hold such hearings, sit and act at such times and places, take such testimony, and receive such evidence as the Commission considers advisable to carry out its duties under this section.

(2) WITNESS EXPENSES- Witnesses requested to appear before the Commission shall be paid the same fees as are paid to witnesses under section 1821 of title 28, United States Code. The per diem and mileage allowances for witnesses shall be paid from funds appropriated to the Commission.

(h) INFORMATION FROM FEDERAL OR STATE AGENCIES- The Commission may secure directly from any Federal department or agency such information as the Commission considers necessary to carry out its duties under this section. The Commission may request the head of any State or local department or agency to furnish such information to the Commission.

(i) PERSONNEL MATTERS-

(1) TRAVEL EXPENSES- The members of the Commission shall be allowed travel expenses, including per diem in lieu of subsistence, at rates authorized for employees of agencies under subchapter I of chapter 57 of title 5, United States Code, while away from their homes or regular places of business in the performance of service for the Commission.

(2) DETAIL OF FEDERAL EMPLOYEES- With the affirmative vote of 2/3 of the Commission, any Federal Government

employee, with the approval of the head of the appropriate Federal agency, may be detailed to the Commission without reimbursement, and such detail shall be without interruption or loss of civil service status, benefits, or privileges.

(3) PROCUREMENT OF TEMPORARY AND INTERMITTENT SERVICES- Upon the request of the Commission, the Attorney General shall provide reasonable and appropriate office space, supplies, and administrative assistance.

(j) CONTRACTS FOR RESEARCH-

(1) NATIONAL INSTITUTE OF JUSTICE- With a 2/3 affirmative vote, the Commission may select nongovernmental researchers and experts to assist the Commission in carrying out its duties under this Act. The National Institute of Justice shall contract with the researchers and experts selected by the Commission to provide funding in exchange for their services.

(2) OTHER ORGANIZATIONS- Nothing in this subsection shall be construed to limit the ability of the Commission to enter into contracts with other entities or organizations for research necessary to carry out the duties of the Commission under this section.

(k) SUBPOENAS-

(1) ISSUANCE- The Commission may issue subpoenas for the attendance of witnesses and the production of written or other matter.

(2) ENFORCEMENT- In the case of contumacy or refusal to obey a subpoena, the Attorney General may in a Federal court of appropriate jurisdiction obtain an appropriate order to enforce the subpoena.

(3) CONFIDENTIALITY OF DOCUMENTARY EVIDENCE- Documents provided to the Commission pursuant to a subpoena issued under this subsection shall not be released publicly without the affirmative vote of 2/3 of the Commission.

(l) AUTHORIZATION OF APPROPRIATIONS- There are authorized to be appropriated such sums as may be necessary to carry out this section.

(m) TERMINATION- The Commission shall terminate on the date that is 60 days after the date on which the Commission submits the reports required by this section.

(n) EXEMPTION- The Commission shall be exempt from the Federal Advisory Committee Act.

Sec. 8. Adoption and Effect of National Standards

(a) PUBLICATION OF PROPOSED STANDARDS-

(1) FINAL RULE- Not later than 1 year after receiving the report specified in section 7(d)(3), the Attorney General shall

publish a final rule adopting national standards for the detection, prevention, reduction, and punishment of prison rape.

(2) INDEPENDENT JUDGMENT- The standards referred to in paragraph (1) shall be based upon the independent judgment of the Attorney General, after giving due consideration to the recommended national standards provided by the Commission under section 7(e), and being informed by such data, opinions, and proposals that the Attorney General determines to be appropriate to consider.

(3) LIMITATION- The Attorney General shall not establish a national standard under this section that would impose substantial additional costs compared to the costs presently expended by Federal, State, and local prison authorities. The Attorney General may, however, provide a list of improvements for consideration by correctional facilities.

(4) TRANSMISSION TO STATES- Within 90 days of publishing the final rule under paragraph (1), the Attorney General shall transmit the national standards adopted under such paragraph to the chief executive of each State, the head of the department of corrections of each State, and to the appropriate authorities in those units of local government who oversee operations in one or more prisons.

(b) APPLICABILITY TO FEDERAL BUREAU OF PRISONS- The national standards referred to in subsection (a) shall apply to the Federal Bureau of Prisons immediately upon adoption of the final rule under subsection (a)(4).

(c) ELIGIBILITY FOR FEDERAL FUNDS-

(1) COVERED PROGRAMS-

(A) IN GENERAL- For purposes of this subsection, a grant program is covered by this subsection if, and only if—

(i) the program is carried out by or under the authority of the Attorney General; and

(ii) the program may provide amounts to States for prison purposes.

(B) LIST- For each fiscal year, the Attorney General shall prepare a list identifying each program that meets the criteria of subparagraph (A) and provide that list to each State.

(2) ADOPTION OF NATIONAL STANDARDS- For each fiscal year, any amount that a State would otherwise receive for prison purposes for that fiscal year under a grant program covered by this subsection shall be reduced by 5 percent, unless the chief executive of the State submits to the Attorney General—

(A) a certification that the State has adopted, and is in full compliance with, the national standards described in section 8(a); or

(B) an assurance that not less than 5 percent of such amount shall be used only for the purpose of enabling the State to adopt, and achieve full compliance with, those national standards, so as to ensure that a certification under subparagraph (A) may be submitted in future years.

(3) REPORT ON NONCOMPLIANCE- Not later than September 30 of each year, the Attorney General shall publish a report listing each grantee that is not in compliance with the national standards adopted pursuant to section 8(a).

(4) COOPERATION WITH SURVEY- For each fiscal year, any amount that a State receives for that fiscal year under a grant program covered by this subsection shall not be used for prison purposes (and shall be returned to the grant program if no other authorized use is available), unless the chief executive of the State submits to the Attorney General a certification that neither the State, nor any political subdivision or unit of local government within the State, is listed in a report issued by the Attorney General pursuant to section 4(c)(2)(C).

(5) REDISTRIBUTION OF AMOUNTS- Amounts under a grant program not granted by reason of a reduction under paragraph (2), or returned by reason of the prohibition in paragraph (4), shall be granted to one or more entities not subject to such reduction or such prohibition, subject to the other laws governing that program.

(6) IMPLEMENTATION- The Attorney General shall establish procedures to implement this subsection, including procedures for effectively applying this subsection to discretionary grant programs.

(7) EFFECTIVE DATE-

(A) REQUIREMENT OF ADOPTION OF STANDARDS- The first grants to which paragraph (2) applies are grants for the second fiscal year beginning after the date on which the national standards under section 8(a) are finalized.

(B) REQUIREMENT FOR COOPERATION- The first grants to which paragraph (4) applies are grants for the fiscal year beginning after the date of the enactment of this Act.

Sec. 9. Requirement that Accreditation Organizations Adopt Accreditation Standards

(a) ELIGIBILITY FOR FEDERAL GRANTS- Notwithstanding any other provision of law, an organization responsible for the accreditation of Federal, State, local, or private prisons, jails, or other penal facilities may not receive any new Federal grants during any period in which such organization fails to meet any of the requirements of subsection (b).

(b) REQUIREMENTS- To be eligible to receive Federal grants, an accreditation organization referred to in subsection (a) must meet the following requirements:

(1) At all times after 90 days after the date of enactment of this Act, the organization shall have in effect, for each facility that it is responsible for accrediting, accreditation standards for the detection, prevention, reduction, and punishment of prison rape.

(2) At all times after 1 year after the date of the adoption of the final rule under section 8(a)(4), the organization shall, in addition to any other such standards that it may promulgate relevant to the detection, prevention, reduction, and punishment of prison rape, adopt accreditation standards consistent with the national standards adopted pursuant to such final rule.

Sec. 10. Definitions
In this Act, the following definitions shall apply:

(1) CARNAL KNOWLEDGE- The term 'carnal knowledge' means contact between the penis and the vulva or the penis and the anus, including penetration of any sort, however slight.

(2) INMATE- The term 'inmate' means any person incarcerated or detained in any facility who is accused of, convicted of, sentenced for, or adjudicated delinquent for, violations of criminal law or the terms and conditions of parole, probation, pretrial release, or diversionary program.

(3) JAIL- The term 'jail' means a confinement facility of a Federal, State, or local law enforcement agency to hold—
(A) persons pending adjudication of criminal charges; or
(B) persons committed to confinement after adjudication of criminal charges for sentences of 1 year or less.

(4) HIV- The term 'HIV' means the human immunodeficiency virus.

(5) ORAL SODOMY- The term 'oral sodomy' means contact between the mouth and the penis, the mouth and the vulva, or the mouth and the anus.

(6) POLICE LOCKUP- The term 'police lockup' means a temporary holding facility of a Federal, State, or local law enforcement agency to hold—
(A) inmates pending bail or transport to jail;
(B) inebriates until ready for release; or
(C) juveniles pending parental custody or shelter placement.

(7) PRISON- The term 'prison' means any confinement facility of a Federal, State, or local government, whether administered by such government or by a private organization on behalf of such government, and includes—
(A) any local jail or police lockup; and
(B) any juvenile facility used for the custody or care of juvenile inmates.

(8) PRISON RAPE- The term 'prison rape' includes the rape of an inmate in the actual or constructive control of prison officials.

(9) RAPE- The term 'rape' means—
(A) the carnal knowledge, oral sodomy, sexual assault with an object, or sexual fondling of a person, forcibly or against that person's will;
(B) the carnal knowledge, oral sodomy, sexual assault with an object, or sexual fondling of a person not forcibly or against the person's will, where the victim is incapable of giving consent because of his or her youth or his or her temporary or permanent mental or physical incapacity; or
(C) the carnal knowledge, oral sodomy, sexual assault with an object, or sexual fondling of a person achieved through the exploitation of the fear or threat of physical violence or bodily injury.

(10) SEXUAL ASSAULT WITH AN OBJECT- The term 'sexual assault with an object' means the use of any hand, finger, object, or other instrument to penetrate, however slightly, the genital or anal opening of the body of another person.

(11) SEXUAL FONDLING- The term 'sexual fondling' means the touching of the private body parts of another person (including the genitalia, anus, groin, breast, inner thigh, or buttocks) for the purpose of sexual gratification.

(12) EXCLUSIONS- The terms and conditions described in paragraphs (9) and (10) shall not apply to—
(A) custodial or medical personnel gathering physical evidence, or engaged in other legitimate medical treatment, in the course of investigating prison rape;
(B) the use of a health care provider's hands or fingers or the use of medical devices in the course of appropriate medical treatment unrelated to prison rape; or
(C) the use of a health care provider's hands or fingers and the use of instruments to perform body cavity searches in order to maintain security and safety within the prison or detention facility, provided that the search is conducted in a manner consistent with constitutional requirements.

Sexual Victimization of Prisoners in Local Jails Reported by Inmates, 2007

As a requirement of PREA, prisoners were asked about their experiences with sexual crime behind bars. The 2007 National Inmate Survey (NIS), conducted by the Bureau of Justice Statistics, involved a sample of 40,419 prisoners in 282 local jails. The survey only gathered allegations of attacks made within the prior six months. Weights were applied to the samples to create nationwide estimates. The study found:

- About 1.6 percent of inmates (12,100 nationwide) reported sexual victimization of a prisoner by another prisoner while 2.0 percent (15,200) reported an attack by a staff member.
- Inmates are most likely to be attacked in their own cells (56%) by other prisoners while staff-on-inmate victimization occurred in a closet, office, or other locked room (47%).
- Women are more likely than men to be sexually attacked (5%), largely as the result of attacks by other inmates.
- In total, 0.6 percent of all jail inmates reported an injury related to sexual crime. These injuries included bruises, scratches, anal tearing, stab wounds, broken bones and concussions but most were not reported to authorities as the results of sexual victimization.
- Most injured victims (85%) reported that they had suffered a serious injury.

Rates of Forcible Rape Nationwide

The Federal Bureau of Investigation has published a Uniform Crime Report each year since 1930. The report, which aims to provide reliable crime statistics, collects data submitted by nearly 17,000 law enforcement agencies across the United States. The FBI tries to ensure uniformity of reporting by providing law enforcement agencies with a handbook that explains how to classify and score offenses according to standardized definitions of offenses. Since definitions of criminal offenses may vary according to state or local law, the FBI sets its own definitions of crime for agencies to follow. The numbers in Table 6.3 below are part of a 1.4 percent decrease in violent crime between 2006 and 2007.

TABLE 6.3
Annual Uniform Crime Report, January-December 2007

Offenses reported to law enforcement
by state and by city 100,000 and over in population

State	City		Population[1]	Forcible Rape
Alabama	Birmingham	2006		220
		2007	227,686	229
	Huntsville	2006		100
		2007	169,391	96
	Mobile[3]	2006		50
		2007	253,842	23
	Montgomery	2006		74
		2007	202,062	54
Alaska	Anchorage	2006		248
		2007	284,142	257
Arizona	Chandler	2006		56
		2007	250,868	51
	Gilbert	2006		37
		2007	206,681	23
	Glendale	2006		75
		2007	250,444	58
	Mesa	2006		203
		2007	454,576	175
	Peoria	2006		41
		2007	147,223	41
	Phoenix	2006		550
		2007	1,541,698	509
	Scottsdale	2006		65
		2007	235,243	41
	Tempe	2006		71
		2007	171,320	63
	Tucson[4]	2006		294
		2007	523,299	277
Arkansas	Little Rock	2006		151
		2007	184,594	123
California	Anaheim	2006		107
		2007	335,133	96
	Antioch	2006		35
		2007	101,973	27
	Bakersfield	2006		43
		2007	318,743	41
	Berkeley	2006		22
		2007	101,343	24
	Burbank	2006		10
		2007	104,871	14
	Chula Vista	2006		70
		2007	218,718	57

(*Continued*)

TABLE 6.3
Annual Uniform Crime Report, January-December 2007 (*Continued*)

Offenses reported to law enforcement
by state and by city 100,000 and over in population

State	City		Population[1]	Forcible Rape
	Concord	2006		20
		2007	122,202	13
	Corona	2006		31
		2007	153,518	28
	Costa mesa	2006		30
		2007	109,835	39
	Daly city	2006		18
		2007	100,632	15
	Downey	2006		21
		2007	109,642	17
	Elk Grove[5]	2006		
		2007	138,103	23
	El Monte	2006		25
		2007	124,182	25
	Escondido	2006		33
		2007	133,429	28
	Fairfield	2006		36
		2007	106,098	36
	Fontana	2006		40
		2007	176,490	43
	Fremont	2006		29
		2007	201,318	35
	Fresno	2006		133
		2007	472,170	99
	Fullerton	2006		47
		2007	133,855	41
	Garden Grove	2006		29
		2007	166,414	35
	Glendale	2006		14
		2007	200,049	12
	Hayward	2006		33
		2007	140,603	48
	Huntington Beach	2006		31
		2007	195,067	29
	Inglewood	2006		36
		2007	115,223	19
	Irvine	2006		17
		2007	201,872	19
	Lancaster	2006		56
		2007	144,210	59
	Long Beach	2006		134
		2007	473,959	138

TABLE 6.3
Annual Uniform Crime Report, January-December 2007 (*Continued*)

Offenses reported to law enforcement
by state and by city 100,000 and over in population

State	City		Population[1]	Forcible Rape
	Los Angeles	2006		1,059
		2007	3,870,487	1,004
	Modesto	2006		73
		2007	208,067	65
	Moreno Valley	2006		61
		2007	190,248	66
	Norwalk	2006		21
		2007	105,330	14
	Oakland	2006		306
		2007	396,541	277
	Oceanside	2006		48
		2007	166,424	51
	Ontario	2006		74
		2007	175,537	46
	Orange	2006		13
		2007	135,818	8
	Oxnard	2006		34
		2007	186,367	33
	Palmdale	2006		58
		2007	142,122	34
	Pasadena	2006		19
		2007	145,553	33
	Pomona	2006		17
		2007	155,161	32
	Rancho Cucamonga	2006		25
		2007	177,683	19
	Rialto	2006		30
		2007	100,451	25
	Richmond	2006		41
		2007	102,471	31
	Riverside	2006		83
		2007	299,312	91
	Roseville	2006		24
		2007	111,497	31
	Sacramento	2006		196
		2007	460,546	194
	Salinas	2006		45
		2007	145,251	51
	San Bernardino	2006		50
		2007	200,810	74

(*Continued*)

TABLE 6.3
Annual Uniform Crime Report, January-December 2007 (*Continued*)

Offenses reported to law enforcement
by state and by city 100,000 and over in population

State	City		Population[1]	Forcible Rape
	San Diego	2006		348
		2007	1,261,196	296
	San Francisco	2006		154
		2007	733,799	125
	San Jose	2006		217
		2007	934,553	217
	Santa Ana	2006		73
		2007	340,223	65
	Santa Clara	2006		16
		2007	109,420	32
	Santa Clarita	2006		26
		2007	170,429	22
	Santa Rosa	2006		75
		2007	154,953	65
	Simi Valley	2006		21
		2007	122,677	20
	South Gate	2006		14
		2007	98,701	17
	Stockton	2006		102
		2007	297,170	105
	Sunnyvale	2006		21
		2007	130,326	15
	Thousand Oaks	2006		13
		2007	125,196	19
	Torrance	2006		18
		2007	142,970	21
	Vallejo	2006		31
		2007	116,763	26
	Ventura	2006		24
		2007	104,523	27
	Victorville	2006		26
		2007	104,872	30
	Visalia	2006		50
		2007	116,766	38
	West Covina	2006		13
		2007	108,097	21
Colorado	Arvada	2006		31
		2007	105,197	29
	Aurora	2006		217
		2007	307,621	191
	Centennial	2006		25
		2007	97,746	34

TABLE 6.3
Annual Uniform Crime Report, January-December 2007 (*Continued*)

Offenses reported to law enforcement
by state and by city 100,000 and over in population

State	City		Population[1]	Forcible Rape
	Colorado Springs	2006		250
		2007	374,112	286
	Denver	2006		342
		2007	573,387	296
	Fort Collins	2006		76
		2007	130,935	70
	Lakewood	2006		101
		2007	139,407	81
	Pueblo	2006		49
		2007	103,958	43
	Thornton	2006		75
		2007	113,289	72
	Westminster	2006		39
		2007	106,383	22
Connecticut	Bridgeport	2006		69
		2007	137,655	77
	Hartford	2006		47
		2007	124,558	58
	Stamford	2006		28
		2007	119,510	31
	Waterbury	2006		39
		2007	107,241	18
Florida	Cape Coral	2006		52
		2007	159,936	40
	Clearwater	2006		44
		2007	107,501	34
	Coral Springs	2006		2
		2007	131,307	7
	Fort Lauderdale	2006		83
		2007	187,995	56
	Gainesville	2006		96
		2007	108,289	93
	Hialeah	2006		26
		2007	215,853	42
	Hollywood	2006		58
		2007	146,673	62
	Jacksonville	2006		218
		2007	797,350	249
	Miami	2006		101
		2007	410,252	57

(*Continued*)

TABLE 6.3
Annual Uniform Crime Report, January-December 2007 (*Continued*)

Offenses reported to law enforcement
by state and by city 100,000 and over in population

State	City		Population[1]	Forcible Rape
	Miramar	2006		45
		2007	114,029	26
	Orlando	2006		163
		2007	224,417	162
	Pembroke Pines	2006		15
		2007	151,817	16
	Pompano Beach	2006		54
		2007	104,989	63
	Port St. Lucie	2006		36
		2007	154,036	60
	St. Petersburg	2006		112
		2007	248,069	103
	Tallahassee	2006		155
		2007	159,943	136
	Tampa	2006		133
		2007	337,220	80
Georgia	Athens-Clarke	2006		53
	County	2007	113,389	43
	Atlanta	2006		171
		2007	497,290	148
	Columbus	2006		19
		2007	188,944	57
	Savannah-	2006		65
	Chatham	2007	208,116	78
	Metropolitan			
Hawaii	Honolulu	2006		229
		2007	905,903	226
Idaho	Boise	2006		135
		2007	199,104	122
Illinois[6]	Aurora	2006		
		2007	174,724	
	Chicago	2006		
		2007	2,824,434	
	Joliet	2006		
		2007	148,484	
	Naperville	2006		
		2007	144,933	
	Peoria	2006		
		2007	113,137	
	Rockford[7]	2006		135
		2007	155,713	107
	Springfield	2006		
		2007	117,185	

TABLE 6.3
Annual Uniform Crime Report, January-December 2007 (*Continued*)

Offenses reported to law enforcement
by state and by city 100,000 and over in population

State	City		Population[1]	Forcible Rape
Indiana	Evansville	2006		61
		2007	114,985	56
	Fort Wayne[8]	2006		80
		2007	248,423	85
	Gary	2006		61
		2007	97,048	57
	Indianapolis	2006		549
		2007	797,268	505
	South Bend	2006		67
		2007	104,437	67
Iowa	Cedar Rapids	2006		41
		2007	124,730	34
	Des Moines[4]	2006		
		2007	192,948	185
Kansas	Kansas City	2006		91
		2007	143,371	91
	Overland Park	2006		48
		2007	169,224	35
	Topeka	2006		57
		2007	121,885	47
	Wichita	2006		245
		2007	358,294	266
Kentucky	Lexington	2006		128
		2007	272,815	111
	Louisville Metro	2006		175
		2007	624,030	191
Louisiana	Baton Rouge	2006		93
		2007	228,446	72
	Lafayette	2006		73
		2007	114,212	68
	New Orleans	2006		87
		2007	220,614	115
	Shreveport	2006		140
		2007	199,811	112
Maryland	Baltimore	2006		138
		2007	624,237	146
Massachusetts	Boston	2006		275
		2007	591,855	263
	Cambridge[7]	2006		11
		2007	101,161	12

(*Continued*)

TABLE 6.3

Annual Uniform Crime Report, January-December 2007 (*Continued*)

Offenses reported to law enforcement
by state and by city 100,000 and over in population

State	City		Population[1]	Forcible Rape
	Springfield	2006		115
		2007	151,074	91
	Worcester	2006		126
		2007	175,825	93
Michigan	Ann Arbor	2006		34
		2007	113,011	29
	Detroit	2006		592
		2007	860,971	344
	Flint	2006		143
		2007	116,024	113
	Grand Rapids	2006		66
		2007	192,376	69
	Lansing	2006		116
		2007	113,643	91
	Sterling Heights	2006		17
		2007	128,555	21
	Warren[4]	2006		75
		2007	134,081	71
Minnesota	Minneapolis	2006		453
		2007	371,240	452
	St. Paul	2006		197
		2007	271,662	173
Mississippi	Jackson	2006		160
		2007	175,525	141
Missouri	Independence	2006		61
		2007	108,879	45
	Springfield	2006		82
		2007	150,488	72
	St. Louis	2006		337
		2007	348,197	255
Montana	Billings	2006		28
		2007	101,342	23
Nebraska	Lincoln	2006		100
		2007	243,243	113
	Omaha	2006		187
		2007	431,810	189
Nevada	Henderson	2006		63
		2007	251,270	66
	Las Vegas Metropolitan Police Department	2006		718
		2007	1,341,156	723
	North Las Vegas	2006		57
		2007	211,419	53

TABLE 6.3
Annual Uniform Crime Report, January-December 2007 (*Continued*)

Offenses reported to law enforcement
by state and by city 100,000 and over in population

State	City		Population[1]	Forcible Rape
	Reno	2006		100
		2007	214,197	95
New Jersey	Edison Township	2006		15
		2007	99,082	0
	Elizabeth	2006		35
		2007	125,621	25
	Jersey city	2006		60
		2007	240,718	47
	Newark	2006		87
		2007	280,158	60
	Paterson	2006		37
		2007	148,049	26
	Woodbridge	2006		17
	Township	2007	98,769	14
New Mexico	Albuquerque	2006		286
		2007	513,124	307
New York	Amherst Town	2006		11
		2007	111,622	8
	Buffalo	2006		174
		2007	273,832	164
	New York	2006		1,071
		2007	8,220,196	875
	Rochester	2006		92
		2007	206,686	124
	Syracuse	2006		66
		2007	139,880	67
	Yonkers	2006		31
		2007	198,071	44
North Carolina	Cary	2006		14
		2007	114,221	11
	Charlotte-	2006		346
	Mecklenburg	2007	733,291	282
	Fayetteville	2006		61
		2007	167,157	56
	Greensboro	2006		86
		2007	238,122	94
	Raleigh	2006		97
		2007	367,120	99
Ohio	Akron	2006		163
		2007	208,701	174

(*Continued*)

TABLE 6.3
Annual Uniform Crime Report, January-December 2007 (*Continued*)

Offenses reported to law enforcement
by state and by city 100,000 and over in population

State	City		Population[1]	Forcible rape
	Cincinnati	2006		296
		2007	332,388	313
	Cleveland	2006		455
		2007	439,888	374
	Columbus	2006		598
		2007	735,981	661
	Dayton	2006		125
		2007	155,526	114
	Toledo	2006		169
		2007	296,403	151
Oklahoma	Norman	2006		38
		2007	103,721	35
	Oklahoma City	2006		327
		2007	542,199	326
	Tulsa	2006		289
		2007	381,469	299
Oregon	Eugene	2006		44
		2007	147,458	55
	Portland	2006		293
		2007	538,133	280
	Salem	2006		74
		2007	154,484	58
Pennsylvania	Allentown	2006		42
		2007	107,397	20
	Erie	2006		69
		2007	101,812	75
	Philadelphia	2006		960
		2007	1,435,533	956
	Pittsburgh	2006		102
		2007	312,179	129
Rhode Island	Providence[7]	2006		52
		2007	173,719	43
South Carolina	Charleston	2006		45
		2007	109,382	55
	Columbia	2006		56
		2007	121,674	67
South Dakota	Sioux Falls	2006		120
		2007	144,985	95
Tennessee	Chattanooga	2006		121
		2007	155,043	102
	Clarksville	2006		50
		2007	114,582	64

TABLE 6.3

Annual Uniform Crime Report, January–December 2007 (*Continued*)

Offenses reported to law enforcement
by state and by city 100,000 and over in population

State	City		Population[1]	Forcible rape
	Knoxville	2006		91
		2007	183,319	109
	Memphis	2006		434
		2007	669,264	451
	Nashville	2006		320
		2007	564,169	290
Texas	Abilene	2006		67
		2007	114,644	89
	Amarillo	2006		97
		2007	187,234	127
	Arlington	2006		192
		2007	372,073	156
	Austin	2006		319
		2007	716,817	328
	Beaumont	2006		75
		2007	109,345	71
	Brownsville[4]	2006		
		2007	177,090	21
	Carrollton	2006		6
		2007	123,324	3
	Corpus Christi	2006		167
		2007	286,428	238
	Dallas	2006		665
		2007	1,239,104	511
	Denton	2006		66
		2007	113,936	76
	El Paso[7]	2006		300
		2007	616,029	258
	Fort Worth	2006		251
		2007	670,693	333
	Garland	2006		50
		2007	218,236	52
	Grand Prairie	2006		69
		2007	157,913	74
	Houston	2006		854
		2007	2,169,544	694
	Irving	2006		48
		2007	196,676	30
	Killeen	2006		81
		2007	104,188	82

(*Continued*)

TABLE 6.3
Annual Uniform Crime Report, January-December 2007 (*Continued*)

Offenses reported to law enforcement
by state and by city 100,000 and over in population

State	City		Population¹	Forcible Rape
	Laredo	2006		96
		2007	221,253	81
	Lubbock	2006		98
		2007	213,988	101
	McAllen	2006		28
		2007	129,455	27
	McKinney	2006		50
		2007	118,113	45
	Mesquite	2006		10
		2007	132,399	8
	Midland	2006		58
		2007	103,118	57
	Pasadena	2006		49
		2007	145,235	75
	Plano	2006		41
		2007	259,771	52
	Richardson	2006		12
		2007	100,933	22
	San Antonio	2006		514
		2007	1,316,882	635
	Waco	2006		72
		2007	122,514	95
	Wichita Falls	2006		27
		2007	98,717	31
Utah	Provo	2006		49
		2007	115,264	28
	Salt Lake City	2006		95
		2007	178,449	116
	West Valley	2006		74
		2007	121,447	90
Virginia	Alexandria	2006		27
		2007	137,812	18
	Chesapeake	2006		60
		2007	223,093	78
	Hampton	2006		53
		2007	144,490	52
	Newport News	2006		114
		2007	177,550	91
	Norfolk	2006		105
		2007	227,903	97
	Portsmouth	2006		38
		2007	101,284	36

TABLE 6.3
Annual Uniform Crime Report, January-December 2007 (*Continued*)

Offenses reported to law enforcement
by state and by city 100,000 and over in population

State	City		Population[1]	Forcible Rape
	Richmond	2006		78
		2007	191,785	53
	Virginia Beach	2006		116
		2007	435,943	88
Washington	Bellevue	2006		42
		2007	118,984	29
	Seattle	2006		129
		2007	585,118	90
	Spokane	2006		91
		2007	198,272	88
	Tacoma[7]	2006		142
		2007	196,909	138
	Vancouver	2006		103
		2007	161,092	118
Wisconsin	Green Bay	2006		50
		2007	100,010	67
	Madison	2006		64
		2007	225,370	57
	Milwaukee	2006		220
		2007	572,938	236

Source: Crime in the United States. Preliminary Annual Uniform Crime Report. Department of Justice. Federal Bureau of Investigation, 2007. Available from http://www.fbi.gov/ucr/2007prelim/table4al_ca.htm.

[1]The 2007 population figures are FBI estimates based on provisional data from the U.S. Census Bureau.

[2]The FBI does not publish arson data unless it receives 12 months data from either the agency or the state for 2006 and/or 2007.

[3]The population for the city of Mobile, Alabama, includes 61,856 inhabitants from the jurisdiction of the Mobile County Sheriff's Department.

[4]The FBI determined that the agency did not follow national Uniform Crime Reporting (UCR) Program guidelines for reporting an offense. Consequently, this figure is not included in this table and has been excluded from all *Report* tabulations.

[5]Elk Grove, California, became an incorporated city in July 2006. Therefore, complete January through December data for 2006 are not available.

[6]The data collection methodology for the offense of forcible rape used by the Illinois (with the exception of Rockford, IL) state Uniform Crime Reporting (UCR) Program does not comply with national UCR guidelines. Consequently, their figures for forcible rape and violent crime (of which forcible rape is a part) are not published in this *Report*.

[7]Because of changes in the agency's reporting practices, figures are not comparable to previous years' data.

[8]Due to an annexation, population and figures may not be comparable to previous years' data.

Further Reading

Brownmiller, Susan. *Against Our Will: Men, Women, and Rape.* New York: Simon and Schuster, 1975.

Flowers, R. Barri. *Runaway Kids and Teenage Prostitution: America's Lost, Abandoned, and Sexually Exploited Children.* New York: Praeger, 2001.

Flowers, R. Barri. *Sex Crimes: Perpetrators, Predators, Prostitutes, and Victims.* Springfield, IL: Charles C. Thomas, 2006.

Koss, Mary P. "Hidden Rape: Incidence, Prevalence, and Descriptive Characteristics of Sexual Aggression Reported by a National Sample of Postsecondary Students." In A. W. Burgess, ed. *Sexual Assault,* vol. 2, New York: Garland, 1988.

Warshaw, Robin. *I Never Called It Rape: The* Ms. *Report on Recognizing, Fighting, and Surviving Date and Acquaintance Rape.* New York: Harper Perennial, 1994.

7

Directory of Organizations

Abused Deaf Women's Advocacy Services (ADWAS)
8623 Roosevelt Way NE
Seattle WA 98115
TTY: 206-726–0093 TTY: 1–800–787–3224
Sexual Assault Crisis Line: TTY: 1–888–236–1355
24 hours—7 days a week
Domestic Violence Crisis Line: TTY: 1–888–236–1355
24 hours—7 days a week
E-mail: adwas@ndvh.org
URL: http://www.adwas.org

Abused Deaf Women's Advocacy Services (ADWAS) is the first organization to provide services to deaf victims of crime. It began in 1986 as a support agency for deaf, deaf-blind, and hard-of-hearing victims of sexual assault and domestic violence. ADWAS has since established the nation's first transitional housing program for deaf victims of abuse, "A Place of Our Own." It has branches in 14 cities across the United States. In addition to the crisis lines, services include support groups for both female and male victims of physical, sexual, or emotional abuse and educational programs on date rape and teen battering that are presented to high schools with deaf populations.

AdvocateWeb
P.O. Box 202961
Austin, TX 78720
Phone: 512–249–1217
E-mail: hope@advocateweb.org
http://www.advocateweb.org

AdvocateWeb, a Web-only organization in existence since 1998, provides free public information on the Web about sexual abuse or exploitation by someone in a position of trust, such as a teacher, physician, or member of the clergy. The organization serves as a resource for victim/survivors, their families and friends, the general public, and for victim advocates and professionals.

Association for Women's Self-Defense Advancement (AWSDA)
556 Route 17 North, Suite 7–209
Paramus, NJ 07652
Phone: 1–888-STOP RAPE or 201–794–2153.
Fax: 201–791–6005.
E-mail: info@awsda.org
URL: http://www.awsda.org/

When a serial rapist is active, many communities respond by promoting women's self-defense courses. The Association for Women's Self-Defense Advancement (AWSDA) is dedicated to year-round promotion of the best self-defense techniques. It began in 1990 to provide women with practical self-defense training and information about legal rights in regard to self-defense. Members, who are generally in law enforcement or antirape work, are expected to promote women's self-defense in their local communities by making use of the organization's newsletter advice and its annual training seminar.

Association for the Treatment of Sexual Abusers
4900 S.W. Griffith Drive, Suite 274
Beaverton, Oregon U.S.A. 97005
Phone: 503–643–1023
Fax: 503–643–5084
E-mail: atsa@atsa.com
URL: http://www.atsa.com

The challenging problem of what to do with sex offenders has bedeviled communities across the country. The Association for the Treatment of Sexual Abusers (ATSA) is a professional association that focuses on sexual offender identification and treatment. It grew out of a series of conferences in the late 1970s. ATSA helps with the effective management of sex offenders by providing the latest research on current issues. ATSA has issued several policy statements, on civil commitment of sexually violent offenders and chemical castration among others, to provide state and local government bodies with formulating public policy on sex offenders.

American Civil Liberties Union
733 15th Street NW, Suite 620
Washington, DC 20005
Phone: 202–393–4930
Fax: 202–393–4931
URL: http://www.aclu.org

The American Civil Liberties Union (ACLU) established two projects in 1972 that address sexual crime as part of their broader missions. The National Prison Project seeks to protect prisoners from rape, while the Women's Rights Project seeks to empower female victims of sexual abuse. The National Prison Project, the only national litigation program on behalf of prisoners, seeks to create constitutional conditions of confinement and strengthen prisoners' rights through class action litigation and public education. The Project also publishes a semi-annual journal, coordinates a nationwide network of litigators, conducts training and public education conferences, and provides expert advice and technical assistance to local community groups and lawyers throughout the country. The Women's Rights Project uses litigation, community outreach, advocacy and public education to advance battered women's civil rights and challenge the housing and employment discrimination experienced by so many battered women, especially low-income and women of color.

American College of Obstetricians and Gynecologists (ACOG)
409 12th Street SW
Washington, DC 20024
Phone: 202–638–5577
Fax: 202–484–3917
URL: http://www.acog.org

The American College of Obstetricians and Gynecologists (ACOG), founded in 1951, is the nation's leading group of professionals providing health care for women. To promote quality health care for women and increase awareness about women's health care, ACOG produces publications on violence against women (intimate partner violence, sexual assault, adolescent dating violence) and materials for patient education in English and Spanish.

**American Professional Society on the Abuse
of Children (APSAC)**
350 Poplar Avenue
Elmhurst, IL 60126
Phone: 630–941–1235, Toll Free: 1–877–402–7722
Fax: 630–359–4274
E-mail: apsac@apsac.org
URL: http://www.apsac.org

The American Professional Society on the Abuse of Children (APSAC), founded in 1987, is a multidisciplinary society of professionals working in the fields of child abuse research, prevention, treatment, investigation, litigation, and policy. It aims to prevent child abuse by eliminating recurrence of child maltreatment, promoting research, educating the public, and connecting professionals to help formulate policy and guidelines.

Campus Outreach Services
109 Summer Hill Lane
St. Davids, PA 19087
Phone: 610–989–0651
Fax: 610–989–0652
E-mail: info@campusoutreachservices.com
URL: http://www.campusoutreachservices.com/contact.html

Campus Outreach Services is the creation of Katie Koestner, who was sexually assaulted by a fellow college student. The organization focuses on the prevention of date rape and other sexual crimes by offering speakers and programs on sexual violence, providing research aid, lobbying for sexual assault related legislation, and collaborating with the association with the National Center for Higher Education Risk Management (http://www.ncherm.org).

Centers for Disease Control and Prevention (CDC)
National Center for Injury Prevention and Control (NCIPC)
4770 Buford Hwy, NE
MS F-63
Atlanta, GA 30341–3717
Phone: 1–800-CDC-INFO (232–4636)
TTY: 1–888-232–6348
Fax: 770–488–4760
E-mail: cdcinfo@cdc.gov
URL: http://www.cdc.gov/ncipc/dvp/SV/default.htm

The U.S. Surgeon General identified violent behavior as a public health concern in 1979. In the following year, the Centers for Disease Control (CDC) began studying patterns of violence. These early activities grew into a national program to reduce the death and disability associated with injuries outside the workplace. In 1992, the CDC established the National Center for Injury Prevention and Control (NCIPC) as the lead federal organization for violence prevention. The Division of Violence Prevention (DVP), one of three divisions within NCIPC, aims to stop violence before it begins. The CDC also tracks violence against women, develops antiviolence prevention programs, and promotes research into violent behaviors directed at women.

Center for Sex Offender Management (CSOM)
c/o Center for Effective Public Policy
8403 Colesville Road, Suite 720
Silver Spring, MD 20910
Phone: 301–589–9383
Fax: 301–589–3505
E-mail: cartermm@cepp.com
URL: http://www.csom.org

The Center for Sex Offender Management (CSOM), part of the U.S. Department of Justice, began in 1997 to manage sex offenders in the community. CSOM provides an information exchange about effective procedures for managing sex offenders and training to those responsible for such individuals.

Childhelp USA
15757 North 78th Street
Scottsdale, AZ 85260
Phone: 480–922–8212
TTD: 1–800–222–4453
National Child Abuse Hotline,
1–800–4-A-CHILD
URL: http://www.childhelpusa.org

Childhelp USA was started in 1959 by Sara O'Meara and Yvonne Fedderson to combat child abuse. The organization seeks to prevent child abuse and promote healing through residential treatment centers, foster care, and group homes. It sponsors the National Day of Hope in April, which is National Child Abuse Prevention Month.

Clan Star, Inc.
P.O. Box 2410
Cherokee, NC 28719
Phone: 828–497–5507, Toll-Free: 1–888-636–4748
Fax: 828–497–5688
URL: http://www.clanstar.org/

Clan Star has begun to strengthen Native American justice systems. It is based on the Indian way of life, which recognizes the unique role of and respect for all living things. Abuse of women and children is not traditional and not acceptable. Clan Star focuses on gender-based crimes such as domestic violence, sexual assault, and stalking.

Coalition to Abolish Slavery and Trafficking (CAST)
042 Wilshire Blvd., #586
Los Angeles CA 90036
Phone: 213–365–1906
Fax: 213–365–5257
E-mail: info@castla.org
URL: http://www.castla.org

The sexual trafficking of women has increased dramatically since the end of the Cold War, yet the issue has attracted comparatively little attention. The Coalition to Abolish Slavery & Trafficking (CAST), established in 1998, helps women who are trafficked for sexual and other purposes by providing legal aid, social services, and police training. CAST opened the first shelter for trafficked women in the United States.

Community United Against Violence
170A Capp Street
San Francisco, CA 94110
Phone: 415–777–5500
Fax: 415–777–5565
24-hour Crisis Line: 415–333-HELP (4357)
E-mail: info@cuav.org
URL: http://www.cuav.org/contact

Founded in 1979 in the wake of the antigay murders of two San Franciscogovernmentofficials,CommunityUnitedAgainstViolence (CUAV) is a multicultural, antioppression organization working to end violence against and within the lesbian, gay, bisexual, transgender, queer, and questioning (LGBTQQ) communities. It focuses on hate violence as well as domestic violence. CUAV was one of the first agencies in the country to realize the gravity of domestic violence in our LGBTQQ communities.

Coordinadora Paz para la Mujer, Inc. [Coordinating Peace for the Woman]
Apartado 193008
San Juan, Puerto Rico 00919–3008
Phone: 787–281–7579
Fax: 787–767–6843
E-mail: pazmujer@prtc.net
URL: http://www.pazparalamujer.org/contacto.html

Coordinadora Paz para la Mujer [Coordinating Peace for the Woman], founded in 1989, is a feminist Latina organization that works to stop violence against women and provide services to female victims of domestic violence and their children. It is the first group to specifically serve the Latina community in the United States. It grew out of Law 54, legislation passed by Puerto Rico in 1989 to combat domestic violence that has served as model for domestic violence legislation throughout Latin America and the Caribbean.

COYOTE and St. James Infirmary
St. James Infirmary
1372 Mission Street
San Francisco, CA 94103
Phone: 415–554–8494
Fax: 415–554–8444
URL: http://www.stjamesinfirmary.org/

Call Off Your Old Tired Ethics, better known as COYOTE, was formed in 1973 to work for the legalization of prostitution laws and an end to the stigma associated with sex work. Margo St. James, who spent five years as a prostitute in the 1960s, began the group in San Francisco, California. Part of the feminist movement, COYOTE is the best known of the groups in the prostitution rights movement. In 1999, St. James and COYOTE founded St. James Infirmary, a free occupational health and safety clinic for current, former, and transitioning sex workers in San Francisco. The infirmary offers primary medical care, harm-reduction help, such as testing for sexually transmitted diseases and mental health counseling, as well as a pretrial diversion program for those charged with prostitution-related crimes.

Faith Trust Institute
2400 N. 45th Street, Suite 10
Seattle, WA 98103
Phone: 206–634–1903 ext. 10
E-mail info@faithtrustinstitute.org
URL: http://www.faithtrustinstitute.org/

Faith Trust Institute, founded in 1977 by the Reverend Marie M. Fortune, is an ecumenical organization that focuses on education, clergy training, and pastoral care of sexual assault victims. It serves as a bridge between religious and secular communities with an emphasis on education and prevention. Accordingly, it has developed education and prevention programs, including a clergy ethics program, for Buddhist, Jewish, Protestant, and Roman Catholic communities.

Federal Bureau of Investigation
Various branch offices
URL: http://www.fbi.gov/hq/cid/cac/crimesmain.htm

The Federal Bureau of Investigation (FBI) is the investigative arm of the U.S. Department of Justice. The FBI has the mission of preventing and investigating crimes that cross state boundaries. Like several other federal agencies, it addresses sexual crime. The FBI's Crimes Against Children (CAC) program seeks to improve the abilities of state and local law enforcement to respond quickly and effectively to child sexual exploitation. CAC offers investigative assistance and training programs.

Feminist Majority Foundation
1600 Wilson Boulevard, Suite 801
Arlington, VA 22209
Phone: 703–522–2214
URL: http://www.feminist.org

The Feminist Majority Foundation (FMF), founded in 1987, seeks to empower women economically, socially, and politically. It has programs related to women and policing, domestic violence, sexual assault, and women's health.

Gift From Within
16 Cobb Hill Rd.
Camden, ME 04843
Phone: 207–236–8858
Fax: 207–236–2818
URL: http://www.giftfromwithin.org/

Gift from Within, founded by Frank M. Ochberg in 1993, is dedicated to those who suffer posttraumatic stress disorder (PTSD), those at risk for developing the ailment, and caregivers. It provides educational materials.

**Hamilton Fish Institute on School
and Community Violence**
2121 K Street NW, Suite 200
Washington, DC 20037
Phone: 202–496–2200
Fax: 202–496–6244
URL: http://www.hamfish.org

The Hamilton Fish Institute on School and Community is a national clearinghouse for K-12 school violence prevention programs. The Institute, administered by George Washington University since its founding in 1997, focuses upon adolescent violence, criminology, law enforcement, substance abuse, juvenile justice, public health, education, behavior disorders, and social skills development as well as prevention programs.

**Higher Education Center for Alcohol and Other
Drug Abuse and Violence Prevention**
55 Chapel Street
Newton, MA 02458
Phone: 800–676–1730
Fax: 617–928–1537
URL: http://www.edc.org/hec

The U.S. Department of Education established the Center in 1993 to serve as the national resource center for institutions of higher education concerned with reducing alcohol, other drug use, and violence. The Center provides training and publications to help colleges universities to develop, implement, and evaluate prevention programs and policies. Date and fraternity rape is often linked to the consumption of alcohol.

Human Rights Watch
350 Fifth Avenue, 34th floor
New York, NY 10118–10118
Phone: 212–290–4700
E-mail: hrwnyc@hrw.org
URL: http://www.hrw.org/

Much of the information about rape around the world is provided by Human Rights Watch, an international human rights organization. Human Rights Watch also sponsors a film festival that has included films about sexual crime.

IAFN Sexual Assault Forensic Examination
Technical Assistance (SAFE TA)
1517 Ritchie Hwy, Ste 208
Arnold, MD 21012–21012
Phone: 410–626–7805
Fax: 410–626–7804
Helpline: 877–819–7278
E-mail: info@safeta.org
URL: http://www.safeta.org/

SAFETA is the main organization for Sexual Assault Nurse Examiners and Sexual Assault Response Team members. Funded by the federal Office on Violence Against Women, it provides a helpline and Website for further information about the National Protocol for Sexual Assault Medical Forensic Examinations.

Illusion Theatre
528 Hennepin Avenue, Suite 704
Minneapolis, MN 55403
Phone: (612)339–4944
E-mail: info@illusiontheater.org
URL: http://www.illusiontheater.org/

Illusion Theater uses drama to teach children about the difficult topic of sexual abuse. The theater's nationally acclaimed sexual abuse prevention play, TOUCH, was created in 1978 by Michel Robins and Bonnie Morris in collaboration with the Child Sexual Abuse Prevention Project of the Hennepin County Attorney's Office to teach young people about personal body safety. TOUCH pioneered the concept of education/prevention plays. Through its Peer Education Program, the theater allows other groups to perform all of its plays. A discussion led by a moderator concludes every performance, allowing children to further explore challenging ideas.

IMPACT International
Various sites
1–800–345-KICK
URL: http://www.wammselfdefense.org/wamm_resources/other_chapters.htm

IMPACT, also known as model mugging, offers self-defense to women and children. Created by law enforcement officers, psychologists, and martial arts experts, it is based on the fact that individuals who appear strong are less likely to be attacked and women who fight back have a significantly better chance of avoiding being raped and murdered. Developed in 1971, IMPACT simulates realistic scenarios to help participants develop the skills necessary to address threats. Participants practice verbal as well as full-contact physical skills on a padded assailant. Maximum retention and muscle memory is obtained when the course is spread out over several weeks, rather than an intensive weekend. Clients learn how to perceive and analyze dangerous situations, use verbal and other interventions for de-escalation and conflict resolution, develop confidence in their ability to avoid or mitigate danger, and deploy physical intervention skills for defense against single or multiple assailants. There are specialized curricula to train adults, teens, children and special needs individuals who are blind or otherwise physically challenged. The IMPACT for Kids program, as one example, offers practical safety skills in a fun, age-appropriate environment for 7–10 year-old girls and boys. Children learn to use their voices for protection and draw attention to an unsafe situation, use physical skills to get away from someone threatening them, remember the details of an altercation, and tell a safe adult what happened.

Incite! Women of Color Against Violence
P.O. Box 226
Redmond, WA 98073
Phone: 484–932–3166
E-mail: incite_national-at-yahoo.com
URL: http://www.incite-national.org/

Incite! formed in 2000 as an outgrowth of a conference on violence against women. The organization argues that women of color and their allies are hungry for a new approach toward ending violence. Incite! has grown into grassroots chapters and affiliates across the country; launched political projects mobilizing women of color against violence; held conferences; and sparked critical dialogue through two anthologies, posters, and other media.

International Association of Chiefs of Police (IACP)
515 North Washington Street
Alexandria, VA 22314
Phone: 703–836–4718
Fax: 703–836–4718, Toll Free: 800–843–4227
URL: http://www.theiacp.org/

The International Association of Chiefs of Police (IACP) Victim Services Committee aims to improve victim awareness training for law enforcement personnel. IACP also lobbies to obtain funding for victim awareness program

International Association of Forensic Nurses (IAFN)
1517 Ritchie Hwy, Suite 208
Arnold, MD 21012
Phone: 410–626–7805
Fax: 410–626–7804
E-mail: info@iafn.org.
URL: http://www.iafn.org/

IAFN is the only international association of registered nurses that focuses on forensic nursing. Forensic nursing is the application of nursing science to public or legal proceedings; the application of the forensic aspects of health care are combined with the biopsychosocial education of the registered nurse in the scientific investigation and treatment of trauma and/or death of victims and perpetrators of abuse, violence, criminal activity, and traumatic accidents.

Legal Momentum
395 Hudson Street, 5th Floor
New York, NY 10014
Phone: 212–925–6635
Fax: 212–226–1066
URL: http://www.nowldef.org/

Legal Momentum (formerly National Organization for Women Legal Defense & Education Fund) provides legal advocacy for female victims of sexual crime. It also offers free, confidential legal information, as well as referrals and legal resource kits.

Male Survivor (formerly National Organization on Male Sexual Victimization)
PMB 103 5505 Connecticut Avenue, NW
Washington, DC 20015–20015
Phone: 800–738–4181
URL: http://www.malesurvivor.org

Male Survivor addresses the sexual victimization of men and boys. It formed in 1995 as an outgrowth of several professional conferences on male sexual victimization. The organization focuses on public education, advocating treatment for victims and perpetrators, and offering voice and experience to those developing prevention programs

Men Can Stop Rape
P.O. Box 57144
Washington, DC 20037
Phone: 202–265–6530
Fax: 202–285–4362
URL: http://www.mencanstoprape.org/

Men Can Stop Rape focuses on changing male attitudes that permit sexual violence against women. It focuses on education and community organizing.

Mending the Sacred Hoop
202 East Superior Street
Duluth, MN 55802
Phone: 218–722–2781, Toll Free: 1–888–305–1650
Fax: 218–722–5775
URL: http://www.msh-ta.org

This organization focuses on stopping domestic violence and sexual assault within Native American communities through training, technical assistance, and resource development.

Miles Foundation, Inc.
P.O. Box 423
Newtown, CT 06470–06470

Phone: 203–270–7861
Advocacy Helpline: 877–570–0688
E-mail: Milesfdn@aol.com or milesfd@yahoo.com
URL: http://www.vva.org/Committees/WomenVeterans/
MilesFoundationSAMM.htm

Targeting sexual harassment and sexual assault within the military, this is a private organization that provides education and training. It also serves as a resource center for the military and civilian communities.

National Alliance to End Sexual Violence
1101 Vermont Street, N.W., Suite 400
Washington, DC 20005
E-mail: info@naesv.org
URL: http://www.naesv.org

The National Alliance to End Sexual Violence, which began in September of 1995, is an organization that focuses on public policy and public education to end sexual violence.

National Association of Counsel for Children
1825 Marion Street, Suite 340
Denver, CO 80218
Phone: 888–828–6222
Fax: 303–864–5351
URL: http://www.naccchildlaw.org/

The National Association of Counsel for Children (NACC) began in 1977 to improve the condition of America's children involved with the legal system. It aims to provide high quality legal representation for children.

National Black Women's Health Imperative
1420 K Street, N.W., Suite 1000
Washington, D.C. 20005
Phone: 202–548–4000
E-mail: info@BlackWomensHealth.ORG
URL: http://www.blackwomenshealth.org/

The National Black Women's Health Imperative, formerly known as the National Black Women's Health Project, is a black feminist group that addresses sexual violence among other health concerns. It began in 1983 under founder Byllye Y. Avery. When the group became the Imperative in 2002, it instituted aggressive national programs in health policy, education, research, knowledge and leadership development and communications to save and extend the lives of black women.

**National Center for Higher Education
Risk Management (NCHERM)**
20 Callery Way
Malvern, PA 19355
Phone: 610–964–9836
Fax: 610–989–0652
URL: http://www.ncherm.org/

The National Center for Higher Education Risk Management (NCHERM) helps colleges and universities to create safe learning environments by providing services and publications. NCHERM typically aids student affairs administrators.

National Center for Injury Prevention and Control
Centers for Disease Control and Prevention
Mailstop K65
4770 Buford Highway NE
Atlanta, GA 30341–30341
Phone: 770–488–1506
Fax: 770–488–1667
URL: http://www.cdc.gov/ncipc

Operated by the Centers for Disease Control, the National Center for Injury Prevention and Control (NCIPC) aims to reduce intentional and unintentional injuries in the United States. As part of its mission, it seeks to stop crime, including intimate partner violence, sexual violence, child maltreatment and other violent acts and preventable injuries.

National Center for Missing & Exploited Children
Chas B. Wang International Children's Bldg.
699 Prince Street
Alexandria, VA 22314–22314
Phone: 703–274–3900
Fax: 703–274–2200
24-Hour Hotline: 800–843–5678
URL: http://www.missingkids.com/

The National Center for Missing & Exploited Children (NCMEC) raises public awareness about ways to help prevent child abduction, molestation, and sexual exploitation. It is the best known organization dedicated to helping missing and exploited children.

National Center for Prosecution of Child Abuse
American Prosecutors Research Institute
99 Canal Center Plaza, Suite 510
Alexandria, VA 22314
Phone: 703–519–1678
Fax: 703–549–6259
URL: http://www.ndaa-apri.org/

Created to improve the prosecution of child abusers, the National Center for Prosecution of Child Abuse is a program of the American Prosecutors Research Institute. It provides training and legal assistance to prosecutors and investigators.

National Center for Victims of Crime
2000 M Street NW, Suite 480
Washington, DC 20036
Phone: 202–467–8700
Fax: 202–467–8701
Helpline: 800–394–2255 Monday through Friday,
8:30 A.M.—8:30 P.M. EST
URL: http://www.ncvc.org/

The National Center for Victims of Crime (NCVC) helps victims recover. The organization operates a toll-free helpline for victims and their advocates.

National Center for Women & Policing
433 South Beverly Drive
Beverly Hills, CA 90212
Phone: 310–556–2526
Fax: 310–556–2509
URL: http://www.feminist.org/police

A division of the Feminist Majority Foundation, the National Center for Women & Policing (NCWP), aims to increase the numbers of women at all ranks of law enforcement to help improve police responses to violence against women.

National Center on Elder Abuse
University of Delaware 297 Graham Hall

Newark, DE 19716 USA
Phone: 302–831–3525
Fax: 302–831–4225
E-mail: ncea-info@aoa.hhs.gov
URL: http://www.ncea.aoa.gov

The National Center on Elder Abuse aims to stop crimes that are rarely reported by providing information, training, and research.

National Children's Alliance
516 C Street, NE
Washington, DC 20002
Phone: 800-239–9950 or 202–548–0090
Fax: 202–548–0099
E-mail: info@nca-online.org
URL: http://www.nca-online.org

The National Children's Alliance (formerly the National Network of Children's Advocacy Centers) is a not-for profit organization that provides training, technical assistance, and networking opportunities to communities that are developing programs to help child victims of crime.

National Children's Advocacy Center
210 Pratt Avenue, NE
Huntsville, AL 35801
Phone: 256–327–3785
Fax: 256–327–3864
URL: http://www.nationalcac.org

The National Children's Advocacy Center (NCAC) is the leading organization in the country for training child abuse professionals. Founded in 1985 by Robert E. Cramer, NCAC sponsors the annual National Symposium on Child; the National Training Center to provide seminars for child abuse professionals; Academy Online, free weeklong classes; and the National Conference on Child Sexual Abuse Prevention. It also sponsors the Southern Regional Children's Advocacy Center (SRCAC). The SRCAC, operating in 17 southern states, provides information, consultation and training and technical assistance, helping to establish child-focused programs that facilitate and support coordination among agencies responding to child abuse.

National Clearinghouse on Child Abuse & Neglect Information
330 C Street SW
Washington, DC 20447
Phone: 703–385–7565, Toll Free: 800–394–3366
Fax: 703–385–3206
URL: http://nccanch.acf.hhs.gov/

The National Clearinghouse on Child Abuse and Neglect Information was established by the Child Abuse Prevention and Treatment Act of 1974. The Clearinghouse helps professionals locate information related to child abuse, neglect, and related child welfare issues.

National Clearinghouse on Marital and Date Rape
URL: http://members.aol.com/ncmdr/index.html

This organization became defunct in 2004 but it has maintained a Webpage for historical purposes. The clearinghouse is best known for a campaign to make marital/cohabitant/date rape a crime, at least where force is used, in all fifty states. All the governments in the U.N. voted in Beijing in 1995 to abolish the marital privilege to sex on demand from wives. The clearinghouse viewed this vote as testimony to its world-wide strength.

National Coalition Against Domestic Violence
1633 Q Street NW, Suite 210
Washington, DC 20009
Phone: 202–745–1211
Fax: 202–745–0088
TTY: 202–745–2042
URL: http://www.ncadv.org/

The National Coalition Against Domestic Violence (NCADV) does not provide direct services but instead focuses on public policy and legislative issues.

National Coalition of Anti-Violence Projects
240 West 35th Street
Suite 200
New York, NY 10001
Phone: 212–714–1184
Fax: 212–714–2627
E-mail: info@ncavp.org
URL: http://www.ncavp.org

The National Coalition of Anti-Violence Programs (NCAVP) targets violence directed at and within the lesbian, gay, bisexual, transgender (LGBT), and HIV-affected communities.

National Coalition for the Protection of Children & Families (NCPCF)
800 Compton Road, Suite 9224
Cincinnati, OH 45231
Phone: 513–521–6227
Fax: 513–521–6337
Helpline: 800–583–2964
URL: http://www.nationalcoalition.org/

The National Coalition for the Protection of Children & Families (NCPCF), formerly the National Coalition Against Pornography, seeks to protect children and families from the dangers posed by pornography.

National Committee for the Prevention of Elder Abuse
1612 K Street, NW, Suite 400
Washington, DC 20006
Phone: 202–682–4140
Fax: 202–682–3984
URL: http://www.preventelderabuse.org/

The National Committee for the Prevention of Elder Abuse publishes the *Journal of Elder Abuse & Neglect* and *NEXUS*.

National Council on Child Abuse and Family Violence (NCCAFV)
1025 Connecticut Avenue NW, Suite 1012
Washington, DC 20036
Phone: 202–429–6695
Fax: 831–655–3930
URL: http://www.nccafv.org

The National Council on Child Abuse and Family Violence (NCCAFV) seeks to stop intergenerational violence. It provides public awareness and educational materials.

National Crime Victim Law Institute
10015 SW Terwilliger Boulevard
Portland, OR 97219–97219
Phone: 503–768–6819

Fax: 503–768–6671
URL: http://www.ncvli.org/

The National Crime Victim Law Institute (NCVLI), established in 2000, is a non-profit research and educational organization at Lewis & Clark Law School, Portland, Oregon. It promotes the rights of victims within the judicial system.

National Crime Victims Research & Treatment Center
Medical University of South Carolina
165 Cannon Street
Charleston, SC 29425
Phone: 843–792–2945
Fax: 843–792–3388
URL: http://www.musc.edu/cvc

The National Crime Victims Research & Treatment Center provides mental health services to crime victims and their families. It also provides educational materials and training about trauma-related topics.

National Indian Child Welfare Association (NICWA)
5100 SW Macadam Avenue, Suite 300
Portland, OR 97201
Phone: 503–222–4044
Fax: 503–222–4007
URL: http://www.nicwa.org/

The National Indian Child Welfare Association (NICWA) provides information, training, and advocacy to benefit Native American child welfare.

National Institute on Drug Abuse
6001 Executive Boulevard
Bethesda, MD 20892–20892
Phone: 301–443–1124
Fax: 301–443–7397
URL: http://www.clubdrugs.org/

The National Institute on Drug Abuse (NIDA), part of the National Institutes of Health, supports research on drug abuse and addiction. It particularly focuses on club drugs such as "Ecstasy," that have also been implicated in date rapes. NIDA's Web site provides scientific information about club drugs.

National Organization for Victim Assistance
510 King Street, Suite 424
Alexandria, VA 22314
Phone: 202–232–6682
24-Hour Information and Referral: 800–879–6682
URL: http://www.try-nova.org/

The National Organization for Victim Assistance (NOVA) is a nonprofit organization of former victims and those who work with victims. It provides lobbying, direct victim assistance, and continuing education for social workers and the like. NOVA coordinates the National Crisis Response Team and the National Crime Victim Information and Referral Hotline.

National Organization of Sisters of Color
Ending Sexual Assault (SCESA)
P.O. Box 625
Canton, CT 06019
Phone: 860–693–2031
URL: http://www.sisterslead.org

Women of color are more likely to be the victims of sexual attacks than white women. The National Organization of Sisters of Color Ending Sexual Assault (SCESA) attempts to guarantee that policymakers consider the point of view of minority women when sexual assault initiatives are created and implemented. The organization also provides training in communities of color.

National Sexual Assault Coalition Resource
Sharing Project
c/o Iowa Coalition Against Sexual Assault 515
28th Street, Suite 107
Des Moines, IA 50312
Phone: 515–244–7424, Toll Free: 800–284–7821
Fax: 515–244–7417
E-mail: rsp@iowacasa.org
URL: http://www.resourcesharingproject.org/

The National Sexual Assault Coalition Resource Sharing Project (RSP) seeks to guarantee that antirape organizations take full advantage of available resources. Many of these groups are grassroots organizations with limited staffing. The RSP provides technical assistance and professional development help. The RSP is funded by the U.S. Department of Justice, Office on Violence Against Women.

National Sexual Violence Resource Center
123 North Enola Drive, Enola, PA 17025
Phone: 717–909–0710
Fax: 717–909–0714, Toll Free: 877–739–3895
TTY: 717–909–0715
E-mail: resources@nsvrc.org
URL: http://www.nsvrc.org/contact.aspx

The National Sexual Violence Resource Center (NSVRC), funded by the Centers for Disease Control and Prevention's Division of Violence Prevention, opened in July 2000 as an information clearinghouse on all aspects of sexual violence. The Center uses the information to assist groups that combat rape and help survivors of sexual attacks. It does not provide services directly to the public but it advise direct callers about the locations and contact numbers for their state antirape coalitions.

National Women's Law Center
11 Dupont Circle NW, Suite 800
Washington, DC 20036
Phone: 202–588–5180
Fax: 202–588–5185
URL: http://www.nwlc.org/

The National Women's Law Center began in 1972 as a means of using the law to assist women and girls in every aspect of their lives. Although sexual crime is not the major focus of the Center, it does focus upon health and education as well as sexual harassment. The Center does not provide legal services to individuals but instead provides information to help formulate public policy. It monitors legal issues relating to women and seeks to educate the public about such issues.

Office for Victims of Crime
U.S. Department of Justice 810 7th Street, NW
Washington, DC 20531
Phone: 202–307–5983
Fax: 202–514–6383
Resource Center: 800–627–6872
URL: http://www.ojp.usdoj.gov/ovc

The Office for Victims of Crime (OVC) is the federal effort to recognize the particular issues of crime victims. It also administers the Crime Victims Fund created by the Victims of Crime Act. These Fund supports victim assistance and victim compensation grants, training and technical assistance to victim service and criminal justice system professionals, and services for federal crime victims and Native American organizations.

Office of Juvenile Justice & Delinquency Prevention
810 7th Street, NW
Washington, DC 20531
Phone: 202–307–5911, Toll Free: 800–638–8736
Fax: 202–307–2093
URL: http://www.ojjdp.ncjrs.org/

The Office of Juvenile Justice & Delinquency Prevention (OJJDP) seeks to prevent juvenile delinquency through intervention programs and rehabilitation. It supports state and local community efforts.

Office of Minority Health Resource Center
P.O. Box 37337
Washington, DC 20013
Phone: 800–444–6472
Fax: 301–230–7198
TTY: 301–230–7199
URL: http://www.omhrc.gov/

The Office of Minority Health Resource Center (OMHRC) is an information clearinghouse and referral center. Operated since 1987 by the U.S. Department of Health and Human Services, OMHRC collects and distributes information on a range of health topics, including sexual violence.

Office on Violence Against Women
810 7th Street NW
Washington, DC 20531
Phone: 202–307–6026
Fax: 202–305–2589
TTY: 202–307–2277
URL: http://www.usdoj.gov/ovw/

The Office on Violence Against Women (OVW), a federal agency, works to improve the ability of state, local, tribal, and nonprofit organizations to provide services to victims of sex crime.

Posttraumatic Stress Disorder Alliance
No street address
Phone: 877–507–7873
Fax: 410–337–0747
URL: http://www.ptsdalliance.org

The Posttraumatic Stress Disorder Alliance (PTSD Alliance) provides educational assistance to healthcare professionals and those individuals suffering from PTSD. It consists of the American College of Obstetricians and Gynecologists, Anxiety Disorders Association of America, the International Society for Traumatic Stress Studies, and the Sidran Traumatic Stress Institute.

Prevent Child Abuse America
200 S. Michigan Avenue 17th Floor
Chicago, IL 60604–60604
Phone: 312–663–3520
Fax: 312–939–8962
URL: http://www.preventchildabuse.org

Founded in 1972, Prevent Child Abuse America is one of the oldest organizations fighting to end child abuse. Headquartered in Chicago, it focuses on public awareness and prevention programs.

Rape, Abuse & Incest National Network (RAINN)
2000 L Street, NW, Suite 406
Washington, GA 20036
Phone: 202–544–1034
Fax: 202–544–3556
24 Hour Hotline: 800–656-HOPE (4673)
URL: http://www.rainn.org/

The Rape, Abuse & Incest National Network (RAINN) is the nation's largest organization against sexual assault. RAINN operates the National Sexual Assault Hotline and the National Sexual Assault Online Hotline at rainn.org. It publicizes the hotline's free, confidential services; educates the public about sexual assault; and leads national efforts to prevent sexual assault, improve services to victims and ensure that rapists are brought to justice.

**Sacred Circle: National Resource Center to
End Violence Against Native Women**
722 St. Joseph Street

Rapid City, SD 57701
Phone: 877–733–7623
Fax: 605–341–2472

Sacred Circle targets violence against Native American women by working with tribes and tribal organizations, especially tribal law enforcement personnel. Unlike organizations that are centered upon whites, Sacred Circle considers the unique historical, jurisdictional, and cultural issues that Native Americans face. It provides culturally appropriate information, training, and materials.

Security on Campus, Inc.
133 Ivy Lane, Suite 200
King of Prussia, PA 19406
Phone: 610–768–9330
Fax: 610–768–0646
Toll Free Hotline: 888–251–7959
URL: http://www.campussafety.org/

Security On Campus addresses safety on college and university campuses. Besides educating parents and students about campus crime, Security on Campus helps victims of such crime and supports programs that reduce alcohol and drug abuse.

SESAME. (Stop Educator Sexual Abuse, Misconduct and Exploitation)
P.O. Box 94601
Las Vegas, NV 89193
Phone: 775–727–5428
URL: http://www.sesamenet.org/

SESAME (Stop Educator Sexual Abuse, Misconduct and Exploitation) addresses sexual abuse at the K-12 level. It seeks to increase public awareness of sexual abuse by teachers and to develop policies that halt such crimes.

Sexual Assault Nurse Examiner/Sexual Assault Response Team Website
Sexual Assault Resource Service
525 Portland Avenue South, #712
Minneapolis, MN 55434
Phone: 612–347–2434
Fax: 612–347–8751
URL: http://www.sane-sart.com/

A Sexual Assault Nurse Examiner (SANE) is specially trained to collect evidence from rape victims at hospitals. This Web site, funded by the Office for Victims of Crime, contains a national database of sexual assault victim information as well as guides to program planning and development.

Sexual Assault Report (SAR)
3097 Ordway Street NW
Washington, DC 20008–3255
Phone: 202–362–3715
Fax: 413–513–8582
URL: http://www.civicresearchinstitute.com

The *Sexual Assault Report* is a newsletter about sexual crime that aims to keep healthcare and law enforcement personnel current on legal developments and medical research.

Sexual Assault Training & Investigations (SATI)
15769 Creek Hills Road
El Cajon, CA 92021–92021
Phone: 619–561–3845
URL: http://www.mysati.com

Sexual Assault Training & Investigations (SATI) offers multidisciplinary training for Sexual Assault Response Teams to encourage the reporting and successful prosecution of sex criminals.

Sexual Information and Education Council
of the United States
130 W. 42nd Street, Suite 350
New York, NY 10036–10036
Phone: 212–819–9770
Fax: 212–819–9776
URL: http://www.siecus.org

The Sexual Information and Education Council of the United States (SIECUS) is an information clearinghouse that focuses on healthy sexual development. It provides sex education and advocates for individuals to make responsible sexual choices.

Sidran Traumatic Stress Institute
200 E. Joppa Road, Suite 207

Towson, MD 21286
Phone: 410–825–8888
Fax: 410–337–0747
URL: http://www.sidran.org/

Sidran Traumatic Stress Institute is one of the major American organizations that addresses posttraumatic stress, a common ailment among victims of sexual crime. Sidran develops books and multimedia materials, assessment and teaching tools, and educational programs that help health care professionals and victims to effectively combat traumatic stress.

SNAP—Survivors Network of those Abused by Priests
P.O. Box 6416
Chicago, IL 60680
Phone: 312–409–2720
Fax: 314–645–2017
URL: http://www.snapnetwork.org/

Survivors Network of those Abused by Priests (SNAP) is one of the more prominent organizations that addresses sexual abuse by Catholic clergy. It is a self-help organization of victims of clergy abuse that includes an online support group with members from around the world.

Speaking Out About Rape
817 Virginia Drive, #A
Orlando, FL 32803
Phone: 407–836–9692
Fax: 407–836–9693
URL: http://soar99.org/

Speaking Out About Rape (SOAR) provides the rape victim's perspective to the general public. The members offer presentations that discuss all aspects of sexual crime.

Stalking Resource Center
2000 M Street, Suite 480
Washington, DC 20036
Phone: 202–467–8700
Fax: 202–467–8701
E-mail: SRC@ncvc.org
URL: http://www.ncvc.org/src

The Stalking Resource Center, part of the National Center for Victims of Crime, provides information, training, and technical assistance to those who work with victims of stalking.

Stop it Now!
351 Pleasant Street, Suite B, #319
Northampton, MA 01060
Phone: 413–587–3500
Fax: 413–587–3505
Helpline: 888–773–8368
E-mail: info@stopitnow.org
URL: http://www.stopitnow.org/

STOP IT NOW!, founded in 1992, offers public education programs that emphasize adult and community responsibility to prevent sex crimes against children.

Stop Prisoner Rape
325 Wilshire Blvd., Ste. 340
Los Angeles, CA 90010
Phone: 213-384-1400
Fax: 213–384–1411
E-mail: info@spr.org
URL: http://www.spr.org/

Stop Prisoner Rape (SPR) was begun in 1980 by Russell Dan Smith, a survivor of rape behind bars. Originally known as People Organized to Stop the Rape of Imprisoned Persons (POSRIP), the group addresses the problems of rape, sexual assault, unconsensual sexual slavery, and forced prostitution in the prison context.

Survivors Take Action Against Abuse
by Military Personnel (STAMP)
Survivors Take Action Against Abuse by Military Personnel
500 Greene Tree Place
Fairborn, OH 45324
Hotline: 1–866–879–2568
URL: http://www.militarywoman.org/stamp.htm

STAMP, Survivors Take Action Against Abuse by Military Personnel, is a grassroots organization dedicated to stopping abusive behavior, including sexual crimes. In partnership with the G.I. Rights Network, STAMP connects active-duty personnel with information, legal representation, and support. It also connects domestic violence survivors with outside, civilian advocates who understand the unique situation of military spouses. Once out of the military, some STAMP members are suing their perpetrators in federal court; still more are marshaling for class action.

Take Back the Night
URL: http://www.takebackthenight.org/

Take Back the Night is a grassroots, somewhat informal, organization of women and male allies who march to protest violence against women. It began in the United States in 1978 when protestors in San Francisco invoked the slogan following an antipornography conference. Today, it is generally antirape activism. Common components of Take Back the Night rallies include candlelight vigils, empowerment marches, and survivor testimonials.

Urban Institute
2100 M Street NW
Washington, DC 20037
Phone: 202–833–7200
Fax: 202–728–0232
URL: http://www.urban.org/

The Urban Institute is a nonpartisan economic and social policy research organization. The scope of the institute includes housing, retirement, and employment issues but it also focuses upon crime, healthcare, and poverty.

V-Day
URL: http://www.vday.org/

V-Day grew out of playwright Eve Ensler's much-produced work *The Vagina Monologues*. It is a global movement to stop violence against women and girls. V-Day promotes creative events, including productions of *The Vagina Monologues* to increase awareness of sexual abuse directed against women and girls. The organization also raises money for existing antirape organizations.

Victims' Assistance Legal Association (VALOR)
8180 Greensboro Drive, Suite 1070
McLean, VA 22102–3823

Phone: 703–748–0811
Fax: 703–356–5085
URL: http://www.valor-national.org

The Victims' Assistance Legal Organization (VALOR), begun in 1979 by victim advocate Frank G. Carrington, advances the legal rights of crime victims in the civil, criminal, and juvenile justice systems. It provides legal counsel to victims' organizations and has filed U.S. Supreme Court briefs on behalf of victims. It also created the National Victim Assistance Academy.

Victim Rights Law Center
18 Tremont Street, Suite 220
Boston, MA 02144
Phone: 617–399–6720
Fax: 617–399–6722
URL: http://www.victimrights.org

The Victim Rights Law Center is the first law center in the United States to focus exclusively on the needs of victims. It provides sexual assault victims with free and confidential legal help.

Voices in Action
8041 Hosbrook Road, Suite 236
Cincinnati, OH 45236
Phone: 800–786–4238
Fax: 513–625–1194
URL: http://www.voices-action.org

VOICES in Action is a national organization for survivors of incest and child sexual abuse as well as family and friends of survivors. It offers a free referral service, a newsletter, an annual conference, and networking.

Wellesley Centers for Women
106 Central Street
Wellesley, MA 02481
Phone: 781–283–2500
Fax: 781–283–2504
URL: http://www.wcwonline.org

Wellesley Centers for Women covers a range of issues that affect women, including education, childcare, and gender violence. It has sponsored research on adult memories of childhood sexual abuse, dating violence prevention programs in public schools, and decriminalizing consensual sex between teenagers.

World Health Organization
URL: http://www.who.int/en/

The World Health Organization (WHO) is a branch of the United Nations and it addresses sex work as a part of its effort to address problems with sexually transmitted diseases. When AIDS was identified as a significant threat to public health in the 1980s, WHO formed a department, the Global Program on AIDS (GPA). This department has developed guidelines on how to organize HIV prevention programs in the context of sex work. It is GPA's position that the people most affected by the epidemic have a crucial role to play in developing an effective response. GPA's approach to prostitution uses a labor perspective by which HIV is addressed as a workplace issue for sex workers. This program later became UNAIDS.

YWCA of the U.S.A.
22 West 26th Street 9-H
New York, NY 10010
Phone: 212–273–7800
Fax: 212–273–7939
URL: http://www.ywca.org/

The YWCA of the U.S.A. is a long-established, national women's organization that aims to empower women and girls. Local YWCAs offer a range of services that may include help for victims of domestic violence and rape, emergency and long term housing, child care and youth development programs, employment training, women's health programs, resource and referral services and advocacy.

State and Territorial Organizations

Alabama Coalition Against Rape
P.O. Box 4091
Montgomery, AL 36102
Phone: 334–264–0123
Toll-free: 888–656–4673
Hotline: 888–725–7273

Fax: 334–264–0128
E-mail: acar@acar.org
URL: http://www.acar.org

Alaska Network on Domestic Violence and Sexual Assault
130 Seward Street
Suite 214
Juneau, AK 99801
Phone: 907–586–3650
Toll-free: 800–520–2666
Fax: 907–463–4493
E-mail: info@andvsa.org
URL: http://www.andvsa.org

American Samoa Coalition Against Domestic and Sexual Violence
P.O. Box 1353
Pago Pago, AS 96799
Phone: 684–633–2696
E-mail: aluifea@yahoo.com

Arizona Sexual Assault Network
1949 East Calle De Arcos
Tempe, AZ 85284
Phone: 480–831–1986
Fax: 602–266–1958
E-mail: info@azsan.org
URL: http://www.ArizonaSexualAssaultNetwork.org

Arkansas Coalition Against Sexual Assault
215 North East Avenue
Fayetteville, AR 72701
Phone: 479–527–0900
Toll-free: 866–632–2272
Fax: 479–527–0902
E-mail: acasa@sbcglobal.net
URL: http://www.acasa.ws/

California Coalition Against Sexual Assault
1215 K Street
Suite 1100
Sacramento, CA 95814

Phone: 916–446–2520
Fax: 916–446–8166
E-mail: info@calcasa.org
URL: http://www.calcasa.org

Colorado Coalition Against Sexual Assault
P.O. Box 300398
Denver, CO 80203
Phone: 303–861–7033
Toll-free: 877–372–2272
Fax: 303–832–7067
E-mail: info@ccasa.org
URL: http://www.ccasa.org

Connecticut Sexual Assault Crisis Services, Inc.
96 Pitkin Street
East Hartford, CT 06108
Phone: 860–282–9881
Toll-free: 888–999–5545
Hotline: 888–999–5545
Fax: 860–291–9335
E-mail: info@connsacs.org
URL: http://www.connacs.org

CONTACTLifeline, Inc. (Delaware)
P.O. Box 9525
Wilmington, DE 19809
Phone: 302–472–1841
Toll-free: 800–262–9800
Fax: 302–761–4280
URL: http://www.contactlifeline.org

Day One—Sexual Assault & Trauma Resource Center of Rhode Island
100 Medway Street
Providence, RI 02906
Phone: 401–421–4100
Toll-free: 800–494–8100
Hotline: 800–494–8100
Fax: 401–454–5565
E-mail: info@DayOneRI.org
URL: http://www.dayoneri.org/

DC Rape Crisis Center
P.O. Box 34125
Washington, DC 20043
Phone: 202–232–0789
Hotline: 202–333–7273
Fax: 202–387–3812
E-mail: dcrcc@dcrcc.org
URL: http://www.dcrcc.org/

**Domestic Violence Sexual Assault Council
of the Virgin Islands**
RR #1 Box 10550
Kingshill, VI 00850
Phone: 340–719–0144
Fax: 340–719–5521
E-mail: dvsac@viaccess.net
URL: http://www.dvsac.net

Florida Council Against Sexual Violence
1311 North Paul Russell Road
Suite A 204
Tallahassee, FL 32301
Phone: 850–297–2000
Toll-free: 888–956–7273
Fax: 850–297–2002
E-mail: information@fcasv.org
URL: http://www.fcasv.org

Georgia Network to End Sexual Assault
131 Ponce De Leon Avenue, Suite 131
Atlanta, GA 30308
Phone: 404–815–5261
Toll-free: 866–354–3672
Fax: 404–815–5265
E-mail: gnesa@mindspring.com
URL: http://www.gnesa.com

Hawaii Coalition Against Sexual Assault
P.O. Box 10596
Honolulu, HI 96816
Phone: 808–533–1637
Fax: 808–733–9032

Healing Hearts Crisis Center (Guam)
790 Governor Carlos G. Camacho Road
Tamuning, GU 96913
Phone: 671–647–5351
Fax: 671–647–5414
URL: http://www.pmcguam.com

Idaho Coalition Against Sexual and Domestic Violence
300 East Mallard Drive
Suite 130
Boise, ID 83706
Phone: 208–384–0419
Toll-free: 888–293–6118
Fax: 208–331–0687
E-mail: ahrensa@idvsa.org
URL: http://www.idvsa.org

Illinois Coalition Against Sexual Assault
100 North 16th Street
Springfield, IL 62703
Phone: 217–753–4117
Fax: 217–753–8229
E-mail: sblack@icasa.org
URL: http://www.icasa.org

Indiana Coalition Against Sexual Assault
55 Monument Circle Suite 1224
Indianapolis, IN 46204
Phone: 317–423–0233
Toll-free: 800–691–2272
Fax: 317–423–0237
E-mail: incasa@incasa.org
URL: http://www.incasa.org

Iowa Coalition Against Sexual Assault
515 28th Street, Suite 107
Des Moines, IA 50312
Phone: 515–244–7424
Toll-free: 800–284–7821
Hotline: 800–284–7821
Fax: 515–244–7417
URL: http://www.iowacasa.org

Jane Doe Inc.
14 Beacon Street, Suite 507
Boston, MA 02108
Phone: 617–248–0922
Toll-free: 877–785–2020
Hotline: 877–785–2020
Fax: 617–248–0902
Org. E-mail: info@janedoe.org
URL: http://www.janedoe.org

**Kansas Coalition Against Sexual
and Domestic Violence**
634 SW Harrison
Topeka, KS 66603
Phone: 785–232–9784
Fax: 785–266–1874
E-mail: coalition@kcsdv.org
URL: http://www.kcsdv.org

Kentucky Association of Sexual Assault Programs
P.O. Box 4028
83 C. Michael Davenport Boulevard
Frankfort, KY 40604
Phone: 502–226–2704
Toll-free: 866–375–2727
Fax: 502–226–2725
URL: http://www.kasap.org

Louisiana Foundation Against Sexual Assault
1250 SW Railroad Avenue, Suite 170
Hammond, LA 70403
Phone: 985–345–5995
Toll-free: 888–995–7273
Fax: 985–345–5592
E-mail: resource@lafasa.org
URL: http://www.lafasa.org

Maine Coalition Against Sexual Assault
83 Western Avenue, Suite 2
Augusta, ME 04330
Phone: 207–626–0034
Toll-free: 800–871–7741

Hotline: 800–871–7741
Fax: 207–626–5503
E-mail: info@mecasa.org
URL: http://www.mecasa.org

Maryland Coalition Against Sexual Assault
1517 Governor Ritchie Highway, Suite 207
Arnold, MD 21012
Phone: 410–974–4507
Toll-free: 800–983–7273
Fax: 410–757–4770
E-mail: info@mcasa.org
URL: http://www.mcasa.org

Michigan Coalition Against Domestic and Sexual Violence
3893 Okemos Road, Suite B2
Okemos, MI 48864
Phone: 517–347–7000
Fax: 517–347–1377
E-mail: general@mcadsv.org
URL: http://www.mcadsv.org

Minnesota Coalition Against Sexual Assault
161 St. Anthony Avenue, Suite 1001
St. Paul, MN 55103
Phone: 651–209–9993
Toll-free: 800–964–8847
Fax: 651–209–0899
URL: http://www.mncasa.org

Mississippi Coalition Against Sexual Assault
P.O. Box 4172
Jackson, MS 39296
Phone: 601–948–0555
Toll-free: 888–987–9011
Fax: 601–948–0525
URL: http://www.mscasa.org

Missouri Coalition Against Domestic and Sexual Violence
217 Oscar Drive, Suite A

Jefferson City, MO 65101
Phone: 573–634–4161
Fax: 573–636–3728
E-mail: mocadsv@mocadsv.org
URL: http://www.mocadv.org

**Montana Coalition Against Domestic
and Sexual Violence**
P.O. Box 818
Helena, MT 59624
Phone: 406–443–7794
Toll-free: 888–404–7794
Hotline: 888–404–7794
Fax: 406–443–7818
E-mail: mcadsv@mt.net
URL: http://www.mcadsv.com

Nebraska Domestic Violence Sexual Assault Coalition
1000 O Street, Suite 102
Lincoln, NE 68508
Phone: 402–476–6256
Fax: 402–476–6806
E-mail: info@ndvsac.org
URL: http://www.ndvsac.org

Nevada Coalition Against Sexual Violence
P.O. Box 620716
Las Vegas, NV 89162
Phone: 775–828–1115
URL: http://www.ncasv.org

**New Hampshire Coalition Against Domestic
and Sexual Violence**
P.O. Box 353
Concord, NH 03302
Phone: 603–224–8893
Toll-free: 800–277–5570
Fax: 603–228–6096
URL: http://www.nhcadsv.org

New Jersey Coalition Against Sexual Assault
2333 Whitehorse Mercerville Road Suite J

Trenton, NJ 08619
Phone: 609–631–4450
Toll-free: 800–601–7200
Fax: 609–631–4453
E-mail: mail@njcasa.org
URL: http://www.njcasa.org

New Mexico Coalition of Sexual Assault Programs
3909 Juan Tabo Boulevard, NE, Suite 6
Alburquerque, NM 87111
Phone: 505–883–8020
Toll-free: 888–883–8020
Fax: 505–883–7530
E-mail: nmcaas@swcp.com
URL: http://www.swcp.com/nmcsaas/

New York State Coalition Against Sexual Assault
28 Essex Street
Albany, NY 12206
Phone: 518–482–4222
Fax: 518–482–4248
E-mail: info@nyscasa.org
URL: http://www.nyscasa.org

North Carolina Coalition Against Sexual Assault
183 Windchime Court
Suite 100
Raleigh, NC 27615
Phone: 919–870–8881
Toll-free: 888–737–2272
Fax: 919–870–8828
E-mail: nccasa@nccasa.org
URL: http://www.nccasa.org

North Dakota Council on Abused Women's Services
418 East Rosser Avenue, # 320
Bismarck, ND 58501
Phone: 701–255–6240
Toll-free: 888–255–1904
Hotline: 888–255–1904
Fax: 701–255–1904
URL: http://www.ndcaws.org

Oklahoma Coalition Against Domestic Violence and Sexual Assault
3815 North Santa Fe Avenue, Suite 124
Oklahoma City, OK 73118
Phone: 405–524–0700
Fax: 405–524–0711
E-mail: info@ocadvsa.org
URL: http://www.ocadvsa.org

Oregon Coalition Against Domestic and Sexual Violence
380 SE Spokane Street, Suite 100
Portland, OR 97202
Phone: 503–230–1951
Toll-free: 800–622–3782
Fax: 503–230–1973
URL: http://www.ocadsv.com

Pennsylvania Coalition Against Rape
125 North Enola Drive
Enola, PA 17025
Phone: 717–728–9740
Toll-free: 800–692–7445
Hotline: 888–772–7227
Fax: 717–728–9781
URL: http://www.pcar.org

South Carolina Coalition Against Domestic Violence and Sexual Assault
P.O. Box 7776
Columbia, SC 29202
Phone: 803–256–2900
Toll-free: 800–260–9293
Hotline: 800–260–9293
Fax: 803–256–1030
URL: http://www.sccadvasa.org

South Dakota Coalition Against Domestic Violence and Sexual Violence
P.O. Box 141
Pierre, SD 57501
Phone: 605–945–0869
Toll-free: 800–572–9196

Fax: 605–945–0870
URL: http://www.southdakotacoalition.org

**South Dakota Network Against Family
Violence and Sexual Assault**
P.O. Box 90453
Sioux Falls, SD 57106
Phone: 605–731–0041
Toll-free: 800–670–3989
Fax: 605–977–4742
URL: http://www.sdnafvsa.com

**Tennessee Coalition Against Domestic
and Sexual Violence**
2 International Plaza Drive, Suite 425
Nashville, TN 37217
Phone: 615–386–9406
Fax: 615–383–2967
E-mail: tcadsv@tcadsv.org
URL: http://www.tcadsv.org

Texas Association Against Sexual Assault
6200 La Calma Drive, Suite 110
Austin, TX 78752
Phone: 512–474–7190
Toll-free: 888–918–2272
Fax: 512–474–6490
E-mail: taasa@taasa.org
URL: http://www.taasa.org

Utah Coalition Against Sexual Assault
284 West 400 North
Salt Lake City, UT 84103
Phone: 801–746–0404
Hotline: 888–421–1100
Fax: 801–746–2929
E-mail: info@ucasa.org
URL: http://www.ucasa.org

**Vermont Network Against Domestic Violence
and Sexual Assault**
P.O. Box 405
Montpelier, VT 05601

Phone: 802–223–1302
Hotline: 800–489–7273
Fax: 802–223–6943
E-mail: vtnetwork@vnetwork.org
URL: http://www.vtnetwork.org

Virginia Sexual and Domestic Violence Action Alliance
5008 Monument Avenue, Suite A
Richmond, VA 23230
Phone: 804–377–0335
Toll-free: 800–838–8238
Hotline: 800–838–8238
Fax: 804–377–0339
E-mail: info@vsdvalliance.org
URL: http://www.vsdvalliance.org

Washington Coalition of Sexual Assault Programs
4317 6th Avenue SE, Suite 102
Olympia, WA 98503
Phone: 360–754–7583
Toll-free: 800–775–8013
Fax: 360–786–8707
E-mail: wcsap@wcsap.org
URL: http://www.wcsap.org

West Virginia Foundation for Rape Information and Services
112 Braddock Street
Fairmont, WV 26554
Phone: 304–366–9500
Fax: 304–366–9501
E-mail: fris@labs.net
URL: http://www.fris.org

Wisconsin Coalition Against Sexual Assault
600 Williamson Street, Suite N-2
Madison, WI 53703
Phone: 608–257–1516
Fax: 608–257–2150
E-mail: wcasa@wcasa.org
URL: http://www.wcasa.org

8

Resources

The following is a list of print and video resources compiled with the intention of providing the reader with a guide for further research.

Print Sources

Child Sexual Abuse

Ainscough, Carolyn, and Kay Toon. *Surviving Childhood Sexual Abuse: Practical Self-Help for Adults Who Were Sexually Abused As Children.* Boulder, CO: Da Capo Press, 2000.

The authors are clinical psychologists who provide suggestions and techniques for coping with and overcoming sexual abuse.

Aptheker, Bettina F. *Intimate Politics: How I Grew Up Red, Fought for Free Speech, and Became a Feminist Rebel.* San Francisco: Seal Press, 2006.

The daughter of famed Communist Party member and history professor Herbert Aptheker, Bettina Aptheker repressed memories of being sexually abused by her father. She recounts her abuse in this memoir, which also covers her political activism in the 1960s.

Bass, Ellen, and Laura Davis. *The Courage to Heal 4e: A Guide for Women Survivors of Child Sexual Abuse 20th Anniversary Edition.* New York: Collins Living, 2008.

This is the classic guide to overcoming sexual abuse. It uses first-person narratives to illustrate healing while describing the effects of abuse, the stages that survivors pass through, and warnings about self-defeating behaviors.

Brady, Katherine. *Father's Days: A True Story of Incest.* New York: Seaview Books, 1979.

Brady tried to maintain the façade of a happy family as a model student while struggling privately with her father's sexual abuse and the associated stresses. She underwent years of depression and therapy before finding happiness.

Burgess, Ann Wolbert, and Christine A. Grant. *Children Traumatized in Sex Rings.* Philadelphia: National Center for Missing & Exploited Children, 1988.

After providing an overview of child sexual abuse, the authors discuss the response patterns of traumatized children and treatment issues.

Butler, Sandra. *Conspiracy of Silence: The Trauma of Incest.* San Francisco: New Glide, 1978.

Butler attributes incestuous relationships to the socialization of men and women. Socialized to believe that power is a man's natural right, men who become aggressors are despotic and tyrannical at home while powerless in the outside world.

Cossins, Anne. *Masculinities, Sexualities, and Child Sexual Abuse.* The Hague, Netherlands: Kluwer Law International, 2000.

This book focuses on the motivations of men who abuse children. It covers the criminalization of incest in Australia and England, the characteristics of child sex offenders, and the role of power in such abuse.

Davis, Laura. *Allies in Healing: When the Person You Love Was Sexually Abused as a Child.* New York: Harper, 1991.

Still readily available in print almost two decades after its publication, this remains as the standard guide for spouses, lovers, girlfriends, and boyfriends who are trying to help their partners overcome sexual abuse. Davis covers intimacy and communication, sex, and family issues through a number of stories from partners.

Echols, Mike. *I Know My First Name is Steven: The True Story of the Steven Stayner Abduction Case.* New York: Pinnacle, 1999.

Kenneth Parnell, a convicted child kidnapper and rapist, kidnapped seven-year-old Steven and held him prisoner as a sex slave for seven years. Stayner managed to obtain help when Parnell brought home a second young boy to abuse.

Finkelhor, David. *Sexually Victimized Children.* New York: The Free Press, 1979.

Finkelhor argues that child abuse is fundamentally different from the rape of an adult because of the victim's youth, naivete, and relationship to the older person.

Gillham, Bill. *The Facts About Child Sexual Abuse.* London: Cassell Educational, 1991.

This book provides a general introduction to child sexual abuse with a section dedicated to protecting children from such abuse.

Gilmartin, Pat. *Rape, Incest, and Child Sexual Abuse: Consequences and Recovery.* New York: Garland, 1994.

The author discusses the immediate and long-term consequences of sexual victimization along with treatment issues.

Grevatt, Marge, et al. *We Can Break the Cycle: A Mother's Handbook for Sexual Abuse Survivors.* Cleveland: Orange Blossom Press, 1999.

This pamphlet is aimed at survivors of childhood sexual abuse who are mothers. It is written by survivors/mothers who are aware that that carry-over symptoms of abuse, such as depression, can negatively impact the parenting skills of sexual abuse victims.

Human Rights Watch. *Scared at School: Sexual Violence Against Girls in South African Schools.* New York: Human Rights Watch, 2001.

This report examines sexual abuse of students by teachers and various forms of sexual violence committed by students against other students in South Africa.

Justice, Blair, and Rita Justice. *The Broken Taboo: Sex in the Family.* New York: Human Sciences Press, 1979.

This book is based on a survey by the authors of 112 families in which incest had occurred. It is, therefore, one of the very few sources of direct information about incest.

May, John P., and Khalid R. Pitts, eds. *Building Violence: How America's Rush to Incarcerate Creates More Violence.* Thousand Oaks, CA: Sage Publications, 2000.

In this collection of essays, Randy Blackburn provides a personal account of his experiences after being accused of sexually assaulting a nine-year-old girl.

Meiselman, Karin. *Incest: A Psychological Study of Causes and Effects with Treatment Recommendations.* San Francisco: Jossey-Bass, 1979.

Meiselman summarizes anthropological and sociological views about the origin and maintenance of the incest taboo. She also discusses various strategies for researching incest before focusing on the psychological causes and long-term effects of father-daughter, mother-son, and sibling incest.

Salter, Anna C. *Transforming Trauma: A Guide to Understanding and Treating Adult Survivors of Child Sexual Abuse.* Thousand Oaks, CA: Sage, 1995.

While geared towards treating victims, this book is also helpful for treating attackers. It covers the different thought patterns of sadistic and nonsadistic offenders along with the resulting effects upon the victims. Salter discusses how trauma affects the world views of survivors and advises on the best treatment plans for survivors.

Turner, Jonathan H., and Alexandra Maryanski. *Incest: Origins of the Taboo.* Boulder, CO: Paradigm, 2005.

The authors, defining incest as sexual relations between family members such as brother and sister, review anthropological and evolutionary explanations for the origins of the taboo.

Walsh, John. *Tears of Rage*. New York: Pocket Books, 2008.

Walsh, the founder of the National Center for Missing and Exploited Children and host of *America's Most Wanted*, lost his six-year-old son, Adam, to a killer in 1981. In this autobiography, Walsh traces the steps that took him from being a grieving father to an activist for children.

Date or Acquaintance Rape

Fisher, Bonnie S., and John J. Sloan, III. *Campus Crime: Legal, Social, and Policy Perspectives*. Springfield, IL: Charles C. Thomas, 2008.

Chapters address the implications of the Jeanne Clery Act, intimate partner abuse of female college students, and the evolution of campus policing.

Levy, Barrie, ed. *Dating Violence: Young Women In Danger*. New York: Seal Press, 1998.

Levy provides first-person accounts from abused teens as well as essays on the social context of dating violence. The focus is not exclusively on rape.

Lindquist, Scott. *The Date Rape Prevention Book: The Essential Guide for Girls and Women*. Napierville, Il: Sourcebooks, 2000.

This book contains the usual advice on techniques to avoid becoming a victim of date rape. It also contains a chapter advising men to take responsibility to stop the violence

McGregor, Joan. *Is It Rape?: On Acquaintance Rape and Taking Women's Consent Seriously*. Burlington, Vermont: Ashgate, 2005.

McGregor examines the ethical and legal problems that arise in connection with acquaintance rape. She argues that rape laws need to be remodeled to recognize that victims do not always resist and perpetrators do not always use physical violence.

Parrot, Andrea, and Laurie Bechofer, eds. *Acquaintance Rape: The Hidden Crime*. New York: Wiley, 1991.

This is an overview for educators, psychologists, and law enforcement professionals on acquaintance and date rape.

Sanday, Peggy Reeves. *Fraternity Gang Rape: Sex, Brotherhood, and Privilege on Campus.* New York: New York University Press, 2007.

The author explores the ways in which all-male organizations on college campuses, such as fraternities and athletic teams, promote the exploitation and sexual degradation of women.

Warshaw, Robin. *I Never Called It Rape: The Ms. Report of Recognizing, Fighting, and Surviving Date and Acquaintance Rape* (Harper, 1988).

This is the first major study on date and acquaintance rape.

Wiehe, Vernon R., and Ann L. Richards. *Intimate Betrayal: Understanding and Responding to the Trauma of Acquaintance Rape.* Thousand Oaks, CA: Sage, 1995.

After defining the nature and scope of acquaintance rape, the authors cover the impact of the assault on the survivor and the recovery process. A chapter by Patricia Lynn Peacock covers marital rape.

Williams, Mary E., ed. *Date Rape.* San Diego: Greenhaven, 1998.

The book contains a series of essays by such authors as Katie Roiphe and Camille Paglia that debate the risk of rape and whether antirape policies are effective.

Domestic Violence

Bergen, Raquel Kennedy. *Wife Rape: Understanding the Response of Survivors and Service Providers.* Thousand Oaks, CA: Sage, 1996.

Bergen provides a brief legal history of wife rape, addresses women's experiences of wife rape, and discusses how to end this form of sexual violence.

Finkelhor, David, and Kersti Yllo. *License to Rape: Sexual Abuse of Wives.* New York: Holt, Rinehart & Winston, 1985.

This book contains the results of a child sexual abuse questionnaire distributed in 1980s Boston to over 300 women who had had a child between 6 and 14 living with them, as well as interviews conducted with 50 Boston-area women. The authors aim to show the prevalence of marital rape and the fact that it has been traditionally minimized.

Frieze, Irene Hanson. *Hurting the One You Love: Violence in Relationships.* Belmont, CA: Thomson Wadsworth., 2005.

This book addresses how pornography teaches youths that violence against women is acceptable. The author largely focuses on biological factors in aggression and reactions to victimization.

Knopp, Fay Honey. *When Your Wife Says No: Forced Sex in Marriage.* Brandon, VT: Safer Society Press, 1994.

A good study of marital rape that helped persuade legislators to take this issue seriously.

Leventhal, Beth, and Sandra E. Lundy, eds. *Same-Sex Domestic Violence: Strategies for Change.* Thousand Oaks, CA: Sage, 1999.

Many of these essays address sexual abuse. The survivor stories and the essays that contrast same-sex domestic violence with heterosexual battering are especially powerful.

Roberts, Albert R., ed. *Battered Women and Their Families: Intervention Strategies and Treatment Programs.* New York: Springer, 2007.

Sexual abuse is often part of domestic violence, as several of the essays in this collection acknowledge. Nicky Ali Jackson's essay on same-sex domestic violence is one of the few works to address same-sex rape.

Russell, Diana. *Rape in Marriage.* Bloomington: Indiana University Press, 1990.

This landmark book on marital rape helped persuade several states to criminalize sexual assaults by husbands. Russell found that one in seven women had been raped within marriage.

History of Sexual Assault

Cameron, Deborah, and Elizabeth Frazer. *The Lust to Kill: A Feminist Investigation of Sexual Murder.* Cambridge, England: Polity Press, 1987.

The authors examine the history and philosophy of sexually motivated murder. The book is wide-ranging, with chapters devoted to the literary works of the Marquis de Sade and the murders committed by Britons Myra Hindley and Dennis Nilsen.

Carter, Dan T. *Scottsboro: A Tragedy of the American South.* Baton Rouge: Louisiana State University Press, 1979.

The Scottsboro Boys were African American teenagers falsely accused of rape in 1931 in Alabama. This is arguably the best book on the rape case by one of the leading historians of the American South.

Carter, John Marshall. *Rape in Medieval England: An Historical and Sociological Study.* Lanham, MD: University Press of America, 1985.

Carter covers rape from 1208 to 1321 and provides one of the very few studies of medieval sexual assault.

Clinton, Catherine, and Michele Gillespie, eds. *The Devil's Lane: Sex and Race in the Early South.* New York: Oxford University Press, 1997.

The contributors to this book examine sex in the colonial and early U.S. South. A chapter by Diane Miller Sommerville covers rape and castration in slave law while Jane Landers looks at rape in Spanish-held St. Augustine.

Dolan, Frances E. *Marriage and Violence: The Early Modern Legacy.* Philadelphia: University of Pennsylvania Press, 2008.

Dolan argues that present-day marriage so often leads to violence because of the lingering impact of 16th- and 17th-century English theories about marriage.

Dorr, Lisa Lindquist. *White Women, Rape, and the Power of Race in Virginia, 1900–1960.* Chapel Hill: University of North Carolina Press, 2004.

The charge of rape made by a white woman has resulted in the lynching of many a black man in the South. This book examines the history of black-on-white rape in Virginia as well as the issue of consent, the problem of false accusations, and African American strategies of resistance.

Drzazga, John. *Sex Crimes*. Springfield, IL: Charles C. Thomas, 1960.

This book, written by a police officer, provides a look into mid-century American thought about prohibited sexual conduct.

Dusky, Lorraine. *Still Unequal: The Shameful Truth About Women and Justice in America*. New York: Crown, 1996.

This book focuses on the challenges that women have faced while pursuing legal careers. The chapter on sexual assault covers the historical tradition of failing to believe women claiming rape, the prejudices of judges against rape victims, and the ineffectiveness of rape shield laws.

Goodman, James. *Stories of Scottsboro*. New York: Pantheon Books, 1994.

Good account of the Scottsboro Boys rape case.

Langbein, John H. *Prosecuting Crime in the Renaissance: England, Germany, France*. Cambridge, MA: Harvard University Press, 1974.

Langbein covers the prosecution of sex crimes.

Lefowitz, Bernard. *Our Guys: The Glen Ridge Rape Case and the Secret of the Perfect Suburb*. Berkeley: University of California Press, 1997.

This book examines the connection between sports and violence against women.

Marquart, James W., Sheldon Ekland-Olson, and Jonathan R. Sorensen. *The Rope, the Chair, and the Needle: Capital Punishment in Texas, 1923–1990*. Austin: University of Texas, 1998.

The authors argue that black men convicted of raping white women were more likely to be sentenced to death than white men charged with a similar crime.

National Institute of Mental Health. *Victims of Rape*. Washington, DC: Department of Health, Education, and Welfare, 1976.

This slim book contains the conclusions of the 27-month Philadelphia Assault Victim Study conducted from 1973–1975.

Norris, Clarence, and Sybil D. Washington. *The Last of the Scottsboro Boys.* New York: G. P. Putnam's Sons, 1979.

Norris, one of the accused rapists and the last survivor among the boys, tells his life story.

Ohio Youth Services Network. *Sexual Offenses by Adolescents in Ohio.* Columbus, OH: Ohio Youth Services Network, 1989.

Ohio became one of the first states to compile data on juvenile sexual offenders and to recommend policy changes such as increased funding for specific programs for adolescent sexual offenders.

Read, Jacinta. *The New Avengers: Feminism, Femininity and the Rape-Revenge Cycle.* Manchester, England: Manchester University Press, 2000.

This is a fascinating study of rape in films from the silent era to the present. It would be a useful accompaniment to a class that examined portrayals of women in film.

Royster, Jacqueline Jones, ed. *Southern Horrors and Other Writings: The Anti-Lynching Campaign of Ida B. Wells, 1892–1900.* Boston: Bedford Books, 1997.

Wells, an investigative journalist and African American, exploded the popular notion that lynchings only happened to black men who were accused of raping white women.

Sanday, Peggy Reeves. *A Woman Scorned: Acquaintance Rape on Trial.* New York: Doubleday, 1996.

The author examines British and American landmark rape cases to argue that, with the exception of the Colonial era, rape victims have always been placed on trial as gold diggers, false accusers, or scorned women.

Sielke, Sabine. *Reading Rape: The Rhetoric of Sexual Violence in American Literature and Culture, 1790–1990.* Princeton, NJ: Princeton University Press, 2002.

This book examines discussion of rape in such works as Thomas Dixon's *The Clansmen*, Frances E. W. Harper's *Iola Leroy*, and Upton Sinclair's *The Jungle.*

Sommerville, Diane Miller. *Rape and Race in the Nineteenth-Century South.* Chapel Hill: University of North Carolina Press, 2004.

This is one of the few books to address slave rape and, quite possibly, the only book to examine the sexual assault of white children in the antebellum South. The breadth of the book is impressive as it covers the South through the entire 19th century

Soothill, Keith, and Sylvia Walby. *Sex Crime in the News.* London: Routledge, 1991.

This study of 5,000 newspapers spanning 40 years finds that while the number of sex crimes reported to the police has risen dramatically, the media ignore the wider issues related to sexual assault in favor of focusing on a few unusual cases.

Prison Rape

May, John P., and Khalid R. Pitts, eds. *Building Violence: How America's Rush to Incarcerate Creates More Violence.* Thousand Oaks, CA: Sage Publications, 2000.

While the focus is generally on violence behind bars, two chapters address prison rape. Joanne Mariner covers the trauma of prison rape and JoAnne Page explains how male victims of prison rape are shunned by other prisoners for being weak.

Pinar, William F. *The Gender of Racial Politics and Violence in America: Lynching, Prison Rape, and Violence in America.* New York: Peter Lang, 2001.

Pinar argues that racial subjugation can be seen in prison rape.

Prostitution

Batstone, David. *Not for Sale: The Return of the Global Slave Trade—and How We Can Fight It.* New York: HarperOne, 2007.

Journalist Batstone reports on the efforts of human rights activists to stop forced prostitution. He includes accounts from victims and activists.

Bullough, Vern, and Bonnie Bullough. *Women and Prostitution: A Social History.* New York: Prometheus Books, 1987.

Vern and Bonnie Bullough pioneered the field of the history of sexuality. This book is a study of prostitution over the centuries and around the world. It is the best general history of prostitution.

Delacoste, Frederique, and Priscilla Alexander, eds. *Sex Work: Writings by Women in the Sex Industry.* New York: Cleis Press, 1998.

First published in 1987, this is a pioneering collection of essays by street prostitutes, pornography actors, and other sex workers. The 1998 edition includes legal and health surveys as well as a listing of resources.

Farr, Kathryn. *Sex Trafficking: The Global Market in Women and Children.* New York: Worth, 2004.

A thorough examination of the women and children who are trafficked into the sex industry as well as the organized criminals who promote the sex trade and the economic conditions that foster it.

Flowers, R. Barri. *Runaway Kids and Teenage Prostitution: America's Lost, Abandoned, and Sexually Exploited Children.* Westport, CT: Greenwood, 2001.

Uses a criminological, sociological, and psychological approach to examine prostitution among runaway girls and boys. It covers child sexual abuse and child pornography as well as teenage prostitution across the globe.

Hennig, Jana, et al. *Trafficking in Human Beings and the 2006 World Cup in Germany.* Geneva, Switzerland: International Organization for Migration, 2007.

Many individuals suggest that major sporting events contribute mightily to a rise in prostitution. This report found that the number of victims of human trafficking for sexual exploitation did not increase during the major international soccer event of 2006.

Kempadoo, Kamala, and Jo Doezema, eds. *Global Sex Workers: Rights, Resistance, and Redefinition.* New York: Routledge, 1998.

This collection of essays by scholars and activists examines male and female sex workers in Third World countries. It is especially useful for presenting a full portrait of prostitution, including discussions of the effect of AIDS and the major organizational efforts of sex workers.

Kempadoo, Kamala, ed. *Trafficking and Prostitution Reconsidered: New Perspectives On Migration, Sex Work, And Human Rights.* St. Paul, MN: Paradigm, 2005.

A collection of scholarly essays that link trafficking to a lack of employment opportunities, a lack of freedom of movement, and globalization. The focus of this book is on Asia.

King, Gilbert. *Woman, Child for Sale: The New Slave Trade in the 21st Century.* New York: Chamberlain Bros., 2004.

This book includes case studies in modern slavery, global trafficking hotspots, and profiles of slave traders.

Malarek, Victor. *The Natashas: Inside the New Global Sex Trade.* New York: Arcade, 2005.

Malarek, a Canadian journalist reports, on the rise of sex trafficking from Eastern and Central Europe in the years since the 1991 collapse of the Soviet Union. Just under a million young women have been tricked by organized criminals with promises of legitimate jobs into working in massage parlors or brothels in Asia, the Middle East, or Europe. Malarek uses first-person accounts from the women.

Mam, Somaly. *The Road of Lost Innocence.* London: Virago, 2007.

This is the autobiography of a Cambodian woman who was sold into prostitution at 15 years of age. After years of abuse, she escaped and founded Acting for Women in Distressing

Situations (AFESIP) in 1996 to combat sexual slavery. This French edition of this book won the Le Cannet Truth Prize in 2005.

Parrot, Andrea, and Nina Cummings. *Sexual Enslavement of Girls and Women Worldwide.* Westport, CT: Praeger, 2008.

This should become the standard reference on sexual slavery. The authors put the situation in context, discuss types of sexual slavery, and examine attempts to combat it.

Ringdal, Nils Johan. *Love For Sale: A World History of Prostitution.* New York: Grove Press, 2005.

Traces prostitution across the globe from ancient times to the present. Ringdal argues that different cultures have different definitions for what constitutes prostitution.

Van den Anker, Christien L., and Jeroen Doomernik, eds. *Trafficking and Women's Rights.* Basingstoke, England: Palgrave Macmillan, 2006.

The authors examine female sexual slavery in Europe.

Williams, Phil, ed. *Illegal Immigration and Commercial Sex: The New Slave Trade.* London: Frank Cass, 1999.

This is a good general account of the global trafficking in women and children.

Yadav, C. P. *Encyclopedia on Women and Children Problems: Sexual Abuse and Commercial Sex Exploitation.* New Delhi, India: Anmol, 2008.

This reference examines the causes of sexual trafficking of women and girls as well as preventive measures. It is one of the few readily available works to examine trafficking from the perspective of India, a nation with a very high percentage of victims.

Runaway Sexual Abuse

Schaffner, Laurie. *Teenage Runaways: Broken Hearts and "Bad Attitudes".* New York: Routledge, 1999.

Based on a study of 26 New England runaways, this book examines the why these children left home, often to escape sexual abuse.

Slesnick, Natasha. *Our Runaway and Homeless Youth: A Guide to Understanding.* Westport, CT: Praeger, 2004.

Summarizes the current research on runaway and homeless children, including factors common to these children and their lives after leaving home. The author interviews three runaways and the parent of a runaway.

Sexual Abuse—General

Ageton, Suzanne S. *Sexual Assault Among Adolescents.* Lexington, MA: Lexington Books, 1983.

One of the first books to address juvenile sexual offenders, this book is still often cited in the literature. Very little empirical research had been completed on juvenile sexual offenders by 1983.

Barbaree, Howard E., Stephen M. Hudson, and William L. Marshall, eds. *The Juvenile Sex Offender.* New York: Guilford Press, 1993.

This book is widely acknowledged as the best source on juveniles who commit sex crimes. The authors summarize the current theoretical and clinical knowledge about juvenile offenders while suggesting directions for future research.

Allison, Julie A., and Lawrence S. Wrightsman. *Rape: The Misunderstood Crime.* Newbury Park, CA: Sage, 1993.

The authors provide a general discussion of rape from stranger rape to the treatment of victims.

Bart, Pauline, and Eileen Geil Moran, eds. *Violence Against Women: The Bloody Footprints.* Thousand Oaks, CA: Sage, 1992.

Originally published as a special issue of *Gender & Society*, this book focuses on policy. It is aimed at undergraduate and graduate readers.

Benedict, Helen. *Recovery: How to Survive Sexual Assault for Women, Men, Teenagers, and Their Friends and Families.* New York: Doubleday, 1985.

Benedict provides a practical guide for victims seeking to help themselves and those nonprofessionals seeking to help victims. She includes a focus on the gay and lesbian subjects of sexual assault.

Bessmer, Sue. *The Laws of Rape.* New York: Praeger, 1984.

Despite its age, this remains the best study of the history of rape laws. It covers the double standard between rape victims, the resistance requirement, and the admissibility of chastity.

Bevacqua, Maria. *Rape on the Public Agenda: Feminism and the Politics of Sexual Assault.* Boston: Northeastern University Press, 2000.

Bevacqua provides a superb survey of the feminist efforts to make rape into a matter of public policy concern. The appendices in the book are usually strong, including a time line of antirape events and the bylaws of a Washington, D.C., rape crisis center.

Bode, Janet. *Rape: Preventing It, Coping With the Legal, Medical, and Emotional Aftermath.* New York: Franklin Watts, 1979.

Bodes uses case histories and interviews to discuss the myths surrounding rape and the challenges faced by rape victims.

Bohmer, Carol, and Andrea Parrot. *Sexual Assault on Campus: The Problem and the Solution.* New York: Lexington Books, 1993.

This handbook examines how colleges have handled sexual assault cases, with a focus on the errors that college administrators have made. The authors suggest specific steps that administrators can take to avoid creating a hostile climate for those who report rape.

Bourke, Joanna. *Rape: Sex, Violence, History.* London: Shoemaker & Hoard, 2007.

This book focuses on the rapist to determine why some people sexually attack others. Bourke discusses how military culture influences sexual assault, with coverage of the sexual humiliation of prisoners at the Abu Ghraib prison during the Second Gulf War. The author's discussion of the legal and cultural differences between indecent exposure and exhibitionism is especially interesting.

Braen, G. Richard. *The Rape Examination*. North Chicago, IL: Abbott Laboratories, 1976.

Braen uses nonspecialist language to describe the steps involved in the medical treatment of a victim of rape.

Braswell, Linda. *Quest for Respect: A Healing Guide for Survivors of Rape*. Oxnard, CA: Pathfinder, 1992.

A popular guide to recovery for victims of rape and incest as well as the families and friends of sexual assault victims.

Brownmiller, Susan. *Against Our Will: Men, Women, and Rape*. New York: Simon & Schuster, 1975.

Arguably the most significant book ever written about rape, this classic work opened a public discussion about sexual assault. Brownmiller traces the history of rape through the ages, including sexual assaults by military personnel. Some of the language reflects the feminist movement of the 1970s, including Brownmiller's claim that rape is a conscious effort by all men to keep all women in a state of fear.

Buchwald, Emilie, Pamela R. Fletcher, and Martha Roth, eds. *Transforming a Rape Culture*. Minneapolis, MN: Milkweed, 2005.

The essays in this collection discuss the refusal of society to recognize the violence inherent in rape, the weak response of the institutional church to rape, sexual attacks by soldiers, sexual violence in Latino marriages, and establishing rape as a war crime.

Budrionis, Rita, and Arthur E. Jongsma, Jr. *The Sexual Abuse Victim and Sexual Offender Treatment Planner*.

The authors provide assistance to professional therapists who need to develop formal treatment plans for offender issues such as anger management, empathy deficits, and deviant sexual arousal, as well as victim issues such as eating disorders, self-blame, and social withdrawal.

Burgess-Jackson, Keith, ed. *A Most Detestable Crime: New Philosophical Essays on Rape.* New York: Oxford University Press, 1999.

Philosophers discuss definitions of rape, the persistence of rape, responsibility for rape, and why the legal system continues to fail rape victims.

Burns, Catherine. *Sexual Violence and the Law in Japan.* London: Routledge Curzon, 2005.

The author examines how Japanese judges consider cases of sexual violence.

Cahill, Ann J. *Rethinking Rape.* Ithaca, NY: Cornell University Press, 2001.

This book takes a feminist theoretical approach to rape by addressing such topics as feminist theories of the body and feminist theories of rape.

Campbell, Terence W. *Assessing Sex Offenders: Problems and Pitfalls.* Springfield, IL: Charles C. Thomas, 2004.

This book reviews the scientific evidence about the likelihood that a sex offender will reoffend. It includes guided clinical risk assessments and actuarial instruments for assessing recidivism risk.

Chaka-Makhooane, Lisebo, et al. *Sexual Violence in Lesotho: The Realities of Justice for Women.* Morija, Lesotho: Women and Law in Southern Africa Research and Education Trust, 2002.

This report finds that rape is not viewed as a serious crime by authorities in Lesotho, with the result that judicial structures do not respond appropriately to women's problems and needs. In this country, there is a heightened risk that rape may be linked with the transmission of HIV/AIDS.

Chappell, Duncan, Robley Geis, and Gilbert Geis, eds. *Forcible Rape: The Crime, the Victim, and the Offender.* New York: Columbia University Press, 1977.

This collection of essays is now useful chiefly as a historical source about attitudes and laws regarding rape in the dark ages of the 1970s.

Curran, Bronwyn. *Into the Mirror: The Untold Story of Mukhtar Mai.* New Delhi, India: UBS, 2008.

Mai, a Pakistani woman, became the victim of a gang rape in 2002 on the orders of an informal village tribal council because of a crime allegedly committed by her teenage brother. The incident brought worldwide condemnation of Pakistan's treatment of women.

Daka, Joseph. *Sexual Offenses in Zambia and How the Police Deal with Them.* Lusaka, Zambia: Joseph Daka, 2004.

This is the only book to address sexual crime in Zambia and one of the few to examine how an African nation attempts to protect victims of rape and incest. In this exceptional work, the author not only acknowledges the existence of male rape but argues that Zambian law needs to take measures to protect boys from sexual abuse.

Durham, Andrew. *Young Men Who Have Sexually Abused: A Case Study Guide.* Chichester, England: John Wiley, 2006.

Durham covers the theories relating to abusers before discussing the cases of adolescent males who engaged in sexually inappropriate behaviors.

Estrich, Susan. *Real Rape: How the Legal System Victimizes Women Who Say No.* Cambridge, MA: Harvard University Press, 1987.

Estrich argues that the legal system has not fully recognized acquaintance or date rape as an actual sexual assault, with prosecutors reluctant to prosecute such attacks. The book contains a wealth of historical information about how judges and juries have required victims to use as much physical force as possible to demonstrate that a "real rape" took place.

Fairstein, Linda. *Sexual Violence: Our War Against Rape.* New York: William Morrow, 1993.

Fairstein, the longtime director of the Sex Crimes Prosecution Unit for New York County, argues that legal changes have ended the era when women charging rape were victimized a second time by the legal system. The book is a good historical source for the difficulties faced by victims who had to prove "earnest resistance," reveal their sexual histories, and endure harsh interrogations.

Ferguson, Robert, and Jeanine Ferguson. *A Guide to Rape Awareness and Prevention: Educating Yourself, Your Family, and Those in Need.* Hartford, CT: Turtle Press, 1994.

This basic guide covers safety while traveling, while on the street, and while on campus.

Fischer, Linda A. *Ultimate Power: Enemy Within the Ranks* N.P.: Linda A. Fischer, 1999.

Written by a U.S. Army veteran who experienced sexual harassment while in uniform, this book is a useful study of sexual trauma from the victim's perspective.

Flora, Rudy. *How to Work with Sex Offenders: A Handbook for Criminal Justice, Human Service, and Mental Health Professionals.* New York: Haworth Clinical Practice Press, 2001.

This manual provides techniques for interviewing sex offenders and outlines treatment options, such as family therapy, group therapy, and pharmacology. It includes sections on female sexual offenders and developmentally disabled sexual offenders.

Foubert, John D. *The Men's Program: A Peer Education Guide to Rape Prevention.* New York: Taylor & Francis, 2005.

This is the most popular guide for training men to be antirape peer educators. It covers recruitment, training, advice from men who are peer educators, and sample documents.

Flowers, R. Barri. *Sex Crimes: Perpetrators, Predators, Prostitutes, and Victims.* Springfield, IL: Charles C. Thomas, 2006.

This textbook covers every aspect of sex crimes, including homicides, rape, incest, child molestation, sex trafficking, and theories about sexual criminality.

Francisco, Patricia Weaver. *Telling: A Memoir of Rape and Recovery.* New York: Harper, 2000.

The memoir of the victim of a 1981 stranger rape. Francisco underwent counseling and had the support of her husband but still struggled mightily to recover from the trauma.

Funk, Rus Ervin. *Stopping Rape: A Challenge for Men.* Philadelphia: New Society, 1993.

The author uses a conversational style to persuade men to examine their personal beliefs about sexual violence and to confront sexism in other men. It is most useful for advice about establishing and maintaining men's groups, responding to sexual assault survivors, and specific exercises for consciousness-raising workshops.

Gavey, Nicola. *Just Sex?: The Cultural Scaffolding of Rape.* New York: Routledge, 2005.

Gavey examines the psychosocial context of rape to argue that the blurred line between rape and "just sex" does not mean that coercive sex should be tolerated as simply part and parcel of the natural dynamics of sexual relations.

Graney, Dawn J., and Bruce A. Arrigo. *The Power Serial Rapist: A Criminology-Victimology Typology of Female Victim Selection.* Springfield, IL: Charles C. Thomas, 2002.

This book helps readers understand how a serial rapist chooses his victims by focusing on the case of Gilbert Escobedo, the Ski Mask Rapist.

Groth, A. Nicholas, and H. Jean Birnbaum. *Men Who Rape: The Psychology of the Offender.* New York: Plenum Press, 1979.

Based on 15 years' experience with over 500 sexual offenders, the authors examine the factors that predispose a man to react to situational and life events with sexual violence. The book covers the selection of victims, determination of the sexual act, the offender's reaction during the assault, the role of alcohol, and sexual dysfunction.

Geen, Russell G. *Human Aggression.* Pacific Grove, CA: Brooks/ Cole, 1990.

Geen, a professor of psychology, reviews the major theories and research on human aggression. He discusses the increased aggression by men against women that is fostered by the rape myth, the idea promoted by violent pornography that women secretly like to be sexually abused and assaulted by men.

Gerdes, Louise I., ed. *Sexual Violence*. Detroit: Greenhaven Press, 2008.

Part of the *Opposing Viewpoints* series, this book consists of essays on whether sexual violence is exaggerated or a serious problem.

Hickey, Eric W., ed. *Sex Crimes and Paraphilia*. Upper Saddle River, NJ: Pearson Education, 2006.

The collection of essays covers a full range of forms of sexually unhealthy behavior from voyeurism to pedophilia to rape.

Hodgson, James, and Debra S. Kelley, eds. *Sexual Violence: Policies, Practices, and Challenges in the United States and Canada*. Westport, CT: Praeger, 2002.

This collection of essays addresses such topics as cyber rape, chemical castration, and prison rape.

Holmes, Stephen T., and Ronald M. Holmes. *Sex Crimes: Patterns and Behavior*. Thousand Oaks, CA: Sage, 2002.

This is a textbook that provides a broad overview of sexual deviance.

Holmes, Ronald M., and Stephen T. Holmes, eds. *Current Perspectives on Sex Crimes*. Thousand Oaks, CA: Sage, 2002.

This wide-ranging anthology, a companion to *Sex Crimes: Patterns and Behavior*, offers excepts from book and journal articles.

Johnson, Jerry L., and George Grant, Jr., eds. *Sexual Abuse*. Boston: Pearson, 2007.

This textbook uses case studies to study the work of experienced social workers as they practice in various settings with sexually abused clients and their families.

Katz, Jackson. *The Macho Paradox: Why Some Men Hurt Women and How All Men Can Help*. Napierville, IL: Sourcebooks, 2006.

In this engaging book, Katz looks at the cultural factors that lead men to be tolerant of sexual abuse directed at women.

Katz, Judith H. *No Fairy Godmothers, No Magic Wands: The Healing Process After Rape.* Saratoga, CA: R & E Publishers, 1993.

The author addresses recovery from rape, the impact of rape upon significant others, and the decision to testify in court.

Katz, Sedelle, and Mary Ann Mazur. *Understanding the Rape Victim: A Synthesis of Research Findings.* New York: John Wiley & Sons, 1979.

Despite the age of this work, it remains a good scientific study of the risk of rape, family and social background of the victim and attacker, the situation surrounding the attack, and the effects of rape on the victim.

Kilmartin, Christopher, and Alan D. Berkowitz. *Sexual Assault in Context: Teaching College Men About Gender.* Mahway, NJ: Lawrence Erlbaum Associates, 2005.

This small guide offers strategies for delivering information about sexual assault to men and ideas about involving men in antiviolence work.

Koch, Patricia Barthalow, and David L. Weis, eds. *Sexuality in America: Understanding Our Sexual Values and Behavior.* New York: Continuum, 1999.

This survey of sexuality sets the topic of sex crimes in biological, psychological, social, and spiritual perspective.

Koss, Mary P., and Mary R. Harvey. *The Rape Victim: Clinical and Community Interventions.* Newbury Park, CA: Sage, 1991.

This especially informative book covers the National Crime Survey techniques that undermine rape disclosure, the personal characteristics that affect rape response, and group treatment for survivors.

Krivacska, James J., and John Money, ed. *The Handbook of Forensic Sexology: Biomedical and Criminological Perspectives.* Amherst, NY: Prometheus, 1994.

This book addresses the link between the study of sexuality and criminology in chapters that address sadomasochism and rape, voyeurism, the manufacture of sexual abuse memories, and the alleged link between pornography and violence against women.

Lalumiere, Martin L., et al. *The Causes of Rape: Understanding Individual Differences in Male Propensity for Sexual Aggression.* Washington, DC: American Psychological Association, 2005.

Aimed at a professional audience, this is an excellent survey of current thinking on rape in the animal kingdom, psychological characteristics of rapists, and clinical treatment of rapists.

Lauer, Teresa M. *The Truth About Rape.* N.P.: RapeRecovery.com, 2002.

The author discusses surviving rape though a 40-question and answer format.

LeBeau, Marc A., and Ashraf Mozayani, eds. *Drug-Facilitated Sexual Assault: A Forensic Handbook.* San Diego: Academic Press, 2001.

This book covers everything relating to date rape drugs from the modus operandi of the perpetrators to the drugs to collection of evidence.

Macdonald, John M. *Rape Controversial Issues: Criminal Profiles, Date Rape, False Reports, and False Memories.* Springfield, IL: Charles C. Thomas, 1995.

The author includes an account by a victim of rape and attempted murder before covering interviews with over 200 rape offenders, including 10 who killed their victims. This is one of the few books to include accounts of women who rape men and women who rape women.

Martin, Patricia Yancey. *Rape Work: Victims, Gender, and Emotions in Organization and Community Context.* New York: Routledge, 2005.

This book describes organizations and jobs that deal with rape, showing how some organizations, such as hospitals, orient their workers to provide unresponsive treatment even when the workers feel empathetic and are inclined to be helpful. In essence, the author analyzes practices that produce a second assault of rape victims

Martinez, Manuela, ed. *Prevention and Control of Aggression and the Impact on Its Victims*. New York: Kluwer Academic/Plenum Publishers, 2001.

This book contains the proceedings of the World Meeting of the International Society for Research on Aggression: Prevention and Control of Aggression and the Impact on Its Victims, held in 2000. Scientists from backgrounds as varied as genetics and human relations discuss ways to prevent violence through such means as pharmacology and the promotion of respect.

Matsakis, Aphrodite. *The Rape Recovery Handbook: Step-By-Step Help for Survivors of Sexual Assault*. Oakland, CA: New Harbinger, 2003.

Matsakis is a psychotherapist specializing in Posttraumatic Stress Disorder (PTSD). Rape victims are second only to survivors of war in suffering from PTSD. Matsakis focuses on helping survivors develop a safety plan, develop supportive networks, and diffuse the emotional impact of the sexual assault to regain power.

McEvoy, Alan W., and Jeff B. Brookings. *If She is Raped: A Book for Husbands*. Homes Beach, FL: Learning Publications, 1984.

This book provides information for the friends and family members of rape victims—male or female—to help them assist with the victim's recovery. The authors identify common reactions, suggest appropriate responses, and emphasize good communication.

Mezey, Gillian C., and Michael B. King, eds. *Male Victims of Sexual Assault*. Oxford, England: Oxford University Press, 2000.

This is one of the very few books to examine male rape. Chapters address prison rape, sexual torture, child victims, and historical aspects of male sexual assault.

Mills, Patrick, ed. *Rape Intervention Resource Manual*. Springfield, IL: Charles C. Thomas, 1977.

This guide helps activists assess the need for a rape crisis center, establish a center, and create a training program for center workers.

Morneau, Robert H., Jr., and Robert R. Rockwell. *Sex, Motivation, and the Criminal Offender.* Springfield, IL: Charles C. Thomas, 1980.

The authors cover types of sex crimes commonly encountered by police.

Nelson, Terri. *For Love of Country: Confronting Rape and Sexual Harassment in the U.S. Military.* New York: Routledge, 2002.

Military personnel discuss their experiences with sexual crimes while in uniform, blaming the problem on a failure of leadership and a breakdown in values. The author, a psychotherapist and U.S. Army veteran, includes responses from military and legislative leaders as well as Pentagon data.

Odem, Mary E., and Jody Clay-Warner, eds. *Confronting Rape and Sexual Assault.* Wilmington, DE: Scholarly Resources Books, 1998.

This book provides general coverage of the major issues surrounding rape, including the effects of sexual assault upon men, why rape happens, and the effects of resistance strategies upon rape.

O'Toole, Laura L., and Jessica R. Schiffman, eds. *Gender Violence: Interdisciplinary Perspectives.* New York: New York University Press, 1997.

This collection includes essays on sexual coercion in American life, sexual terrorism, cross-cultural views about rape, and the global health burden of rape.

Owen, David. *Criminal Minds: The Science and Psychology of Profiling.* New York: Barnes & Noble Books, 2004.

Owen describes the different types of criminals whose work is studied by profilers, including anger-excitation rapists, compensatory rapists, power-assertive rapists, power-reassurance rapists, pseudo-unselfish rapists, sadistic rapists, selfish rapists, regressed child molesters, and those who kill their victims.

Palermo, George B., and Mary Ann Farkas. *The Dilemma of the Sexual Offender.* Springfield, IL: Charles C. Thomas, 2001.

This book synthesizes clinical research on sexual offenders. It addresses the conceptualization of sexual offenders, the management and control of sexual offenders, and legal policies related to sexual offenders.

Paludi, Michele Antoinette, ed. *The Psychology of Sexual Victimization: A Handbook.* Westport, CT: Greenwood Press, 1999.

This general history covers incest, stranger rape, and the responses of the U.S. Congress to sexual victimization.

Prentky, Robert Alan, and Ann Wolbert Burgess. *Forensic Management of Sexual Offenders.* New York: Kluwer Academic, 2000.

This scientific study focuses on the best known methods of legal disposition and management of sex offenders.

Rathus, Jill H., and Eva L. Feindler. *Assessment of Partner Violence: A Handbook for Researchers and Practitioners.* Washington, DC: American Psychological Association, 2004.

This book is useful for its Rape Myths Acceptance Scale (RMA), which is a 20-minute self-quiz that measures victim-blaming attitudes.

Raine, Nancy Venable. *After Silence: Rape & My Journey Back.* Pittsburgh: Three Rivers Press, 1999.

The victim of a 1985 stranger rape, Raine describes the steps that she took to recover from the assault.

RAINN Speaker's Bureau. *Yes, You Do Know One of Us: Stories of Everyday Heroes.* New York: Authorhouse, 2009.

This is a collection of personal accounts and poems that has been compiled by the largest organization against sexual assault in the United States.

Roesch, Ronald, Donald G. Dutton, and Vincent F. Sacco, eds. *Family Violence: Perspectives on Treatment, Research, and Policy.* Burnaby, British Columbia, Canada: British Columbia Institute on Family Violence, 1990.

Chapters in this edited collection cover the impact of childhood sexual abuse on adult mental health and the prevalence of the sexual abuse of female children and adolescents.

Rosenberg, Jean. *Fuel on the Fire: An Inquiry into "Pornography" and Sexual Aggression in a Free Society.* Orwell, VT: Safer Society Press, 1989.

Examines the link between sexually explicit material and sexual assault. Rosenberg reviews the major theories of antipornography activists and collects the findings of 20 major sex offender treatment specialists. The title of this book reflects the general consensus that pornography does not cause sexual violence but may prompt already disturbed individuals to attack, thereby adding "fuel to the fire."

Russell, Diana, ed. *Making Violence Sexy: Feminist Views on Pornography.* New York: Taylor and Francis, 1993.

Russell addresses the connection between pornography and rape.

Ryan, Gail, and Sandy Ryan, eds. *Juvenile Sexual Offending: Causes, Consequences, and Correction.* San Francisco: Jossey-Bass, 1997.

This textbook defines sexually abusive youth, discusses the theories of juvenile sexual offending, and addresses the treatment of juvenile criminals.

Saward, Jill, and Wendy Green. *Rape: My Story.* London: Bloomsbury, 1990.

Saward, the Ealing Vicarage Rape Victim, experienced a highly publicized attack at her home in London, England. She has since become one of Great Britain's best known antirape activists.

Scarce, Michael. *Male on Male Rape: The Hidden Toll of Stigma and Shame.* Cambridge, MA: Perseus Publishing, 1997.

This comprehensive survey of male rape is a landmark book. It covers every aspect of male-male sexual assault from medical sensitivity to sexual identity and policing issues.

Schultz, Leroy G., ed. *Rape Victimology.* Springfield, IL: Charles C. Thomas, 1975.

The book examines social and legal aspects of rape victimization. It includes autobiographical essays by three female rape victims.

Schwartz, Martin D., ed. *Researching Sexual Violence Against Women: Methodological and Personal Perspectives.* Thousand Oaks, CA: Sage, 1997.

In this collection, writers examine the role that emotion plays in research about sex crimes.

Scott, Kay. *Sexual Assault: Will I Ever Feel Okay Again?* Ada, MI: Bethany House, 1993.

The author, raped while working in a Christian ministry, takes a Christian-focused approach to healing.

Scully, Diana. *Understanding Sexual Violence: A Study of Convicted Rapists.* New York: Unwin Hyman, 1990.

Scully published this work before the FBI released its profile of serial rapists.

Searles, Patricia, and Ronald J. Berger, eds. *Rape and Society: Readings on the Problem of Sexual Assault.* Boulder, CO: Westview Press, 1995.

This collection of essays is especially useful for interviews with a police officer who investigated sex crimes, a public defender who has defended rapists, a rapist, and the victims of rapes, including a male survivor.

Smith, Merril D. *Encyclopedia of Rape.* Westport, CT: Greenwood, 2004.

This reference covers the history of rape and the issues related to sexual assault.

Smith, Susan E. *Fear or Freedom: A Woman's Options in Social Survival and Physical Defense.* Racine, WI: Mother Courage Press, 1986.

Smith, a martial artist who has created the White Lotus system of self-defense, has written a self-defense manual for women. By combining self-defense tips with attack deterrents and attacker habits, Smith has created a guide that remains an exceptionally useful book despite its age.

Spencer, Alec. *Working with Sex Offenders in Prisons and Through Release to the Community: A Handbook.* London: Jessica Kingsley, 1999.

The author discusses his experiences in creating a multiagency sex offender treatment program in England.

Stevens, Dennis J. *Inside the Mind of a Serial Rapist.* San Jose, CA: Authors Choice Press, 2000.

After seeing a sign that said, "All men are potential rapists, beware!," the author decided to try to shift discussion of rape from a political focus to a criminological one. This book is based on interviews with 61 men who participated in at least 400 sexual assaults.

Stout, Karen, and Beverly McPhail, eds. *Confronting Sexism and Violence Against Women: A Challenge for Social Work* (Longman, 1998).

This collection of essays is aimed at social work professionals.

Swindle, Howard. *Trespasses: Portrait of a Serial Killer.* New York: Penguin, 1997.

The author, a *Dallas Morning News* reporter, provides a biography of Gilbert Escobedo, the Ski Mask Rapist. Escobedo confessed to 48 rapes in Dallas between 1985 and 1990, though he is suspected of committing twice that number.

Thornhill, Randy, and Craig T. Palmer. *A Natural History of Rape: Biological Bases of Sexual Coercion.* Cambridge, MA: MIT Press, 2000.

The authors, both evolutionary psychologists, controversially argue that men rape for reasons related to the evolution of the human species. They suggest that many rape prevention strategies will fail because they rely more on assumptions about human behavior than scientific research about human nature.

Trumpe, Pauline. *Doctors Who Rape.* Wakefield, NH: Longwood Academic, 1991.

The author is an attorney who specializes in the sexual abuse of patients, overwhelmingly female, by physicians.

United States Government. *21st Century Veterans Health: Military Sexual Trauma (MST), Assault and Harassment, Intimate Partner Violence, Rape, Veterans Administration Independent Study Course.* New York: Progressive Management, 2007.

Reproduces the 2004 Veterans Administration Independent Study Course on sexual crimes. It is aimed at helping military veterans who are suffering from mental and physical injuries sustained during military service. It includes a discussion of compensation issues associated with Military Sexual Trauma (MST).

Ward, Tony, Devon Polaschek, and Anthony R. Beech. *Theories of Sexual Offending.* New York: John Wiley, 2005.

This is a comprehensive examination of the key theories about sexual crime. It focuses on putting theories into practice.

Weinrott, Mark R. *Juvenile Sexual Aggression: A Critical Review.* Boulder, CO: Center for the Study and Prevention of Violence, 1996.

This pamphlet describes what is known about juvenile sex offenders, what remains unknown, and what appears to be the best means of treating such offenders.

Winick, Bruce J., and John Q. LaFond, eds. *Protecting Society from Sexually Dangerous Offenders: Law, Justice, and Therapy.* Washington, DC: American Psychological Association, 2003.

In this collection of essays, the authors discuss sexually violent predator laws, when a sexual offender should still be regarded as dangerous, and alternative strategies for protecting the community such as chemical castration.

Wolfthal, Diane. *Images of Rape: The "Heroic" Tradition and Its Alternatives.* London: Cambridge University Press, 1999.

This is the first in-depth exploration of rape in Western art but it does not include a discussion of rape on film and in music.

Zorza, Joan, ed. *Violence Against Women: Victims and Abusers, Legal Issues, Interventions and Treatment.* Kingston, NJ: Civic Research Institute, 2006.

This book contains almost all of the articles that appeared from January 2003 to December 2004 in *Sexual Assault Report.* It covers mother-daughter incest, sexual abuse of women by clergy, cultural differences in reporting sexual abuse, and military rape cases.

War-Related Rape

Amnesty International and CODESRIA. *Monitoring and Investigating Sexual Violence.* Amsterdam, The Netherlands: Amnesty International, 2000.

This slim volume is a companion to *UKWELI: Monitoring and Documenting Human Rights Violations in Africa.* It discusses when sexual violence is a crime under international human rights law, how to monitor sexual violence, and how to assess evidence.

Barstow, Anne Llewellyn, ed. *War's Dirty Secret: Rape, Prostitution, and Other Crimes Against Women.* Cleveland, OH: Pilgrim Press, 2000.

This book covers the modern history of sex crimes during war from the rape of Nanking in the 1930s to the Korean comfort women of World War II, to Nicaragua in the 1980s, and Yugoslavia in the 1990s.

Frederick, Sharon, and The Aware Committee on Rape. *Rape: Weapon of Terror.* River Edge, NJ: Global Publishing, 2001.

The Association of Women for Action and Research (AWARE) produced this general history of rape as an instrument of terror in situations of war and civil conflict. The book covers both World Wars, as well as conflicts in Haiti, Bosnia, Rwanda, Afghanistan, Myanmar, and Indonesia.

Human Rights Watch. *The War Within the War: Sexual Violence Against Women and Girls in Eastern Congo.* New York: Human Rights Watch, 2002.

Examines the frequent and systemic use of violence by Rwandan, Congolese, Mai Mai, and Burundian soldiers in the war in the

Democratic Republic of Congo. The war has proceeded intermittently since 1996.

Stiglmayer, Alexandra, ed. *Mass Rape: The War Against Women in Bosnia-Herzegovina.* Lincoln: University of Nebraska Press, 1994.

In the civil war in the former Yugoslavia in the 1990s, rape became an instrument of war.

Multimedia Sources

Date or Acquaintance Rape

20/20: The Toughest Call. ABC News, 2008. DVD.

This episode of the 20/20 news magazine discusses the case of Kimberly Scott, who struggled to tell her husband that she had become pregnant as the result of an acquaintance rape.

Date Rape: The Ultimate Violation of Trust. Educational Video Network, 2002. DVD and VHS.

This is a 23-minute introduction to date rape that focuses on a failure to communicate effectively as the major cause of such assaults.

Date Rape: No Means No! Phoenix Learning Group, 2008. DVD.

This short video emphasizes to students that girls who say "no" mean it.

Heart on a Chain: The Truth About Date Violence. Phoenix Learning Group, 2008. DVD.

Short film that introduces high school students to the issue of domestic violence, including date rape.

Real Life Teens: The Dark Side of Dating. TMW Media Group, 2008. DVD.

This 20-minute video discusses sexual pressure during a date and how girls should make their desires clear.

Scoring: A Story About Date Rape. Phoenix Learning Group, 2008.

Aimed at students, this 19-minute video is an introduction to the issues surrounding date rape.

History of Sexual Assault

60 Minutes – Innocent. CBS News, 2007.

This 19-minute segment on the Duke University lacrosse rape case originally aired on April 15, 2007. Three white Duke lacrosse players were charged with raping an African American stripper hired to perform at a party. The men were declared innocent and the case dismissed, with the prosecutor, Michael Nifong, ultimately being disbarred for abusing the rights of the men. The lacrosse players discuss the impact of false rape charges on their lives.

The Accused. Paramount, 1988. DVD and VHS.

Probably the best known film about a gang rape, this is a fictionalized account of the real-life attack that took place at Big Dan's Tavern in New Bedford Falls, Massachusetts, in 1983. The victim, played by Jodie Foster, came to the bar to have a drink. When she attempted to leave, a group of men raped her on a pool table while other men cheered the rapists. No one, including the bartender, notified the police. The case quickly drew national attention as one of the crimes of the century. Meanwhile, the community of New Bedford Falls divided over the prosecution of the alleged rapists. Protesters charged that the prosecutor displayed anti-Portuguese prejudice since the attackers were Portuguese by heritage. Other protestors waved placards proclaiming that "rape is not a spectator sport." Four men were ultimately convicted. This film shows the difficulties of prosecuting rape and the character assassination faced by victims in the 1980s. Foster won an Oscar for her portrayal.

Girl 27. Westlake, 2006. DVD.

The documentary focuses on the history of sexual assault. In 1937, the movie studio Metro Goldwyn Mayer tricked 120 underage girls into attending a stag party for visiting salesmen. One of the girls, dancer Patricia Douglas, was beaten and raped when she attempted to leave the gathering. She sued MGM and the studio embarked on a cover-up that involved the district attorney and the media. Director David Stenn interviews the now-elderly Douglas as well as legal analysts and victims of Hollywood sexual harassment.

The Massie Affair. PBS, 2005.

Part of the *American Experience* series, this documentary explores the 1931 case of a troubled white woman who charged that a group of Hawaiian men had raped her. The case inflamed race relations in Hawaii for decades to follow.

No!: Confronting Sexual Assault in Our Community. California Newsreel, 2006. DVD.

This superb film focuses on sexual assaults upon women of color. It includes segments on "gay-baiting" in the civil rights and black power movements as well as efforts by men to stop violence against women.

Rape in Connecticut: The Alex Kelly Story. A & E, 1999. VHS.

Alex Kelly committed two rapes in Darien, Connecticut, in 1986. While awaiting trial in 1987, he fled to Europe and spent the next seven years on the run. After surrendering in Switzerland, Kelly was convicted on one count of rape and pleaded no contest to another count. He left prison in 2007.

Rape Prevention – He Loves Me Not and *Rape Prevention – It's Not Always Somebody Else.* National Archives and Records Administration, 2008. 2 DVD.

These films were created by the U.S. Army in the 1970s to train military personnel and their dependents about the advantages of immediately reporting rape and the dangers that all women face from rape. The National Archives has released the films because of their historical significance.

Roman Polanski: Wanted and Desired. Velocity/Thinkfilm, 2008.

This is a documentary about the film director who was arrested in 1977 for unlawful sexual intercourse with a minor. Polanski then fled the United States and has yet to return. The film, which never received Polanski's cooperation, raises considerable doubt about the director's guilt.

Scottsboro: An American Tragedy. PBS, 2000. DVD.

The Scottsboro Boys were a group of nine African American youths who became an international cause célèbre when they were charged with raping two white women in Alabama in 1931. On the basis of extremely flimsy evidence, most of the defendants received death sentences. The scheduled executions were overturned but the young men served prison terms for a crime that likely never took place.

Searching for Angela Shelton. Hillhopper Productions, 2004. DVD.

This film demonstrates the prevalence of sexual assault. Filmmaker Angela Shelton travels throughout the United States to meet other women with her same name to survey a cross-section of American women. She discovers that 25 out of 40 Angela Sheltons have been raped, beaten, or sexually molested. One Shelton tracks sexual predators.

V-Day—Until the Violence Stops. New Video Group, 2003.

Playwright Eve Ensler, creator of *The Vagina Monologues*, established V-Day as an international grassroots movement to stop violence against women. This documentary traces the birth of the movement and includes celebrity women speaking about their personal experiences of abuse.

Prison Rape

Turned Out: Sexual Assault Behind Bars. Interlock Media, 2003. DVD and VHS.

This documentary on prison rape focuses on the stories of five men imprisoned in Alabama. They report that "turning out" or sodomizing prisoners is common. Prison administrators ignore such assaults, with some claiming that it helps to create a more peaceful and thus more manageable prison environment.

Prostitution

ABC News Primetime: Sex Trafficking in America. ABC News, 2006 DVD.

Examines the cases of two American teenagers who were forced into prostitution.

American Justice – Prostitution: Sex and the Law. DVD.

A & E Television Networks, 2008. Examines prostitution in the age of AIDS as well as the new emphasis on prosecuting the clients

History's Mysteries: History of Prostitution: Sex in the City. A & E Home Video, 2000. DVD.

Entertaining look at the history of prostitution that does not fully examine the dark side of the profession.

Prostitution: Beyond the Myths. Twin Cities Public Television, 2007. DVD.

This 30-minute documentary looks at the lives of three women who left prostitution. It also includes the views of pimps, law enforcement personnel, and social workers. The documentary is especially useful for its coverage of a recovery program that has helped women to get out of sex work.

Storyville: The Naked Dance. Shanachie, 1997. DVD and VHS.

Storyville is the famous section of New Orleans where prostitution was legalized from 1898 until 1917. The history of Storyville began with an effort to combat prostitution by restricting it to a 16-block area. However, about 2000 prostitutes subsequently found work everywhere from elaborate bordellos to the streets of the neighborhood. This film is for mature audiences because it includes turn-of-the-century erotica and period photographs.

Rape in Popular Films

Birth of a Nation. Alpha Video, 1915. DVD.

D. W. Griffith's blockbuster silent film contains two scenes of attempted rapes. One potential rapist is a black man while the other is a mixed-race man. The black man is based on the myth of the black male rapist. He is shown chasing—on all fours and virtually foaming at the mouth—a young white girl. The film, widely regarded as one of the most significant in American history, helped lead to the revival of the Ku Klux Klan in large part because of the rape scenes.

Broken Blossoms. Kino Video, 1919. DVD.

In this D. W. Griffith film, Lucy, played by Lillian Gish, is murdered by her father, Battling Burrows, for having a sexual relationship with the Yellow Man, a Chinese immigrant. The incestuous rape is symbolic but film scholars argue that this is the only way that the codes of silent film and melodrama would allow the depiction of a sexual assault. Standards of decency of the early 20th century limited the extent to which rape could be fully represented.

Death Wish. Paramount, 1974. DVD.

The vigilante hero, played by Charles Bronson, embarks on a murderous rampage after his wife and daughter are raped. When the movie was shown in theaters, audiences famously cheered when street thugs were killed.

Deliverance. Warner Home Video, 1972. DVD.

This movie, about four businessmen from Atlanta who take a camping trip into the wilderness, is one of the key films of the 1970s. It famously features a male rape scene. It stars Ned Beatty, Burt Reynolds, and Jon Voight.

Extremities. MGM, 1986. DVD and VHS.

Marjorie, played by Farrah Fawcett, narrowly escapes being raped but is left in fear that her attacker knows her address. Soon enough, the would-be rapist begins to terrorize Marjorie. When he invades her home, she disarms him and plots her revenge. The film received much critical acclaim, especially for Fawcett's performance.

Eye for an Eye Paramount, 1996. DVD.

When a rapist-killer is released on a technicality, the grieving mother, played by Sally Field, seeks revenge. This is a good thriller but it does not venture into a particularly nuanced discussion of the effects of rape upon the family.

Handgun. Starz/Anchor Bay, 1983. DVD.

When a young Dallas woman is raped, she seeks revenge with a handgun. This low-budget film is more of a discussion about gun control than sexual assault.

I Spit on Your Grave. Elite Entertainment, 1977. DVD.

This low-budget yet still enormously popular horror film, directed by Meir Zarchi, is part of the rape-revenge genre. The heroine tracks down and executes the four men who gang-raped her. The film is extremely graphic. While some reviewers have categorized it as exploitative, others view it as a examination of the psychology of violence.

Johnny Belinda. Warner Home Video, 1948. DVD and VHS.

Jean Negulesco's movie focuses on a deaf and mute woman who is rejected by her family. She is helped by a male physician to make the transformation from a dirty and disheveled girl into a beautiful woman. As a consequence of this transformation, she is raped by a local workman. Belinda responds by rejecting the symbols of heterosexual femininity.

Outrage 1950. This is a significant American movie that is currently not available on DVD or VHS.

It is a rape-revenge film by one of the few women directors, Ida Lupino, who worked in the mid-20th century. Typical of Lupino's film work, the movie is a melodrama that focuses on a social problem and possesses elements of film noir.

Positive ID. Starz/Anchor Bay, 1986. DVD.

A suburban housewife, played by Stephanie Rascoe, struggles to cope as a survivor of a sexual assault. The film appeared on many top 10 lists when it came out.

She Said No. Allumination, 1990. DVD.

In this John Patterson film, the victim of a date rape unsuccessfully prosecutes her attacker and then turns her gun on herself.

Thelma and Louise. MGM. 1991. DVD and VHS.

This classic female-buddy film involves two women who flee when one of them shoots a man attempting to date rape her friend. The film, starring Geena Davis and Susan Sarandon, became one of most popular films in history among women largely because it portrayed two women who fought against gender stereotypes.

A Time to Kill. Warner Home Video, 1996. DVD and VHS.

In Joel Schumacher's film, a young lawyer defends a black man who is accused of killing the men who raped his daughter.

Rape Prevention

Fight Like a Girl: The Rape Escape Method. CustomFlix, 2006. 3 DVD.

Teaches methods of self-defense for women, including fending off an attacker from a prone position, stopping date rape or acquaintance rape, and effectively using pepper spray. The instructor is Brad Parker, an experienced martial artist with a law enforcement background who serves as the executive director of the Women's Self-Defense Institute and is the president of Defend University, an online school focused on self-defense, security, and defensive tactics.

Rape Awareness and Prevention For Women. Black Belt Communications, 2005. DVD.

Provides a basic introduction to sexual assault prevention.

Rape Prevention. Educational Video Network, 2004. DVD.

This 27-minute film is an introduction to rape prevention and rape reporting.

SMART Self-Defense for Women. Greg Mosley's Self-Defense and Wellness, 2008.

This 30-minute video introduces the Simple Martial Arts Reality Training (SMART) developed by Kenpo black belt Greg Mosley to help women fight off attackers. It is marketed as a cheap and quick way of learning self-defense.

Rape Recovery

Nightline: Men and Rape. ABC News, 2007. DVD.

This episode of the news program, *Nightline,* looks at couples who are coping with the sexual assault of the woman. It focuses on the difficulties of husbands and boyfriends in handling the aftermath of a rape.

ABC News Primetime: Rape Survivor: Bridget Kelly. ABC News, 2007. DVD.

A 12-minute report of a rape survivor who decided to go public about being the victim of a sexual assault.

Speak. Showtime Entertainment, 2003. DVD.

This is fictional film based on the novel by Laurie Halse Anderson. It focuses on a high school freshman who becomes silent after being raped at a party. She recovers through the help of a teacher who uses art therapy. The film stars Kristen Stewart, Elizabeth Perkins, and Michael Angarano.

Surviving Rape: A Journey Through Grief. AIMS Multimedia, 1992. VHS.

This program covers the five stages of the grieving process that rape victims encounter: denial, anger, depression, bargaining, and acceptance.

Sexual Orientation Issues

She Stole My Voice: A Documentary About Lesbian Rape.

The American Academy for Film and Gender Studies, 2007. DVD. Many people think that women cannot be rapists. Filmmakers Justine Chang and Armand Kaye are gay rights activists who have created this film to bring attention to a topic that is typically ignored by both the lesbian community and law enforcement. The documentary blends expert commentary with graphic reenactments to show the prevalence of this type of sexual assault.

World History

60 Minutes—The War Against Women. CBS News, 2008. DVD.

This 13-minute film addresses the use of rape as a weapon of war in the African Congo.

Bangkok Girl: A Documentary About Thailand's Night Life. High Banks Entertainment, 2005. DVD.

This film addresses sex tourism through a biography of a 19-year-old bar girl who has worked since age 13 but still makes the somewhat dubious claim that she has never participated in prostitution.

Darfur Diaries: Message From Home. Cinema Libre, 2004. DVD and VHS.

Examines the human rights tragedy in the Darfur region of Africa. The Sudanese government has encouraged the Janjaweed militias to rape women of all ages while looting and murdering. The film allows victims to give their stories. This documentary has been used by Amnesty International to educate its members about the Darfur crisis villages

Rape Recovery Video Program. TeresaLauer.com, 2008. DVD.

This set of 35 short videos is designed to help rape victims address issues resulting from sexual assault such as eating disorders, self-injury, substance abuse, flashbacks, anxiety, depression, intrusive thoughts, nightmares, denial, numbness, and avoidance. It suggests steps to take to get support from family members and a therapist. This documentary is one of the very few films on rape to address expressive therapies, such as art, dance, drama, and music therapy.

Glossary

Acquaintance Rape   When a victim is raped by a person known to him or her. Most rapes are acquaintance rapes.

Brothel   A building devoted to prostitution in which a madam has control over a group of prostitutes. There are numerous slang terms for brothel including cathouse. Brothels are legal in some areas, notably parts of Nevada.

Capital Offense   A criminal act punishable by the death sentence. Rape was a capital offense in the United States for many, many years. Dropping the death penalty is thought to have increased prosecutions for rape, as women were more likely to pursue prosecution and prosecutors more willing to accept the cases.

Chaste   Morally pure. A chaste woman does not engage in sexual activities with anyone except her husband.

Chemical Castration   The use of prescribed drugs to reduce levels of testosterone in a convicted rapist. The drug usually given has the brand name Depo-Provera. It is depot medroxyprogesterone acetate (DMPA), which is a birth control drug that is prescribed to women under normal circumstances.

Chlamydia   A bacterial infection that is spread by sexual contact. Chlamydia can be found in the cervix and urethra as well as the throat and rectum. Women who have recently been infected typically have no symptoms so the infection may go untreated. Chlamydia destroys the fallopian tubes, causing infertility. It is major cause of pelvic inflammatory disease and has been linked to an increased risk of cervical cancer. The infection can be passed from mother to child during birth.

Concubine   A woman who lives with and has sexual relations with a man but who is not married to him. Historically, many concubines have been sex slaves.

Corroboration Requirements   Independent proof, generally a witness, that a woman has been raped. Such requirements imply that women cannot be trusted, especially since victims of armed robberies or other violent crimes are not required to provide proof of their victimization. American law no longer contains corroboration requirements.

Date Rape   A form of acquaintance rape in which a romantic relationship leads to an attack.

Femicide   When a girl or woman is murdered because of her gender. When a man rapes a woman and then kills her, it is femicide. Such a killing is often part of rape as a war crime.

Gang Rape   When two or more individuals commit sexual assaults. Rape as a war crime is typically a form of gang rape.

Gonorrhea   An infection caused by bacterium *Neisseria gonorrhea* that is spread by sexual contact. The gonorrhea bacterium can only survive in moist areas of the body, such as the vagina, urethra, and rectum. More than half of women have no symptoms in the early stages of gonorrheal infection. Those with symptoms may suffer burning urination, frequent urination, yellowish vaginal discharge, vaginal itching, and genital redness or swelling. Gonorrhea can lead to pelvic inflammatory disease, a major cause of infertility in women, as well as heart problems and arthritis. Gonorrhea and chlamydia are often found in the same person.

Grand Jury   A collection of at least 12 people who determine in private whether a prosecutor has sufficient evidence against a person or persons to proceed to trial. A rapist is indicted by a grand jury before his or her guilt is determined by a petit jury.

Hallucinogens   These are drugs that create a false or distorted impression of objects or events. It is a myth that many rapes involve subduing a victim with hallucinogenic drugs.

Indentured Servants   Individuals who agreed to work for a set amount of time, usually four to seven years, in exchange for passage to British America. Agreeing to an indenture provided poor English men and women with a chance at a better future. They did not have such a chance in England. Indentured servants became less common after Bacon's Rebellion in 1676, in which the poor colonists of Virginia fought the rich colonists.

Lynching   An execution that is not approved by the legal system. Prior to the civil rights legislation of the 1960s, black men accused of rape in the South were commonly lynched, usually by hanging, before their guilt or innocence could be determined in a court of law.

Madam   A woman who manages a house of prostitution.

Natasha   The nickname for a prostitute of Eastern European origin. The prostitutes, who are typically girls or women who have been forced into prostitution, notoriously dislike the nickname.

Pedophilia   Sexual abuse of a child.

Petit Jury   Also called a trial jury, such a jury determines the guilt or innocence of a suspect. Most criminal prosecutions never go to a jury because of plea bargaining and guilty pleas.

Recidivism   When a person convicted of a crime commits another crime after being released from prison. The rate of recidivism among sexual criminals, especially pedophiles, is notoriously high.

Sexual Coercion   Using the threat of punishment or the promise of a reward to force someone to engage in sexual activity. Not all force used in a rape is necessarily physical.

Sexual Harassment   Unwanted sexual advances, requests for sexual favors, and other verbal, physical, or any other conduct of a sexual nature.

Sexual Revictimization   When a survivor of childhood sexual abuse or rape is sexually attacked again in adulthood. Sexual revictimization is not uncommon.

Slave Codes   Laws that regulated the lives of slaves. Such codes made slave women into the property of their masters, who could legally use their property for sexual purposes. The codes made slave masters legally exempt for raping their slaves, though they still could be charged with damaging the property of other masters.

Sodomy   Anal intercourse. The term is usually used to designate sexual intercourse between men. Until late in the 20th century, sodomy in the United States was criminalized because of its connection with homosexuality. It remains criminalized in many other countries.

Speakout   A public protest that involves many people speaking publicly. The term, common in the 1960s and 1970s, dates to the first efforts of American feminists to campaign against rape.

Statutory Rape   Sexual intercourse with a person who is not old enough to legally consent to having sex. The age of consent varies from state to state and country to country. Statutory rape is different from other types of rape in that force and lack of consent are not necessary for conviction. The relationship is presumed to be abusive because of the age discrepancy.

Syphilis   A sexually transmitted disease in which *Treponema pallidum*, a microscopic organism burrows into the moist areas of the mouth or genitals. The first symptom is a nonpainful ulcer known as a chancre. Contact with the ulcer spreads the organism. The second stage of syphilis may include headaches, rash, fever, and hair loss. In the third stage, the only step that is not highly infectious, the disease destroys the major organs and the brain. In pregnant women, syphilis, if untreated, is passed on to the baby who will not live long.

Trafficking   The recruitment, transportation, transfer, harboring, or receipt of people, by means of coercion or payment for the purpose of sexual exploitation. Trafficking is a particular problem in economically depressed regions, such as parts of Asia and Eastern Europe.

Victim   A person who been hurt physically, psychologically, socially, intellectually, and/or financially.

Voyeur   A person who receives sexual gratification from observing the sexual activities of others.

White Slavery   Forcing women of European ancestry into prostitution. The term is generally viewed as archaic since it implies a difference between enslaving whites and enslaving people of other races.

Index

About the Author

CARYN E. NEUMANN is a visiting assistant professor of history at Miami University of Ohio. A graduate of Florida Atlantic University and The Ohio State University, she is a past managing editor of the *Journal of Women's History* and has published several articles on the feminist movement.